SONGS

IN

Action

44

SONGS IN *Action*

R. PHYLLIS GELINEAU

Department of Music
Southern Connecticut State College

McGRAW-HILL BOOK COMPANY

New York St. Louis San Francisco Düsseldorf Johannesburg
Kuala Lumpur London Mexico Montreal New Delhi
Panama Paris São Paulo Singapore Sydney Tokyo Toronto

Library of Congress Cataloging in Publication Data

Gelineau, R   Phyllis.
    Songs in action.

    "Resource materials":   p.
    1. School music—Instruction and study.   2. Children's
Songs.   I. Title.
MTL.G35   372.8'7'044   73-6679
ISBN 0-07-023071-4

Songs in Action

    4567890 VHVH 798765

This book was set in IBM Univers by John T. Westlake Publishing
Services. The editor was Robert P. Rainier; the designer was
John T. Westlake Publishing Services; the production supervisor
was Judi Frey.
Von Hoffmann Press, Inc., was printer and binder.

5

To My Three R's — Ruth, Ray and Robin

TABLE OF CONTENTS

ACKNOWLEDGMENTS

The author is deeply indebted to all who so kindly gave permission to reprint copyrighted and other material. In a few instances, even careful research failed to uncover the source of some of the songs. The efforts in this direction were most extended and sincere, and should there be a lack of acknowledgment in the proper place, it is only because the source is unknown. The author would very much appreciate being informed about such materials so that proper acknowledgment may be made in future editions and so that the appropriate arrangements may be secured.

R. Phyllis Gelineau

PREFACE

If you believe—

- that every child should have a chance to taste success during his classroom career,

- that success should not always have to be dependent upon mental ability,

- that achievement of success makes a child feel better about himself (and hopefully, better about others)

- that any subject which can guarantee success in some form deserves a place in the classroom curriculum—

then you believe in music, for this is what music does: provides opportunities for all children to succeed.

Unlike most other subjects, music is many things. The term "music" embraces such a broad range of activities—singing, playing, listening, creating (and more)—suited to so many diverse interests and abilities, that every child can be assured of success in at least one and often more than one musical experience.

The suggested activities related to the songs in this book encompass not only music but also other areas of the curriculum, thus enabling each teacher to choose those best suited to the needs and interests of his class. If you are or ever have been approaching the teaching of music with something less than zest (that's short for "knocking knees") because you think you can't sing, whistle, plunk, or toot, please take heart in the assurance that herein lies something for everyone.

PART I
THE SONGS AND THE ACTION

GUIDELINES

From the SONG comes the ACTION and from the ACTION comes LEARNING. This is the assumption on which this book is based.

Whereas learning a song can be a pleasurable experience in itself, the intent here is to increase that pleasure even more through the use of additional song-related activities which cover a wide range of classroom experiences, not only in music but in other subject areas. This is what is meant by ACTION.

Action

Specifically, ACTION includes suggestions for a variety of musical experiences such as using rhythm and "found" instruments, body movement, harmonization, and many others, as well as ways of encouraging the learner's own creations in all areas. In addition, under the Related Activities and Materials for each song, ACTION also encourages further delightful pursuits which may range in content from a list of recommended recordings for related *listening* experiences (representing a broad range of musical literature) to a project involving another area of the curriculum such as social studies, art, science, or language arts.

From the ideas proposed, a teacher may select the ones he deems appropriate for his class. "Appropriate" may mean any or all of the following:

a. whether the activity will help to increase the child's joy in music

b. whether it is within the child's level of understanding and interest

c. whether it fits into a particular learning sequence at the time, either in music or other related subject areas

d. whether it will help to broaden, deepen, or reinforce the understanding of some particular concept under study

e. some other reason, hitherto unexplored

The songs

The broad repertoire of song material seeks to provide for all levels of interest and achievement and to embrace a wide variety of traditional, contemporary, and world folk music (some with native text).

Many of the songs are in unison, while others are in two and three parts. Ways of creating harmony through various devices are suggested, as are chord accompaniments for use with piano, resonator bells, autoharp, ukulele, and guitar.

Starting tones and keys are indicated for all songs. If a song has been found to be a successful *program* song, it is so classified.

Songs are also classified by suggested levels, indicated by the letter U (upper) and L (lower) on the song page. Some songs show both letters—U *and* L. When this appears, it may be assumed that the reason was one or both of the following: (a) some songs are sung at all levels simply because children of all ages enjoy singing them; (b) the activities listed for the given song may include some for both levels.

Arbitrary classifications of certain kinds of materials into levels is frequently fraught with peril since obviously classes will differ as will the musical purpose of each song. A teacher usually judges the suitability of any given activity on the basis of experience with his particular class. What may be "primary" for one may be "sophisticated" for another. The best that may be said here is that the designations U and L are meant to be merely broad and flexible guidelines.

The *musical learnings* to be derived from each song experience are also part of the ACTION and are pointed up under the heading FOR STUDY. These include musical elements present in the song, which the learner may wish to study in more depth. The "learner" could be the teacher in training, the teacher in service, or the children in an elementary classroom, depending on the level of skill involved. For example, the inclusion of "compound time" in the For Study section of the song "Here We Go Round the Mulberry Bush" is certainly not intended for study by the children at the level commonly associated with learning the song. The very familiarity of the song, however, makes it a good vehicle for practice in learning to feel, recognize, and execute rhythms in compound meter at a higher level.

Other musical aspects of given songs such as minor, chromatics, phrase repetition and contrast, and various musical symbols, also appear under FOR STUDY.

Occasionally the reader will find a suggestion to "chant the rhythm and sing the syllables" (or numbers or letters, if preferred) of certain songs. This implies that the song's level of difficulty (melodically and rhythmically) is such that it may be considered suitable for practice in learning to read music at sight. Assuming that no skill can be achieved without sufficient practice, and that learning to read music requires practice at graded levels, sample pages of rhythm patterns and simple melodies are included in Part III. "Sufficient practice," as mentioned above, means that the learner has had enough singing or playing experiences containing the element under study to enable him not only to recognize the element when he meets it but also to reproduce it accurately when it appears in a new song setting.

It is assumed that the instructor will provide additional practice materials sufficient to accomplish his own purposes wherever necessary.

Further dimensions

In addition to the activities, related materials, and musical learnings suggested for each song, a brief overview of general information pertaining to the teaching of music in the elementary classroom may be found under such headings as Planning a Music Period, Teaching a Song, Helping Out-of-Tune Singers, and others in Part II.*

Part II also contains instructional sections on playing the harmonica, piano, autoharp, and ukulele. It may be helpful to the instructor who wishes to introduce these instruments to his class or to himself.

To assure adequate background information in the fundamentals of music, a complete Review

of Fundamentals, a Glossary of Musical Terms, plus brief sections on related areas which may require further explanation—transposition, selecting chords for accompaniment, etc.—are all included in Part III.

In summary, then, SONGS and ACTION constitute the heart of this literary effort, with additional information included for support.

The action material is designed to help heighten the enjoyment of each song, deepen musical understanding, and hopefully, in the process, contribute toward a more successful music teaching experience for the classroom teacher.

It is hoped that the use of this book will spark more ideas for structuring activities so that musical learning may emerge, as well as further explorations into ways of extracting musical knowledge from given activities.

The following abbreviations may be found throughout the text:

Books

ABC	American Book Company
CRS	Cooperative Recreation Service
DMT	Discovering Music Together series, Follett
EIM	Experiences in Music, McGraw-Hill
EM	Exploring Music series, Holt, Rinehart and Winston
GWM	Growing With Music series, Prentice-Hall
MNAF	Music Near and Far (Music for Living series), Silver Burdett
MMYO	Making Music Your Own series, Silver Burdett
MYA	Music for Young Americans series, American Book Co.
MOM	The Magic of Music series, Ginn and Co.
NDM	New Dimensions in Music series, American Book Co.
NMH	New Music Horizons series, Silver Burdett
TIM	This Is Music series, Allyn and Bacon

Records

AM	Adventures in Music series, RCA Victor
BOL	Bowmar Orchestral Library, Bowmar Records

*Further in-depth information in these areas may be found in Gelineau, *Experiences in Music,* New York: McGraw-Hill, 1970, and other professional publications. See Professional Reading, p. 291.

CRG	Children's Record Guild	Elementary Schools
KP	Keyboard Publications	EIM Experiences in Music records, Custom Recording Consultants
L or R	with number following, e.g., L2, R5, refers to either the listening (1) series or the rhythms (R) series of the RCA Basic Record Library for	CRC Custom Recording Consultants
		YPRC Young People's Record Club

THE SONGS

1. PLACE TO BE

Words and music by Malvina Reynolds

Level: L
Key of F: start F (do)

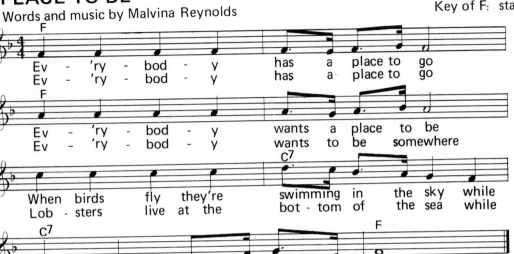

Ev - 'ry - bod - y   has a place to go
Ev - 'ry - bod - y   has a place to go

Ev - 'ry - bod - y   wants a place to be
Ev - 'ry - bod - y   wants to be somewhere

When birds   fly they're   swimming in the sky while
Lob - sters   live at the   bot - tom of the sea while

fish   are   swim ming in the sea.
I'm   at the   bot - tom of the air.

Words and music by Malvina Reynolds, copyright 1958 by Schroder Music Co. (ASCAP), used by permission.

The action
1. Assign solos to individual children on the *first* measure of each line, with class joining in on the second measure.
2. Tap the basic meter of the measure with the feet while clapping the melody rhythm, or let one group tap while another claps and a third group listens.
3. The teacher claps the rhythm of the first line, then the class claps the second line, and so on, alternating lines throughout the song.
4. Choose a different rhythm instrument to play on each line. All play together on the last line.

5. Choose a different rhythm instrument to play each time the word "ev-'ry-bod-y" occurs. Substitute the sound of the instrument for the voice on the word. Let voices come in on time to complete the phrase.
6. Sound four different rhythm instruments on the four syllables of "ev-'ry-bod-y" each time the word occurs, for example:

ev-	drum
ry-	sticks
bod-	wood blocks
y	cymbals

On the final note (whole note) of the song, make the four separate sounds with the rhythm instruments suggested above.

Related activities and materials
1. Look up where people and creatures live, for example, den, nest, igloo, hut; then create some new verses about them.
2. Draw or paint some of the places where these people and creatures live.
3. Film: "Shelter: Almost Anyone Can Build a House," color, 15 minutes, Learning Corporation of America.
4. Filmstrip: "Homes Around the World," Denoyer-Geppert AV.

5. Other songs about homes:
   "My Ranch" (Allá en el rancho grande), MMYO 5, Silver Burdett.
   "My Nipa Hut," NMH 5, Silver Burdett.
   "Home on the Range," MNAF, Silver Burdett.
   "The Homeland" (Cain-Burnet), Investigating Music, NDM Series, American Book Co.

For study
    Even and uneven rhythm patterns
    Sequence
    Chant rhythm pattern, then sing with syl-
    lables (See pp. 277-273)
    Conduct in 4-bt. pattern   (See p. 269)

left-hand piano

F   C7

bells
F = F A C
C7 = C E G Bb

Autoharp
F, C7

ukulele
Tune: G C E A key of F tuning (See p. 240)

F   C7

2. GOIN' TO THE ZOO

Words and music by Tom Paxton

Level: L
Key of F: start F (do)

2. See the elephant with the long trunk swingin'
   Great big ears and long trunk swingin'
   Sniffin' up peanuts with the long trunk swingin'
   We can stay all day.

   Refrain: We're goin' to the zoo etc.

3. See all the monkeys scritch, scritch, scratchin'
   Jumpin' round scritch, scritch, scratchin'
   Hangin' by their long tails scritch,
     scritch, scratchin'
   We can stay all day

   Refrain: We're goin' to the zoo etc.

4. Big black (brown) bear all huff, a-puffin'
   Coat's too heavy, he's a puffin'
   Don't get too near the huff a-puffin'
   You can't stay all day

   Refrain: We're goin' to the zoo etc.

5. Seals in the pool all honk, honk, honkin'
   Catchin' fish and honk, honk, honkin'
   Little seals honk, honk, a-honkin'
   We can stay all day

   Refrain: We're goin' to the zoo etc.

6. We stayed all day and I'm gettin' sleepy
   Gettin' sleepy, gettin' sleepy
   Home all ready and I'm sleep, sleep, sleepy
   We have stayed all day

   Refrain: We're goin' to the zoo etc.

The action

1. Create movement for each animal in the different verses of the song, then adapt the tempo and dynamics of that verse to the animal.
2. Contrast the word content of verse 1 and verse 6, then explore possible variations in tempo and dynamics to create appropriate mood.
3. Explore the timbre of various rhythm instruments, then choose the instrument best suited for each different animal to accompany the movements.
4. Create additional verses about other animals seen at the zoo, then add movement and accompany with rhythm instruments as in numbers 1 and 3 above. Vary activity by letting the class guess which animal is being portrayed.
5. Create original words about zoo animals to familiar tunes, for example:

   "Farmer in the Dell"

   a. the keeper of the zoo, etc.
   b. the keeper takes the lion, etc.

Related activities and materials

1. Explore the living habits and native origin of various zoo animals.
2. Explore differences between zoo animals and farm animals.
3. "Dance-A-Story of Noah's Ark," RCA.
4. Go on a "Bear Hunt" (see no. 39).
5. Sing other songs about animals; see Classified Index.
6. Listening:
   Selections from "Carnival of the Animals," EIM and BOL #51.
   "Bear Dance," Bartok, AM 3, vol. 2.
   "Of a Tailor and a Bear," L2 RCA Basic Record Library and BOL *Small Listener*.
   "Jumbo's Lullaby," BOL #63.
   "Tame Bears," L2 RCA Basic Record Library.

For study
  Tonic chord beginning
  Syncopation
  Tie
  See Action for suggestions related to tempo,
  mood, and dynamics

left-hand piano

F   C7

bells   Autoharp
F = F A C   F, C7
C7 = C E G B♭

ukulele
Tune: G C E A key of F tuning (See p. 240)

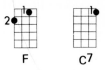

F   C7

---

3. MISS POLLY HAD A DOLLY

English folk song

Level: L
Key of G: start D (low sol)

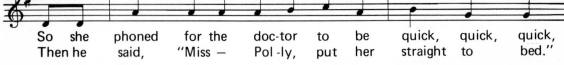

G   D7

1. Miss   Pol - ly   had   a   dol - ly   who was   sick,   sick,   sick,
2. He   looked—   at   the   dol - ly   and he   shook   his   head,

So   she   phoned   for the   doc-tor   to   be   quick,   quick,   quick,
Then he   said,   "Miss — Pol - ly, put her straight to   bed."

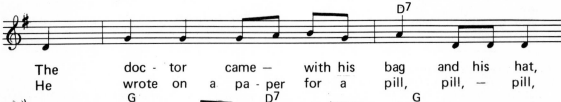

The   doc - tor   came —   with his   bag   and his   hat,
He   wrote   on   a   pa - per   for   a   pill,   pill, —   pill,

And   he   rapped —   at   the   door —   with   a   rat — tat — tat.
"I'll be   back —   in   the   morn-ing with   my   bill,   bill,   bill.

The action

1. Dramatize. Let the children select their own ways of acting out the parts of dolly, Miss Polly, and the doctor.
2. Discuss possible changes in tempo and dynamics in the first two lines of the second verse to highlight the mood.
3. Clap or play a different rhythm instrument on the  rhythm pattern each time it recurs throughout the song. Selection of the rhythm instrument should be based on a discussion of what seems most appropriate for the character in that particular place in the song.
4. Without singing, the teacher claps the first line and the class claps the second (melody rhythm), alternating throughout the song.
5. Show different kinds of dolls in movement (rag, wind-up, etc.).
6. As a relaxing exercise, have class be wooden soldiers (tightened muscles, body stiff), then relax immediately into being limp rag dolls. Alternate between one and the other at a signal from the music—high sound for wooden soldiers, low sound for the rag doll cue.
7. Following a discussion of the importance of health care (which might include the function of doctors and nurses, what to do in emergencies, and so forth), create some original verses for this or another familiar tune about how to keep well.

Related activities and materials

1. "Dance-A-Story of Flappy and Floppy," RCA.
2. Sing other doll songs, for example "Teru, Teru Bozu," MMYO 3, Silver Burdett.
3. Listening:
   "Sleeping Time," L1 RCA Basic Record Library.
   "Serenade of the Doll," BOL #63.
   "Sick Doll, Doll's Burial, New Doll," Tchaikovsky, BOL #68.
   "Baby's Family," Villa Lobos, Keyboard Publications.

For study

Even rhythm pattern
Chant rhythm and sing with syllables (See pp. 277-278)
Conduct in 4-bt. pattern (See p. 269)

left-hand piano

G   D⁷

bells
G = G B D
D⁷ = D F♯ A C

Autoharp

G, D⁷

ukulele

Tune: A D F♯ B key of G tuning (See p. 225)

G   D⁷

4 HELLO EVERYBODY
Words and music by Charity Bailey

Level: L
Key of C: start G (sol)

Briskly   C   C

1.Hel - lo   ev – ry – bod – y;   yes   in – deed;—
2.Good – bye   ev – ry – bod – y;   yes,   in – deed;—

G7   C   C

yes,   in – deed;—   yes,   in – deed,—   Let's – make   mu – sic;
yes,   in – deed;—   yes,   in – deed;— Stay   Well   and   hap – py;

C   dm   G7   C

yes,   in - deed;—   yes,   in – deed, my   dar   –   ling.
yes,   in – deed;—   yes,   in – deed, my   dar   –   ling.

Copyright © 1955 by Plymouth Music Co. Inc., 17 West 60th Street, New York, N.Y., used by permission.

The action
1. Assign the solo, with the class coming in on "Yes indeed."
2. Add rhythm instruments as desired or create an original percussion score to play with the song.
3. Use for tone-matching game in lower grades, for example, the child sings "My name is___." The class answers "Yes, indeed." As the song progresses, different children (indicated by the teacher) sing their names, with the class answering "Yes indeed" each time and "Yes indeed, my darling" sung by everybody at the end. (See Helping Out-of-Tune Singers, p. 225.)
4. Create some new verses dealing with varied subject matter as desired, for example, "The sun is shining, yes indeed," or "We're going on a bus ride."

Related activities and materials
1. Suggest other ways of expressing "hello" and "goodbye" in action (bow, nod, wave, shake hands).
2. Find out ways of greeting in other parts of the world and learn some greetings in other languages, for example:

Spanish	buenos dias	(bway-nos-dee-ahs)
Hebrew	shalom	(shah-lome)
Japanese	moshi	(mo-shee)
Hawaiian	aloha	(ah-low-ha)
French	bon jour	(bon-szhoor)

For study
Syncopation
Sequence

Like phrases
Conduct in 4-bt. pattern (See p. 269)

left-hand piano

C   G7   dm

bells

C = C E G
G7 = G B D F
dm = D F A

Autoharp

C, G7, dm

5. HAD A LITTLE ROOSTER

American folk song

Level: L
Key of C: start middle C (do)

Had a lit-tle roost-er by the gar-den gate, And
that lit-tle roost-er was my play-mate, And
that lit-tle roost-er said, "Cock-a-doo-dle doo, Doo,
doo, doo, doo, doo, doo, doo, doo doo doo."

2. Had a lit-tle hen — And
3. Had a lit-tle duck — by the barn-yard gate. And
4. Had a lit-tle pig — And

that lit-tle hen —
that lit-tle duck — was my play-mate,
that lit-tle pig —

And that lit-tle hen — said, "Chick, chick, chick."
And that lit-tle duck — said, "Quack, quack, quack."
And that lit-tle pig — said, "Oink, oink, oink,"

And that lit-tle roost-er said, "Cock-a-doo-dle doo, Doo,
doo, doo, doo, doo, doo, doo, doo, doo, doo."

From Harry R. Wilson, Walter Ehret, Alice M. Knuth, Edward J. Hermann, and Albert A. Renna, *Growing with Music,* Book 2, Related Arts edition, © 1970 by Prentice-Hall, Inc., Englewood Cliffs, N.J., reprinted by permission.

The action
1. Have individual children take the part of each animal and make the appropriate sounds as they occur in the song.
2. Have the children draw pictures of the animals with the sound they make written out, then hold up each picture as the animal occurs in the song.
3. Add new verses with new animals.
4. Choose a rhythm instrument for each animal and sound as the animal occurs in the song.

Related activities and materials
1. "Dance-A-Story of Little Duck," RCA LC #R66-3272.
2. See Classified Index for other animal songs.
3. Listening:
   "Chicken Little," BOL #52.

"White Cat," AM 3 vol. 1.
"Sounds of Animals," Folkways Records, vol. 1 #6121.
"Hens and Cocks," from "Carnival of the Animals," EIM and BOL #51.

For study
$\frac{3}{4}$ meter
Repeat sign :‖
Cumulative song
Conduct in 3-bt. pattern (See p. 269)

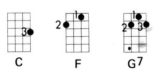

left-hand piano

C   F   G⁷

bells

C = C E G
F = F A C
G⁷ = G B D F

Autoharp

C, F, G⁷

ukulele

Tune: G C E A key of F tuning (See p. 240)

C   F   G⁷

6. MY LITTLE PUPPY

Words and music by Elizabeth Deutsch
With pride

Level: L
Key of G: start B (mi)

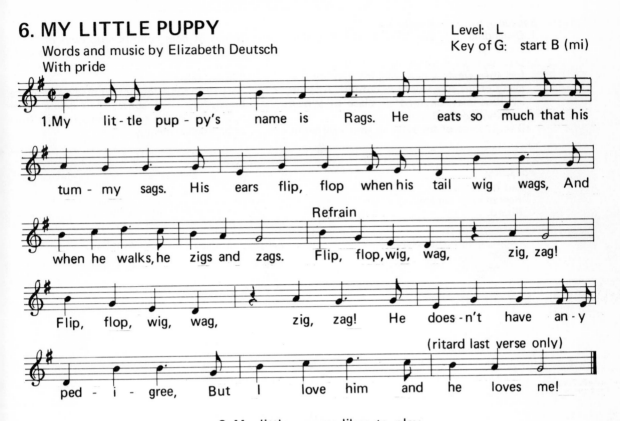

1. My lit-tle pup-py's name is Rags. He eats so much that his
tum-my sags. His ears flip, flop when his tail wig wags, And
when he walks, he zigs and zags. **Refrain** Flip, flop, wig, wag, zig, zag!
Flip, flop, wig, wag, zig, zag! He does-n't have an-y
(ritard last verse only)
ped-i-gree, But I love him and he loves me!

2. My little puppy likes to play.
   He rolls himself in the grass all day.
   I whistle—but he won't obey.
   He always runs the other way.

Refrain:
   Flip, flop, etc.

The action

1. After the song is well learned, add as follows:
   "sags"—bend over, make believe holding a sagging tummy
   "flip flop"—put hands on each side of head and wave fingers up and down
   "wig wags"—swing hips from one side to the other
   "zig zags"—hold hands in front with palms pressed together, point away from the body, first to left, then right
   "flip flop, wig wag, zig zag"—movements in rapid succession
   "he doesn't have any pedigree"—shake head
   "him"—throw arms to sides in "love" gesture
   "me"—point to self
   "rolls"—make hand-over-hand rolling motion after word "whistle," give a little whistle
   "won't obey"—shake head, followed by "hopeless" palms up gesture on "the other way"

2. Sound a different rhythm instrument for each of these: flip flop, wig wag, zig zag.

3. Discuss some of the characteristic movements of dogs and try to imitate them in body movements.

4. Imitate some of the sounds dogs make, then create body movements that seem to fit the sounds.

Related activities and materials

1. Depending on the class level of understanding:
   - Discuss ways in which dogs should be cared for, then create a new song incorporating as many of the suggestions as possible. A familiar tune may be used in place of a new melody, if desired.
   - Discuss some of the ways in which different breeds of dogs contribute to ways of life in various parts of the world, for example, Eskimo, St. Bernard, bloodhound, sheep, Dalmatian, setter.
   - Portray in some form of art media any of the breeds discussed above, then create some new verses about each, using a familiar tune or an original melody.

For study

Cut time
Rest before "zig zag"
Ritard

left-hand piano

G   C   D^7

bells

G = G B D
C = C E G
D^7 = D F$\sharp$ A C

Autoharp

G, C, D^7

ukulele

Tune: A D F$\sharp$ B key of G tuning (See p. 238)

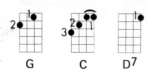

G   C   D^7

7. I KNOW A LITTLE PUSSY

Traditional

Level: L
Key of C: start middle C (do)

The action

1. After the song is learned, add this action: Start in a crouching position and move gradually upward as the tune ascends. When the tune descends on "meow, meow," return to crouching position in little bounces in time to the music. On "scat," jump off the floor.
2. Play the tune on resonator bells with no words. Have children do the movements in number 1 in the proper places just by listening to the tune.
3. Choose one rhythm instrument to accompany the ascending scale, another for the descending, and a third to sound on "scat," as the movements suggested in number 1 are executed.
4. Create some new verses, substituting objects or creatures for the pussy willow, for example, a. I made a little snowman, b. I know a little bunny, his fur is snowy white.
5. Ask children to feel a real pussy willow, then to move the way it makes them feel.
6. Bring in other objects that feel soft. Contrast these with some hard objects. Show the contrast through movement and the choice of rhythm instruments for accompaniment.
7. Discuss other harbingers of spring and create new verses about them.
8. Play on resonator bells, piano, recorder, or other melody instrument, short melodies that go either up or down. Ask the class to listen, but call on individual children to identify the direction verbally or in movement. When all children are asked to respond at the same time, only a few will do the thinking; thus individual responses are preferable to class responses in any kind of ear-training activity.
9. Teach the syllable names of the major scale (*do re mi fa sol la ti do*), ascending and descending by ear only.
10. For practice on the scale in the early grades, try the following:
    a. Write the name of each syllable of the scale on the chalkboard (chart or flannel-board) in the form of a ladder, then have the class sing as each is pointed to. Colored chalk is helpful.
    b. Make eight different colored "lollipops" out of any desired material. Write the name of one syllable on each. Line all syllables (lollipops) up in proper order with low *do* to the left as the teacher faces the line, ascending to high *do* on the right. Have each child hold up his note in turn. The class should respond by singing the tone written on the lollipop. Vary the activity by having the teacher stand behind the line of lollipops, holding his hand over the head of the children in the line in turn. The class should respond by singing the syllable indicated. Children can easily learn to sing short melodic sequences in this manner; *do re mi mi mi fa sol* or *do re mi mi re re do* or *do ti la sol la ti do do*.
11. Sing other songs with scale sequences for example, "Do Re Mi" from "The Sound of Music."

For study

Major scale (See p. 261)
Sing with syllables (See pp. 277-278)

left-hand piano

C   F   G⁷

bells
C = C E G
F = F A C
G⁷ = G B D F

Autoharp
C, F, G⁷

8. THREE BLUE PIGEONS

Traditional

Level: L
Key of C: start E (mi)

1. Three blue pi-geons   sit-ting on the wall,   Three blue pi - geons sit-ting on the wall.

Spoken: One flew away
2. "Two blue pigeons," etc.

Class: sad "ooooh"

Spoken: "Another flew away"
3. "One blue pigeon," etc.

Class: sad "ooooh"

Spoken: "The last one flew away"
4. "No blue pigeons," etc.

Class: sad "ooooh"

Spoken: "One flew back"
5. "One blue pigeon," etc.

Class: happy "wheeee!"

Spoken: "Another flew back"
6. "Two blue pigeons," etc.

Class: happy "wheee!"

Spoken: "The third flew back"
7. "Three blue pigeons," etc.

Class: happy "wheeee!"

(ritard last two measures at conclusion
of song)

The action

1. Dramatize. Let three children be "pigeons"; fly and come back as the song indicates.
2. As an alternative to number 1, use a flannel board or other similar visual on which pigeon figures may be removed and put back as the song indicates.
3. Give a broad sweep (glissando) on bells or piano to indicate the coming and going of the pigeons (upward for flying away—downward for coming back).
4. As each pigeon flies away, the class sighs a sad "oooh." As each pigeon returns, the class cries a happy "wheeee!" Individual children may be assigned the spoken lines.

5. Explore with the class various positions and movements of the body which might best communicate the contrasting feelings in the sad and happy parts.
6. Clap three times or use a different rhythm instrument every time "sitting on the wall" occurs in the song.

If desired, have resonator bells play E D C each time the last measure is sung.
7. Substitute other creatures as desired, for example, "Three Small Bunnies."

Related activities and materials

1. Add more verses with other numbers for counting practice.
2. Represent any portion of the song in some art media.

3. Listening:
"Aviary" from "Carnival of the Animals," BOL #51.
"The Lark Song; Little Bird," BOL #52.

For study:
Chant rhythm pattern and sing with syllables
(See pp. 277-278)

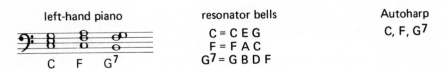

left-hand piano	resonator bells	Autoharp
C F G^7	C = C E G F = F A C G^7 = G B D F	C, F, G^7

9. TEN LITTLE INDIANS

Level: L
Key of G: start G (do)

(John Brown Had a Little Indian)
Traditional

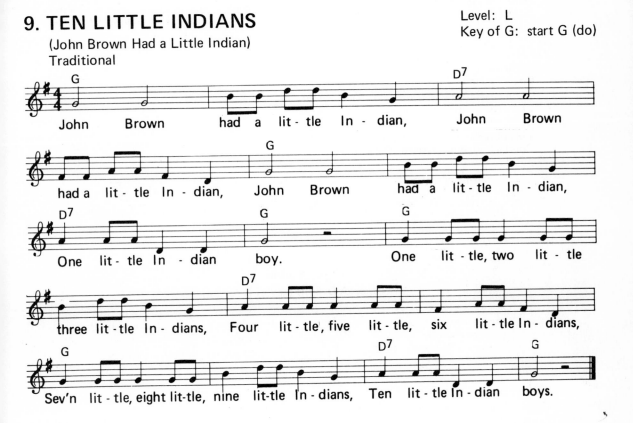

The action
1. Have the class make a circle or stand beside their desks. Assign each child a number from 1 to 10. When that number is heard in the song, the child with that number stoops down. As the numbers are sung backwards (10 little, 9 little, etc.), each child stands up again.
2. Choose a different rhythm instrument or other sound for each number from 1 to 10. Each instrument plays in turn as the numbers are heard in the song. Combine with number 1.
3. Sing as a partner song with "Skip to My Lou."
4. Sing the words in Spanish:
   Uno, dos, tres inditos, cuatro, cinco, seis inditos
   Seite, ocho, nueve inditos, diez indios pequeños

5. Sing a Halloween song to this tune*:

   One little, two little three little witches
   Fly over haystacks, fly over ditches
   Slide down the moon without any hitches
   Hey ho Halloween's here.

   Stand on your head with a lopsided wiggle
   Tickle your little black cats till they giggle
   Swish through the clouds with a higgledy piggle
   Hey ho Halloween's here.

6. Create new verses for other special days or subjects.
7. Make some drums from boxes or cans and beat the rhythm pattern of the melody, then create an Indian dance accompanied by the drums.
8. See "Mos, Mos," no. 56.

*Reprinted with permission of the publisher, The Instructor Publications Inc., Dansville, N.Y. 11437.

For study
Tonic chord (meas. 1 and 2)
Even rhythm
Chant rhythm and sing with syllables (See pp. 277-278)
Sequence
Like phrases
Conduct in 4-bt. pattern (See p. 269)

left-hand piano

G D^7

bottles

G = *do mi sol*
D^7 = *sol ti re fa*

Autoharp

G, D^7

ukulele
Tune: A D F$^\sharp$ B (key of G tuning)

G D^7

10. I'M A LITTLE TEAPOT

Traditional

Level: L
Key of C: start middle C (do)

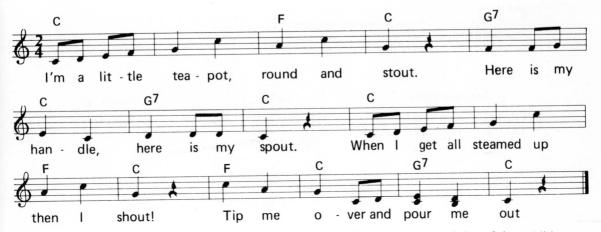

I'm a lit-tle tea-pot, round and stout. Here is my han-dle, here is my spout. When I get all steamed up then I shout! Tip me o-ver and pour me out

From Book 1, *Exploring Music* Series (teachers' edition), © 1966, by special permission of the publisher, Holt, Rinehart and Winston.

The action

1. When the song is learned, add the following action:

    meas. 1-4: cross arms over chest and bend knees slightly

    meas. 5-6: make handle with left hand on hip and elbow extended

    meas. 7-8: make spout with right hand (hold upper arm and elbow close to body, hand to the side, bend wrist, cup hand with palm facing floor)

    meas. 9-12: stand, holding position of handle and spout

    meas. 13-16: tip body to right side

2. Add a second verse and reverse positions in appropriate places:

I'm a very clever teapot too
Here's an example of what I can do
I can change my handle and my spout
Tip me over and pour me out.

3. Choose a rhythm instrument to play on the like phrases and a different instrument to play on the unlike phrases.

4. Tap the basic meter with the feet while clapping the melody rhythm, or divide the class into groups, letting one tap while the other claps.

5. Create new verses using other subject matter, for example:

    a. I'm a very pretty Christmas tree

    b. I'm a funny baby chimpanzee

    c. I'm a very jolly circus clown

Related activities and materials

1. Discuss what makes a teakettle whistle. Try whistling the tune of the song.

2. Tape the sound of a teakettle whistling, as well as other environmental sounds for identification by the class.

3. Discover other sounds in the environment that have pitch, for example, doorbells, car horns, etc. Discuss each sound in terms of whether it is: (1) one tone sustained or a series of tones repeated, (2) high or low, or (3) short or long. Try to reproduce some of the sounds on the pitched instruments in the classroom.

4. See Ear Training (p. 231).

For study
  Like phrases
  Ascending major scale progression in meas. 1
  and 9
  Chant rhythm pattern and sing with syllables
  (See pp. 277-278)
  Conduct in 2-bt. rhythm pattern (see p. 269)

left-hand piano

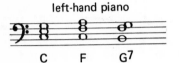

C   F G^7

bells

C = C E G
F = F A C
G^7 = G B D F

Autoharp

C, F, G^7

ukulele

Tune: G C E A (key of F tuning)

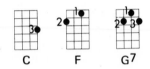

C   F G^7

11. BAA, BAA, BLACK SHEEP

Mother Goose

Level: L
Key of C: start middle C (do)

Playfully

Baa, baa, black sheep, have you a-ny wool?   Yes sir, yes sir, three bags full

Harmonica:

4   6   6   ⑥⑦ 7 ⑥ 6   ⑤   ⑤   5   5   ④   ④   4

One for the mas- ter and one for the dame, and one for the lit-tle boy who lives down the lane.

6   6 6 ⑤ ⑤⑤ 5   5 5 ④   ④   6   6 6 ⑤ 6 ⑥⑤   5   ④④   4

The action

1. Divide the class into two groups and sing as a dialogue song, one group asking the question and the other answering.
2. Use as in number 1 in dialogue, except omit singing and substitute clapping the melody rhythm in questions and answers.
3. Use as in number 2, except choose different rhythm instruments for questions and answers on alternate lines.
4. Dramatize the song or interpret in body movement.
5. Have one group say the words in rhythm while another group says the words to "Peas Porridge" in rhythm at the same time.
   A third group could tap or clap the basic meter while listening to the other two groups.
6. Use as in number 5, except substitute two different rhythm instruments of contrasting timbre for the groups of voices.
7. Play on the harmonica, key of C. See Playing the Harmonica (p. 234). (Appropriate numbers for blowing and drawing are written under the words on the song page.)

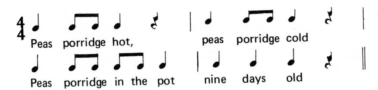

Some like it hot, some like it cold

Some like it in the pot nine days old.

Related activities and materials

1. If raw wool is obtainable, let the children feel it, then have them move the way it makes them feel.
2. Explore the processes involved in making a finished wool product from raw wool, then have the class create some body movements illustrating each process.
3. Listening:
   "The Little Shepherd," BOL #63 and L2 RCA Basic Record Library.
   "Children's Symphony," First movement, AM 3 vol. 2.

For study

Chant rhythm pattern, then sing with syllables (See pp. 277-278)
Conduct in 4-bt. pattern (See p. 269)

left-hand piano

C   F   G7

bells

C = C E G
F = F A C
G7 = G B D F

Autoharp

C, F, G7

12. HICKORY DICKORY DOCK

J. W. Elliott (Mother Goose)

Level: L
Key of F: start A (mi)

Hick - o - ry dick - o - ry   dock,   The mouse   ran up   the   clock;   The

clock struck one,   the   mouse   ran down,   Hick - o - ry   dick - o - ry   dock.

The action

1. Use selected rhythm instruments for sound effects, for example, wood block for steady ticking, triangle or finger cymbals for striking.
2. Chant the words against the words of "Jack and Jill" in rhythm and/or play the melody rhythm of "Jack and Jill" against the melody rhythm of "Hickory Dickory Dock," using two different rhythm instruments.
3. Compose some new verses to the tune.
4. Do the following movements to the song:

   Formation: circle. Bend over from the waist so that the arms hang down to represent the pendulum of the clock.
   On words: "hickory dickory dock" move arms from side to side three counts (L-R-L), then stamp stamp (quickly)
   "mouse ran up the clock" walk three steps to center while raising arms over head, then stamp stamp quickly as before
   "clock struck one" clap hands over head on "one"

   "mouse ran down" walk back two steps while lowering arms
   "hickory dickory dock" repeat pendulum swing (L-R-L) as before, ending with two quick stamps as before

5. Compose some new movements and add rhythm instruments to accompany.
6. Listen to the sounds of different kinds of clocks (wristwatches, clocks in towers, etc.) and try to imitate the sounds. Create movement inspired by the sound of each.
7. As the rhythm of each clock is determined (see number 6) compose a new song about that particular kind of clock, using the rhythm as the clue in determining the basic meter and tempo.
8. Relate ear training activities, for example, play a short series of tones either up or down. Ask the class, "Do you think this sounds like the mouse going up or coming down?" (See Ear Training, p. 231.)

Related activities and materials

1. Dramatize with characters of mouse and clock. Have children make a "living" clock by standing or lying on the floor in position. Show hands at 1 o'clock, then show hands at different times (lunch, recess, end of the day, etc.).
2. Use for counting: "How many times is the clock striking now?" Strike different numbers of times on bells, piano, triangle, etc.
3. Walk the shapes of various kinds of clocks.
4. Listening:
   "The Clock," Kullak, R3 RCA Basic Record Library.
   "Viennese Musical Clock," Kodaly, Keyboard Publications.
   Selections from "Clock Symphony" (No. 101), Haydn, RCA Vic #1262.
   "Syncopated Clock," Anderson, RCA LSC-2638.

For study

$\frac{6}{8}$ (compound) meter. Conduct in 2-bt.
pattern (See p. 269)

Chant rhythm and sing with syllables
(See pp. 277-278)

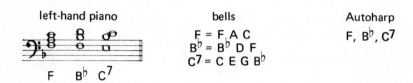

left-hand piano   bells   Autoharp

F = F A C
Bb = Bb D F
C7 = C E G Bb

F, Bb, C7

F   Bb   C7

13. THE FARMER IN THE DELL

Singing game

Level: L

Key of F: start middle C (low sol)

1. The far - mer in the dell, — The farm - er in the dell, —
2. The far - mer takes a wife, — The farm - er takes a wife, —
3. The wife —. takes the child, — The wife — takes the child, —
4. The child — takes the nurse, — The child — takes the nurse, —
5. The nurse — takes the dog, — The nurse — takes the dog, —
6., The dog — takes the cat, — The dog — takes the cat, —
7. The cat — takes the rat, — The cat — takes the rat, —
8. The rat — takes the cheese, — The rat — takes the cheese, —
9. The cheese — stands a - lone, — The cheese — stands a - lone, —

Heigh - ho, the Der - ry O!

The farm - er in the dell. —
The farm - er takes a wife. —
The wife — takes the child. —
The child — takes the nurse. —
The nurse — takes the dog. —
The dog — takes the cat. —
The cat — takes the rat. —
The rat — takes the cheese. —
The cheese — stands a - lone.

The action

1. When the song is learned, play as a singing game with traditional actions:

   Formation: circle with farmer in center.

   Walk around in circle with hands joined singing verse 1. On succeeding verses the farmer chooses a wife who in turn chooses child, etc. When the cheese enters, all return to the outer circle and the cheese stands alone in the center while the last verse is sung.

2. Use rhythm instruments in any of the following ways or as desired:

   a. Play a different instrument for each verse.

   b. Sound a different instrument only on the name as it occurs in the song, for example, "wife," "child."

   c. Choose a rhythm instrument to play only for selected words:

   hi—wood block, one tap (one count)
   ho—drum, one beat (one count)
   derry-o—shake tambourine (two counts)
   farmer in the dell (final words)—strike triangle three times and/or play resonator bells (A G F — *mi re do*).

3. Discuss some of the activities engaged in by farmers. Have different groups portray some of the activities in movement for others to guess. Create new verses about things a farmer does, for example, "The farmer plows his land." Do the movement, then select an appropriate rhythm instrument to accompany the movement.

4. Discuss the activities of farmers in other countries. Portray in movement as in number 3.

5. Add new verses with other subject matter:

   a. the keeper of the zoo, etc.

   b. the leader of the band (the leader takes the drum, etc.)

6. Sing as a partner song with any one or all three of the following:

   a. "Are You Sleeping?"

   b. "Three Blind Mice"

   c. "Row, Row, Row Your Boat" (see Partner Songs, p. 227)

7. Sing or play in a minor key using key signature of F minor:

   Discuss effect of change as to whether this sounds like a happy farmer or a sad farmer and what might make a farmer happy or sad. Create some verses for use with the minor key.

8. Using the same minor key as above, sing some Halloween words.*

   a. The goblin in the dark, etc.

   b. The goblin calls a witch, etc.

   c. The witch calls a bat, etc.

   d. The bat calls a ghost, etc.

   e. The ghost says "boo!" etc.

   f. They all scream and screech, etc.

   Use as a game song as in the original "Farmer in the Dell," with one child in the center as the "goblin."

9. Since this song uses only tones of the pentatonic scale, it may be easily played using all black keys, starting on $D\flat$. Improvise a descant or ostinato on the black keys to play along with the melody.

*From *Sharing Music,* Music for Young Americans Series, by permission of the American Book Company, ©1966.

Related activities and materials

1. Portray some aspect of farm life in any art media.

2. Listening:

   "Children's Symphony," third movement, AM 2 vol. 1.

   "Train to the Farm," YPRC Records.

   "Harvest Song," AM 1 vol. 2.

   See "Old MacDonald," no. 24 for additional related listening selections.

3. See the Classified Index for other singing games and songs related to farm life.

For study
$\frac{6}{8}$ (compound) meter, conduct in 2-bt.
pattern (See p. 269)
Chant rhythm and sing with syllables
(See pp. 277-278)
Tie
Uneven rhythm pattern

left-hand piano

bells

Autoharp

F = F A C
C^7 = C E G B$\flat$

F, C^7

14. HERE WE GO ROUND THE MULBERRY BUSH

Level: L
Key of G: start G (do)

Singing game

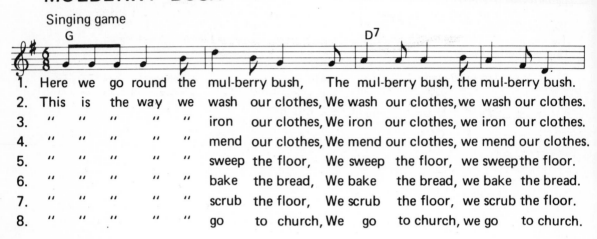

1. Here we go round the mul-berry bush, The mul-berry bush, the mul-berry bush.
2. This is the way we wash our clothes, We wash our clothes, we wash our clothes.
3. " " " " " iron our clothes, We iron our clothes, we iron our clothes.
4. " " " " " mend our clothes, We mend our clothes, we mend our clothes.
5. " " " " " sweep the floor, We sweep the floor, we sweep the floor.
6. " " " " " bake the bread, We bake the bread, we bake the bread.
7. " " " " " scrub the floor, We scrub the floor, we scrub the floor.
8. " " " " " go to church, We go to church, we go to church.

Here we go round the mul - berry bush, So ear - ly in the morn-ing.
This is the way we wash our clothes, So ear - ly Mon - day morn-ing.
" " " " " iron our clothes, " " " Tues - day morn-ing.
" " " " " " mend our clothes, " " " Wednes-day morn-ing.
" " " " " " sweep the floor, " " " Thurs - day morn-ing.
" " " " " " bake the bread, " " " Fri - day morn-ing.
" " " " " " scrub the floor, " " " Sat-ur -day morn-ing.
" " " " " " go to church, " " " Sun - day morn-ing.

The action

1. Add action as suggested by words:
   verse 1: walk in circle with hands joined.
   verses 2-8: stand in place and pantomime washing, ironing, etc.; insert first verse between each of the others, walking in circle each time it is sung.
2. Choose a different rhythm instrument to play with each action.
3. Without singing, the teacher claps the melody rhythm of the first phrase and the class claps the next. Alternate throughout the song.
4. Chant words in rhythm against words of "Hickory Dickory Dock" or "Jack and Jill." Substitute rhythm instruments for chanting, using a different instrument for each melody rhythm. If desired, add a third rhythm instrument to play the basic meter.
5. Create new verses to the same tune, then use

rhythm instruments for accompaniment. Change tempo and timbre of instrument chosen to suit world content and character of each verse, for example:

a. Here we go skipping round the room, etc.
b. This is the way the elephant walks, etc.
c. Dancing 'round the Christmas tree, etc.

6. Create new words about rhythm instruments and/or instruments of the orchestra and pantomime playing while singing, for example:

a. This is the way the triangle sounds, etc.
b. A tambourine can be shaken or rapped, etc.
c. A violin is played with a bow, etc.
   Try a guessing game in which children close their eyes and identify the instrument sounded by the teacher.

7. Sing the following words to the tune for a "stretch" time:
   Head, shoulders, knees and toes (sing three times).
   Clap, clap, bow.
   (Touch each part of the body as it occurs in the song.)

8. Some snowy day, sing the following words to the tune*:

a. Old Mother Goose is picking her geese
   Picking her geese, picking her geese,
   Old Mother Goose is picking her geese
   And throwing the feathers away.
b. Old Mother Goose is making it snow, etc.
   She's making it snow today.
   According to a Scandinavian legend, snowflakes are feathers that are plucked and thrown away by an old woman up in the sky.

9. Play and sing in minor, using the key signature of g minor:

Discuss the effect of the change, then create a new verse in the minor. (See Major and Minor.)

*From *Sharing Music,* Music for Young Americans Series, by permission of the American Book Company, ©1966.

Related activities and materials

1. Find similar singing games played by children in other parts of the world. (See p. 288.)
2. See "Bow, Belinda," no. 15, and "Jingle at the Windows," no. 36. See the classified index for others.
3. Listening:
   "The Sounds of Children," Tony Schwartz, Folkways Records.

"Children's Dance," from "Merry Mount Suite," Hanson, AM 5 vol. 1.
Selections related to "Old Mother Goose Is Picking Her Geese":
   "The Snow Is Dancing," BOL #68
   "Winter Morning," BOL #68.
4. Find a live mulberry bush, if possible, or a picture of one. Learn what the fruit looks and tastes like, as well as the value of the leaves.

For study

Like phrases
$\frac{6}{8}$ (compound) meter, conduct in 2-bt. pattern (See p. 269)
Chant rhythm and sing with syllables (See pp. 277-278)
Slur

left-hand piano

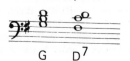

G   D7

bells

G = G B D
D7 = D F# A C

Autoharp

G, D7

15. BOW, BELINDA
Traditional

Level: L
Key of G: start G (do)

G   D⁷   D⁷

1. Bow,   bow,   bow, Be-lin - da,   Bow,   bow,   bow,   Be -lin - da,
2. Right   hand   up, Be-lin - da,   Right   hand   up,   Be -lin - da,

G   D⁷   G

Bow,   bow,   bow, Be-lin - da, Won't you be   my   dar - ling?
Right   hand   up, Be-lin - da, Won't you be   my   dar - ling?

3. Left hand up, Belinda,
   (three times)
Won't you be my darling?

4. Both hands up, Belinda, *etc.*
5. Shake your foot, Belinda, *etc.*
6. Promenade all, O Belinda, *etc.*

From Wilson, Ehret, Knuth, Hermann, and Rena, *Growing with Music*, Book 1, Related Arts edition, ©
1970 by Prentice-Hall, Inc., Englewood Cliffs, N.J., reprinted by permission.

The action

1. Dance as follows:
Formation: two lines of partners facing each other
   a. verse 1—partners walk forward, bow, and walk back to place
   b. verse 2—partners take right hands and turn
   c. verse 3—as in verse 2 with left hands
   d. verse 4—partners take both hands and turn
   e. verse 5—partners remain in place and shake foot or walk forward and pass back to back (do-si-do), then return to place; either movement may be done
   f. verse 6—take hands in skating position (crossed in front) and walk around room (head couple at top of line leads)

2. Create new verses with new actions.
3. Substitute names of class members for "Belinda."
4. Sing in different tempos and change to minor to illustrate various effects. Use key signature of g minor:
5. Sing as a partner song with "Ten Little Indians," no. 9.
6. Add harmony with chord root syllables (see p. 228).
7. Use a different rhythm instrument to accompany each verse.

Related activities and materials

1. Sing other American folk songs (see Classified Index).
2. Learn other American folk dances and singing games. Also:

"Let's Square Dance," RCA.
"Singing Games," RCA Basic Record Library.
"Singing Games," vols. 1, 2, 3, Bowmar.
"Play Party Games," vols. 1 and 2, Bowmar.

For study
    Like phrases
    Cut time
    Quarter rest
    Sequence
    Chant rhythm and sing syllables
    (See pp. 277-278)
    Conduct in 2-bt. pattern (See p. 269)

left-hand piano

G   D^7

bells   Autoharp

G = G B D   G, D^7
D^7 = D F♯ A C

chord root syllables

G = *do*
D7 = *sol*

ukulele

Tune: A D F♯ B (key of G tuning, See p. 238)

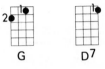

G   D^7

16. MY HANDS

Lucille F. Wood (words by Louise B. Scott)

Level: L

Key of F: start middle C (low sol)

The action

1. Add hand actions as suggested by the words.
2. Play a different rhythm instrument as each part of the body is mentioned in the song, for example, head, shoulders, etc.
3. Discover other sounds that may be made with hands—snapping fingers, tapping forearm, clapping with flat palms, cupped palms, or fingertips.
4. Add new verses using words about the newly discovered sounds in number 3.
5. Select rhythm instruments that sound like the hand sounds and use them to accompany the new verses.
6. Select one rhythm instrument to play on the A part of the song, another instrument to play on the B part, to point up the form of the song.
7. Add new verses, for example, "With my hands my book I'll hold."

Related activities and materials

1. Play a high-low game with hands and music, as follows: Have children stand and close their eyes while the teacher plays music in either a high or a low register (use piano, tape, record, etc.). The children should respond by raising their hands high in response to "high" sounds and stooping or bending over for "low" sounds.
2. See "Bear Hunt," no. 39A, for a story told with body sounds.
3. Sing other songs about parts of the body and do some finger plays. See pp. 38, 57, 144.

For study

Like phrases
Recurrence of *do-mi* skip
Compare dynamics with "Wiggle Song" no. 39 action
Chant rhythm and sing syllables (See pp. 277-278)
Conduct in 4-bt. pattern (See p. 269)

bells

$F = FAC$
$B\flat = B\flat\ D\ F$
$C^7 = C\ E\ G\ B\flat$

Autoharp

F, $B\flat$, C^7

17. I WIGGLE MY FINGERS

Lucille F. Wood (words by Louise B. Scott)

Level: L
Key of G: start low D (low sol)

Reprinted from Lucille F. Wood and Louise B. Scott, *Singing Fun,* © 1954, by permission of McGraw-Hill, Inc.

The action

1. Add the actions as suggested by the words.
2. Find other parts of the body to wiggle and substitute words in appropriate places in the song, for example, elbow, wrist, etc.
3. Divide class into two groups, each singing alternate lines, or have individual children sing one line each. For a variation, try being quiet on the word that indicates the part of the body (fingers, toes, etc.) and simply wiggle that part when the word occurs in the song.
4. Compose new verses to the same tune with actions other than wiggling, for example:
   I snap my fingers, I touch my nose
   I bend way over to look at my toes, etc.
5. Select a different rhythm instrument to play as each part of the body is mentioned—for example, sticks on "fingers," glissando on bells for "toes," shake tambourine for "shoulders," wood black for "nose."
6. Think of some creatures that wiggle all or parts of their bodies, then try to move as they do.
7. Make some body or vocal sounds to accompany the movement of each creature.

Related activities and materials
1. Sing other wiggle songs (p. 79) and other songs that mention parts of the body (p. 31).
2. For more fingerplays, see Scott and Thompson, *Rhymes for Fingers and Flannelboards,* Webster Division, New York: McGraw-Hill Book Co.

For study

Sequence

Insert appropriate dynamics symbols, which will build successively to a climax on "Now no more wiggles," etc.

bells

G = G B D
C = C E G
D7 = D F# A C

Autoharp

G, C, D7

ukulele
Tune: A D F# B (key of G tuning)

G

C

D7

18. EENCY WEENCY SPIDER
Traditional

Level: L
Key of F: start F (do)

Simply

Een - cy ween-cy spi - der went up the wa - ter spout, Down came the rain and

washed the spi-der out; Out came the sun and dried up all the rain, And

een - cy ween - cy spi - der went up the spout a - gain.

The action
1. Add actions as follows:
   - phrase 1—use fingers in climbing motion
   - phrase 2—lower arms from high level to waist level, palms facing down; on word "out" brush hands sideways in opposite directions
   - phrase 3—make big circle overhead with arms
   - phrase 4—repeat climbing motion of line 1
2. Sing first time with words and movement as in number 1. Second time, hum with movement. Third time—no singing or humming—just movement in time—while thinking the tune.
3. Sound a different rhythm instrument on each phrase:
   phrase 1—tap wood block on each beat
   phrase 2—shake tambourine throughout the line and rap on "out"
   phrase 3—strike triangle on each beat
   phrase 4—tap woodblock on each beat as in line 1
   To point up like phrases (1, 3, and 4), if desired, use the same instrument on these phrases and a different instrument on phrase 2, because the melody is different there.
4. Using the instruments and rhythm patterns suggested in number 3, try playing the song through in time, using the instruments only —no singing or playing the melody—just hearing the tune inside.
5. Select other rhythm instruments as desired.
6. Dramatize—letting individual children take the parts of sun, rain, spider, waterspout, etc.
7. Sing as a two-part round. Voice 2 enters when voice 1 begins the third measure.

Related activities and materials
1. Construct a visual (flannelboard, construction paper, etc.) showing waterspout with spider, sun, and rain. Have child add each part as it occurs in the song.
   Relate ear-training activities to the visual, for example, play an ascending series of tones on bells or piano. Ask the class, "Do you think this sounds like the spider climbing *up* or the rain coming *down*?" Let the child put the appropriate object on the picture for his answer. (See Ear Training.)
2. Listening:
   From "The Diary of a Fly," Mikrokosmos Suite No. 2, Bartok AM 1 vol. 2.
3. See Classified Index for other finger plays and songs of creatures.

For study

Uneven rhythm pattern
Like phrases
Sequence
Chant rhythm and sing with syllables (See pp. 277-278)
Conduct in 4-bt. pattern (See p. 269)

left-hand piano

F   C⁷

bottles

F = *do mi sol*
C⁷ = *sol ti re fa*

bells

F = F A C
C⁷= C E G B♭

ukulele

Tune: G C E A (key of F tuning p. 240)

F   C⁷

19. CABIN IN THE WOOD
Traditional

Level: L
Key of G: start D (low so

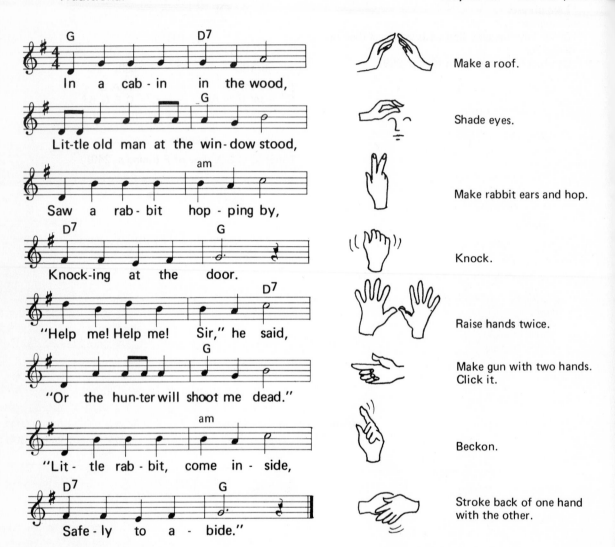

Make a roof.

Shade eyes.

Make rabbit ears and hop.

Knock.

Raise hands twice.

Make gun with two hands. Click it.

Beckon.

Stroke back of one hand with the other.

In a cab-in in the wood,
Lit-tle old man at the win-dow stood,
Saw a rab-bit hop-ping by,
Knock-ing at the door.
"Help me! Help me! Sir," he said,
"Or the hun-ter will shoot me dead."
"Lit-tle rab-bit, come in-side,
Safe-ly to a-bide."

From Edna Doll and Mary Jarman Nelson, *Rhythms Today,* © 1965 by Silver Burdett Co., reprinted by permission of the General Learning Corporation.

The action
1. After the words and melody are learned, add hand movements as shown.
2. Dramatize, using the chorus as narrator and having individual children act the parts of the hunter and the rabbit. The hunter and the rabbit may sing their parts as they occur or they may simply pantomime the actions while the chorus sings. Have another group of children form (outline) the shape of the cabin and window to make a "living" picture.
3. Use selected rhythm instruments to heighten dramatic effects in various places, for example, wood block on "knocking at the door," shake tambourine and rap on "help me," etc.

Related activities and materials
1. Look up the differences between a hare and a rabbit.
2. See "If Rabbit Was Bigger" (no. 32).

3. Listening:
   "Of Brer Rabbit," MacDowell, L3 RCA Basic Record Library.
   "The Hare and the Tortoise," BOL #51.

For study
Even rhythm
Insert appropriate dynamics symbols in selected places
Chant rhythm and sing with syllables (See pp. 277-278)

left-hand piano

G   D⁷   am

bells
G = G B D
D⁷ = D F♯ A C
a min = A C E

Autoharp
G, D⁷, a min.

20. WHEN THE SAINTS GO MARCHING IN

Level: U and L
Key of C: start middle C (do)

Traditional

The action

1. Clap or tap the basic beat of the meter (1-2-3-4, etc.).
2. Clap the rhythm of the melody while tapping the basic meter beat with the feet.
3. Accompany with drum and tambourine in the following rhythm

4. In lower grades sing the following words to the tune:*
   a. Oh when we march around the world
      Oh when we march around the world
      Oh don't you want to march 'round with us

* From *Sharing Music,* Music for Young Americans series, © 1966; by permission of the American Book Company.

When we march around the world?
b. Oh when we clap (x x) our hands like this (x x), etc.
c. Oh when we jump (x x) our feet like this (x x), etc.
d. Oh when we wave our hands up high, etc.
e. Oh when we skip around the moon, etc.
   Create new verses with other actions, then vary the tempo and dynamics of the verses according to the actions suggested in the new verses.
   Beat different rhythm patterns on the drum, characteristic of locomotor movements, such as walking, running, skipping. Have the children identify them by executing the appropriate movement immediately. Change from one to another without pause.
5. Sing as a partner song with verse part only. "Good Night Ladies" and/or "Swing Low Sweet Chariot."
6. Add the harmony part shown below.
7. Create new verses as desired, doing them in the same spirit as the original, for example, "Oh when the chariot comes for me."

Harmony part:

Related activities and materials

1. Research the New Orleans street band and its part in funerals. "When the Saints" was often played on such occasions.
2. Research the evolution of jazz as a unique American contribution. See Listening below, and "Joe Turner Blues" (no. 91).
3. Learn other old gospel tunes and spirituals. (nos. 44, 45, 47, 82)
4. Listening:
   "When the Saints" was recorded by a Dixieland combo (with the parts played by a rhythm section and the solo instruments excerpted for illustration). It may be heard in "Exploring Music," Grade 6 record album, Holt, Rinehart and Winston.
   "The Story of Jazz," Langston Hughes, Folkways.
   "A Child's Introduction to Jazz" Golden Records.
   "America: The Cradle of Jazz," "From Jazz to Rock" (FS and record) Keyboard Publications.

For study

Syncopation
Rests
Gospel songs and spirituals
Conduct in 4-bt. pattern (See p. 269)

left-hand piano

C   F   G⁷

bells

C = C E G
F = F A C
G⁷ = G B D F

Autoharp

C, F, G⁷

ukulele

Tune: G C E A (key of F tuning)

C   G⁷   F

21. THE BROON COO
Scottish folk song

Level: U and L
Key of F: start C (high sol)

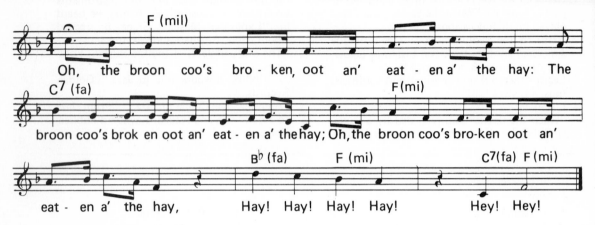

From *Basic Goals in Music,* Book 2, © 1967, McGraw-Hill Book Co. of Canada.

The action

1. After the song is well learned, try any or all of the following:
   a. Tap the basic meter with the feet while clapping the rhythm of the melody.
   b. Tap foot on first and third beats of the measure, clap hands on the second and fourth beats: tap clap tap clap, etc. Continue this throughout the song.
   c. In measure 1—on "broon" and "broken," slap sides
      measure 2—on "eaten" and "hay," clap hands
      measure 3—repeat actions as in measure 1
      measure 4—repeat actions as in measure 2
      measure 5—repeat actions as in measure 1
      measure 6—repeat actions as in measure 2
      measure 7—slap slap slap slap on words "hay hay hay hay"
      measure 8—tap foot on quarter rest, clap hands on "hey hey"
2. Add new verses about other farm animals.
3. Given a choice of *mi* or *fa* as the harmony note, let the class explore the harmonizing possibilities by ear, selecting either one of the notes for each measure or portion of the measure.
4. As an alternative to number 3, if preferred, teach the descant on page 45 or play on resonator bells.
5. Try the following dance steps in time to the music (the "Schottische" step is commonly associated with Scotland):

Position: Right hand on the hip, left hand in the air.
a. Point right toe to the side while hopping on left foot at the same time. One count. Bring right foot to back of left knee, hopping on left foot at the same time. One count.
Point right foot to the side as before, hopping on left foot at the same time. One count.
Bring right foot to front of left knee, hopping on left foot at the same time. One count.
(Chant: "point back, point front" for practice only) 1 2 3 4
b. "Schottische": step to the right on the right foot, bring left foot together with the right, step again to the right with right foot and hop on the right.
(Chant "step together step hop" for practice only.) Repeat Schottische step to the left beginning on the *left* foot.

Descant:

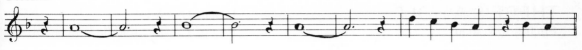

6. Select three different rhythm instruments to play the last two measures:

	measure 7	tambourine	R R R R
	measure 8	wood block	
		cymbals	

Related activities and materials

1. Research the history of the bagpipe and its use during war. Find instruments of other countries which also have a "drone."
2. Listen to a recording of a Scottish bagpipe or, if possible, bring one in for the class to see (some communities have bagpipe groups that perform on special occasions).
3. Listening:
   "Folk Instruments of the World" (record and pictures), Follett.
   "Hi-Fi in the Highlands," The Scots Guards,

Angel Records.
Folkways Records: selections from the following recordings:
"Scottish Bagpipe Music"
"Scottish Songs and Ballads"
"Songs and Ballads of the Scottish Wars"
4. Sing other Scottish songs, for example: "Comin' Thru the Rye," "Loch Lomond," "Weel May the Keel Row."
5. See Classified Index for other songs about farms and farm animals.

For study

Like phrases
Uneven rhythm pattern
Hold ⌒
Quarter rest in final measure (See p. 269)
Conduct in 4-bt. pattern

left-hand piano

F   B♭   C⁷

bells   Autoharp

F = F A C   F, B♭, C7
B♭ = B D F
C7 = C E G B♭

ukulele

Tune: G C E A (key of F tuning)

F   B♭   C7

22. THERE'S A HOLE
English folk song

Level: U and L
Key of F: start middle C (low sol)

1. There's a hole in the bot-tom of the sea, There's a hole in the bot-tom of the sea, There's a hole, There's a hole, There's a hole in the bot-tom of the sea.

2. There's a log in the hole, *etc.*
3. There's a bump on the log in the hole, *etc.*
4. There's a frog on the bump on the log, *etc.*
5. There's a wart on the frog, on the bump on the log, *etc.*

From *Basic Goals in Music,* Book 2, © 1967, McGraw-Hill Book Co. of Canada.

The action

1. Originate some actions for each verse.
2. Sound a different rhythm instrument for each object as it is mentioned in the song, for example: hole—drum; frog—shake tambourine; sea—cymbals.
3. In the early grades use a visual such as flannelboard and have the children add the objects to the scene as they occur in each verse.
4. Tap the basic meter while clapping the rhythm of the melody.
5. Create some new verses about other places, for example, "There's a tree in the middle of the wood."

6. In the middle grades explore simple harmonizing possibilities through the use of chord-root syllables (see p. 228) or by giving a choice of *mi* or *fa* as the harmonizing note for each measure. Find by ear where the change should occur and sing or play the appropriate harmonizing note.
7. Create body movement to represent the following:
   • waves coming in against the shore and receding
   • "underwater walk"
   • surfing
   • water-skiing

Related activities and materials

1. Discuss varying moods of the sea and portray in color to the music of "La Mer," using selected sections as desired.
2. Have the class portray in some art media the way they visualize the bottom of the sea.
3. Try to discover whether there really is a hole in the bottom of the sea.
4. "Dance-A-Story" of "At the Beach," RCA.
5. Listening:
   "Play of the Waves" from "La Mer," De-bussy, AM 6 vol. 2 and EIM.
   "Aquarium" from "Carnival of the Animals," Saint-Saëns, EIM and BOL #51.
   "Sand," AM 2 vol. 2.
   "Sounds of the Sea," vol. 1, Folkways Records #6121.
   "Sea Chanties," Robert Shaw Chorale, RCA LSC #2551.
6. Filmstrip: "The Seas About Us," Denoyer-Geppert AV.

For study

Uneven rhythm pattern
Sequence
Chant rhythm, then sing with syllables (See
p. 277-278)
Conduct in 4-bt. pattern (See p. 269)
Cumulative song

left-hand piano

bells

F = F A C
C7 = C E G Bb

Autoharp

F, C7

ukulele

Tune: G C E A (F tuning)

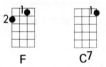

F   C7

23. ALOUETTE

French-Canadian folk song

Level: U and L
Key of G: start G (do)

3. *Le nez.*   4. *Le dos.*   5. *Les pattes.*   6. *Le cou.*

From Choate, Berg, Kjelson, and Troth, *Investigating Music,* New Dimensions in Music Series, © 1970 by the American Book Company, New York.

Gentil' Alouette' means "pretty meadow lark." *Je te plumerai* means "I shall pick off your feathers."
1. *La tête*: head. 2. *Le bec*: beak. 3. *Le nez*: nose.
4. *Le dos*: back. 5. *Les pattes*: feet. 6. *Le cou*: neck.

The action

1. When the song is well learned, have one child take the solo part, with the class joining in on the parts marked *All.*
2. Tap the basic meter with the feet while clapping the melody rhythm.
3. Point to the parts of the body as they occur in the song.
4. Choose a rhythm instrument to represent each part of the body and play it as that part is mentioned in the song. On "Alouette, gentil alouette," etc., together play all of the instruments that have been added in the verses.

5. Each time *Alouette, gentil Alouette,* etc., is sung, add the following action:

march in place	4 counts	♩ ♩ ♩ ♩
slap knees	4 counts	♩ ♩ ♩ ♩
snap fingers	4 counts	♩ ♩ ♩ ♩
clap hands	3 counts	♩ ♩ ♩ 𝄽

6. Write some new verses.

Related activities and materials

1. Sing other songs that mention parts of the body. See "Head, shoulders, knees, and toes," p. 31.
2. Sing other French-Canadian folk songs:
   "Donkey Riding," EM 4.
   "En Roulant ma Boule," MMYO 3.
   "Viva la Canadienne," MMYO 3.

3. Listening:
   "Songs of French Canada," Folkways.
   "Children's Game Songs of French Canada," Folkways #7214.
   "Folk Songs of French Canada," Folkways #3560.
   "Songs and Dances of Quebec," Folkways Records #6951.

For study

Uneven rhythm
D. C. *al Fine*
Repeat sign
mf
Hold ⌒
Conduct in 4-bt. pattern (See p. 269)
Cumulative song

left-hand piano

G   D⁷

bells
G = G B D
D⁷ = D A C

Autoharp
G, D⁷

ukulele
Tune: A D F♯ B (key of G tuning)

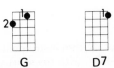

G   D7

24. OLD MACDONALD

Traditional

Level: U and L
Key of G: start G (do)

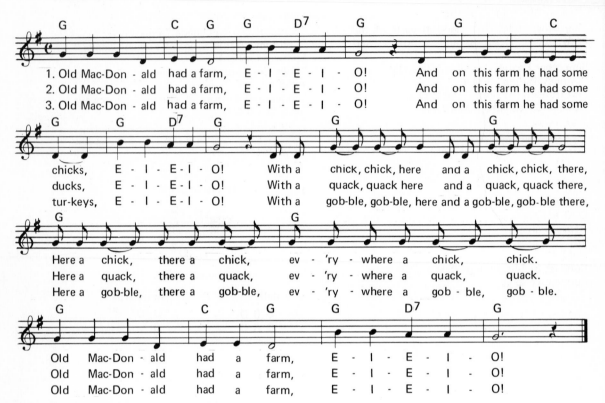

1. Old Mac-Don-ald had a farm, E - I - E - I - O! And on this farm he had some
2. Old Mac-Don-ald had a farm, E - I - E - I - O! And on this farm he had some
3. Old Mac-Don-ald had a farm, E - I - E - I - O! And on this farm he had some

chicks, E - I - E - I - O! With a chick, chick, here and a chick, chick, there,
ducks, E - I - E - I - O! With a quack, quack here and a quack, quack there,
tur-keys, E - I - E - I - O! With a gob-ble, gob-ble, here and a gob-ble, gob-ble there,

Here a chick, there a chick, ev - 'ry - where a chick, chick.
Here a quack, there a quack, ev - 'ry - where a quack, quack.
Here a gob-ble, there a gob-ble, ev - 'ry - where a gob - ble, gob - ble.

Old Mac-Don - ald had a farm, E - I - E - I - O!
Old Mac-Don - ald had a farm, E - I - E - I - O!
Old Mac-Don - ald had a farm, E - I - E - I - O!

The action

1. Select a group of rhythm instruments to play only on "E-I-E-I-O," with the short-sounding instruments, such as sticks and wood blocks, on the "E-I" parts and the longer-sounding instruments, such as triangles and finger cymbals, on the "O" each time it occurs.
2. Add new verses, using:
   a. other animals and their sounds, for example, donkey
   b. rhythm instruments instead of farm objects, for example, "Old MacDonald had a band," and "in his band he had a drum," etc.
   c. some aspects of contrasting city life or other subject matter
3. Create some visuals of the subjects included and display them in the order of their occurrence in the song.
4. Add harmony through the use of chord-root syllables (see p. 228) or choose between *mi* and *fa* as the harmonizing note for each measure.
5. Since this melody is built on the tones of the pentatonic scale (*do re mi sol la*), it may be played on the black keys only (of the piano or song bells). Give the children the starting tone of G♭ and let them find the tune by ear on their instruments.
6. Explore other familiar tunes built on the tones of the pentatonic scale—for example,

"The Farmer in the Dell," "Mary Had a Little Lamb," "Auld Lang Syne." (See p. 266)

7. Create some new tunes using the tones of the pentatonic scale. Add original words if you like.

8. Create some body movement depicting each of the animals.

9. Portray the cycle of a seed in movement.

10. Explore various tasks on a farm. Perform the movements involved. Find the rhythm and tempo of each task, then create a work song about it.

Related activities and materials

1. Listening:
   "Happy Farmer," BOL #64.
   "Children's Symphony," 3rd movement, AM 2 vol. 1.
   "Ballet of the Unhatched Chicks," EIM record album and AM 1 vol. 1.

   "Hens and Cocks: Long-Eared Personages," from "Carnival of the Animals," EIM record album and BOL #51.

2. "Dance-A-Story of Little Duck," RCA.

3. For other songs of the farm and farm animals (See pp. 15, 24, 27)

For study

Tie = Observe when singing one-syllable words. Do not observe when singing two-syllable words

Like phrases

Chant rhythm, then sing with syllables (See pp. 277-278)

Conduct in 4-bt. pattern (See p. 269)

left-hand piano

G   C   D⁷

chord root syllables

G = *do*
C = *fa*
D7 = *sol*

Autoharp

G, C, D7

ukulele

Tune: A D F♯ B (key of G tuning)

G   D7   C

25. SHE'LL BE COMIN' ROUND THE MOUNTAIN

Level: U and L
Key of F: start middle C (low sol)

Traditional

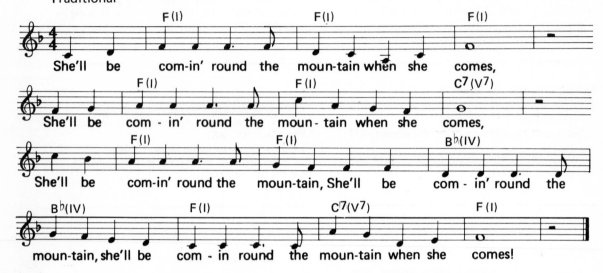

2. She'll be drivin' six white horses when she comes, *etc.*
3. Oh, we'll all go out to meet her when she comes, *etc.*
4. Oh, we'll all have chicken and dumplin's when she comes, *etc.*

The action

1. Add the following sound effects and action at the end of each line:
   a. verse 1—"woo woo" like a train whistle (pull-cord motion)
   b. verse 2—"whoa back" (pull reins back)
   c. verse 3—"hi there" (describe semicircle with hand, palm facing forward, as in greeting)
   d. verse 4—"yum yum" (rub tummy)
2. Add other verses and actions.
3. Choose rhythm instruments for sounds as desired in each verse.
4. Have half of the class sing the root syllable of the given chord while the other half sings the melody of the song. (See p. 228)
5. Have the class find a simple harmony by ear, choosing between *mi* and *fa* as a harmonizing note for each measure.
6. Accompany with bottles or three-part vocal chording.

7. Try the following simple dance:

> Formation: circle; the girls on right of the boys, or simply partners designated by number 1 and number 2.
> measures 1-4: take hands and circle left eight steps (eight counts)
> measures 5-8: circle right eight steps (eight counts)
> measures 9-10: hook right elbows with partner and swing four steps (four counts)
> measures 11-12: hook left elbows with partners and swing four steps (four counts)
> measures 13-16: number 2's (or girls) all move one to the right so that all number 1's will have new partners. Greet new partner with bow or curtsy (seven counts)
> repeat as desired

For study

Chant rhythm pattern and sing with syllables
(See pp. 277-278)
Half rest
Chord root syllables for harmonizing (See p.
228)
Conduct in 4-bt. pattern

left-hand piano

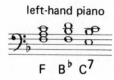

F   B♭ C⁷

bells

F = F A C
B♭ = B♭ D F
C7̄ = C E G B♭

Autoharp

F, B♭, C7

bottles

F = *do mi sol*
B♭ = *fa la do*
C7 = *sol ti re fa*
(See p. 251)

chord root syllables

F = *do*
B♭ = *fa*
C7 = *sol*

ukulele

Tune: G C E A (key of F tuning)

F

C7

B♭

26. BICYCLE BUILT FOR TWO
Words and music by Harry Dacre

Program song
Level: U
Key of G: start D (high sol)

Liltingly

1. Dai - sy,   Dai - sy,   Give me your an - swer do.
2. Mi - chael, Mi - chael, Here is your an - swer true. —

I'm   half   cra - zy,   All for the love of you. —
You're half   cra - zy,   If you think that will do. —

It   won't be a   sty - lish   mar-riage,   I   can't   af -
If   you can't af - ford   a   car- riage, —   There won't be

ford   a   car-riage,   But you'll look sweet   up -
an - y   mar-riage, —   For   I'll   be switched if

on   the   seat Of a bi - cy - cle built for   two. —
I'll get hitched On a bi - cy - cle built for   two. —

From Wilson, Ehret, Knuth, Hermann, and Renna, *Growing with Music*, Book 3, © 1966 by Prentice-Hall, Inc., Englewood Clifs, N.J., reprinted by permission.

The action

1. Reenforce feeling for the three-beat meter by doing one action on the first beat of each measure and two contrasting actions on the second and third beats, for example, tap, clap, clap, etc.
2. Divide the class into boys and girls for one verse each, or assign solo parts.
3. Sing with "Calliope Song" (no. 27) as a descant. Transpose the song into the key of G (see Transposing).
4. Accompany with bottles (p. 252) or three-part vocal chording, using oom-pah-pah rhythm (p. 229).

5. With a little simple costuming such as large hats and parasols for the girls and straw hats for the boys, this can be an appealing program number. A group may sing while four or six couples do the following pantomime (or create some original movement). If space allows, the whole group may participate:
verse 1
meas. 1-8: boy on bended knee in proposing position with hat clasped against chest
meas. 9-16: more ardent and pleading gestures
meas. 17-24: up on feet and turn out pockets

to show that they are empty
meas. 25-32: bow and imitate bicycle riding (hands on handlebars)
verse 2
meas. 1-8: girls rest both hands on parasol, looking haughty
meas. 9-16: shakes head, throws arms out
meas. 17-24: pantomimes riding in carriage (back very straight, head held high), stamps foot, and turns back on "won't"
meas. 25-32: faces boy—hands on hips—still looking haughty—and pantomimes getting "hitched" (hold imaginary wedding bouquet) and riding bicycle.
Add more action and interest with a little more pantomime, for example, boy goes off dejectedly. (The chorus is humming throughout all of this.) Another boy (city slicker) rides up in early vintage automobile (made of cardboard—side view to audience showing wheels, etc.). Girl gets in looking very self-satisfied. Short ride, then sound effect of tire blowing out (slide whistle down). Boy gets out. Makes helpless gesture. Girl looks disgusted. First boy rides by on bicycle (also drawn on cardboard with wheel side to audience). Girl waves eagerly and hopefully—in search of ride. Boy keeps head high and rides by with no backward glance. Girl is properly humbled. All couples take original positions to finish last two lines beginning, "But you'll look sweet."

Related activities and materials

1. Look up other kinds of cycles (tricycles, unicycles, etc.). Create a verse about any of them.

2. Sing other Gay 90's songs, for example, "While Strolling through the Park One Day."

For study

$\frac{3}{4}$ meter

Tie

Chant rhythm and sing with syllables (See pp. 277-278)

Harmonize by ear while listening to Autoharp accompaniment

Conduct in 3-bt. pattern (See p. 269)

left-hand piano

G   C   D7   A7

bells
G = G B D
C = C E G
D7 = D F♯ A C
A7 = A C♯ E G

Autoharp
G, C, D7, A7

ukulele

Tune: A D F♯ B (key of G tuning)

G   D7   C   A7

27. CALLIOPE SONG

Key of F: start F (do)

Oh, haw, haw: Oh, haw, haw.   Tweed-le dee, dee,   Um, paw, paw.

From *Second Fun and Folk Song Proof Book*, Cooperative Recreation Service, Delaware, Ohio, used by permission.

For study

Note: this tune must be transposed into the key of the song with which it is to be used (See Transposing, p. 273)

28. TWINKLE, TWINKLE, LITTLE STAR

Level: U and L
Key of C: start middle C (do)

Traditional

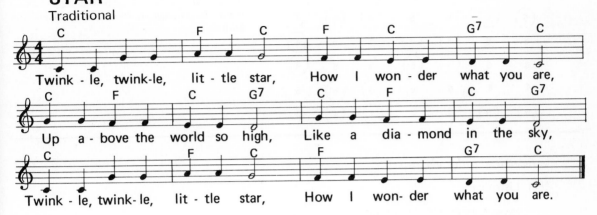

Twink - le, twink-le, lit - tle star, How I won - der what you are,
Up a - bove the world so high, Like a dia - mond in the sky,
Twink - le, twink-le, lit - tle star, How I won- der what you are.

TWINKLE, TWINKLE (in minor key)

Key of c minor: start middle C (la)

The action

1. At the primary level, use this tune for the words of the finger play, "Two Little Blackbirds":
Two little blackbirds sitting on a hill [make two fists with thumbs up]
One named Jack and the other named Jill [wiggle thumbs in turn]
Fly away Jack, fly away Jill [put hands behind back in turn]
Come back Jack, come back Jill [hands in front in turn]
Two little blackbirds sitting on a hill [repeat as in line 1]
One named Jack and the other named Jill [repeat as in line 2]

The same tune may also be used for the "Alphabet Song." (A,B,C,D,E,F,G, etc.)

2. Make up new verses about other heavenly bodies such as the moon.

3. Create an original percussion score to play with rhythm instruments. When determining orchestration, consider using the same instruments for like phrases and different instruments for unlike phrases—in order to emphasize repetition and contrast.

4. Sing as a canon, with the second voice entering as the first voice completes the first measure.

5. Accompany with resonator bells, bottles (p. 251), or vocal chording (p. 229).

6. Play on the harmonica.

4	4	6	6	(6)	(6)	6
(5)	(5)	5	5	(4)	(4)	4
6	6	(5)	(5)	5	5	(4)
6	6	(5)	(5)	5	5	(4)
4	4	6	6	(6)	(6)	6
(5)	(5)	5	5	(4)	(4)	4

7. Change the key signature to C minor (see page 57). Play or sing in a minor key, then discuss the difference in feeling resulting from the change in mode. (See Major and Minor)

Related activities and materials

1. Listening:
   Variations on "Ah Vous Dirai-Je Maman," Mozart, MMYO 6 record album, Silver Burdett.
   Variations on a Nursery Song," Donanhyi.

For study

Like phrases
Chant rhythm and sing with syllables (See pp. 277-278)
Conduct in 4-bt. pattern (See p. 269)

left-hand piano

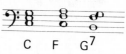

C   F   G⁷

bells
C = C E G
F = F A C
G⁷ = G B D F

Autoharp
C, F, G⁷

bottles
C = *do mi sol*
F = *fa la do*
G⁷ = *sol ti re fa*

vocal chording
(see p. 229)

29. HUSH, LITTLE BABY

American folk song

Level: U and L
Key of F: start middle C (low sol)

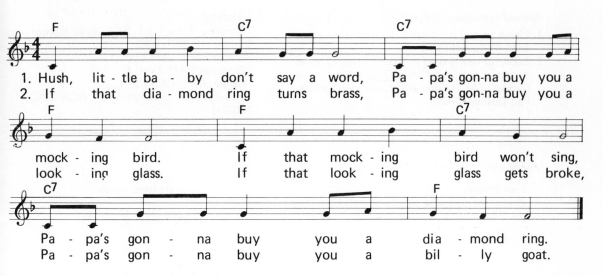

1. Hush, lit - tle ba - by don't say a word, Pa - pa's gon-na buy you a mock - ing bird. If that mock - ing bird won't sing, Pa - pa's gon - na buy you a dia - mond ring.

2. If that dia - mond ring turns brass, Pa - pa's gon-na buy you a look - ing glass. If that look - ing glass gets broke, Pa - pa's gon - na buy you a bil - ly goat.

The action

1. Both "Hush, Little Baby" and "All the Pretty Little Horses" (page 61) are lullabies, yet they have very different sounds. Try to discover what specific musical elements in each song contribute to the difference (tempo, rhythm pattern, mode, etc.).

2. Hold an imaginary baby in arms and sway gently in time to the music, or pretend to sit in a rocking chair with the baby in arms and rock forward and backward in time to the music.

3. "All the Pretty Little Horses"
   a. Choose a suitable accompaniment which will be in keeping with the mood of the song, for example a gentle shake of a tambourine throughout the first two beats of each measure, followed by finger cymbals on the third beat. A soft clip-clop with coconut shells or woodblocks may also be used.
   b. Discuss the colors of the horses mentioned in the song (dapple, bay, etc.). Show pictures, if possible. Look up other unfamiliar colors of horses, such as "strawberry roan."

4. "Hush, Little Baby"
   a. Change the song from F major to f minor by adding three more flats to the one-flat key signature:

   Listen to the way the song sounds in a minor key, then compare it again with "All the Pretty Little Horses."
   b. Sound a different rhythm instrument on each of the objects as they are mentioned in the song (mockingbird, triangle; diamond ring, cymbal; etc.).
   c. Add new verses with new objects.
   d. Add the following descant:

   or let the class discover the *mi fa* changes by ear first, and then create the descant themselves. Accompany with Autoharp.
   e. Accompany with three-part vocal chording or bells.

Related activities and materials

1. Listen to and learn some lullabies from other parts of the world.
2. Look up words used in the language of other countries to lull babies to sleep. (See Leslie Daiken, *The Lullaby Book,* Chester Springs, Pa.: Dufour, 1961.)

3. Listening:
   "Sleeping Time," L1 RCA Basic Record Library and BOL #68.
   "Cradle Song," AM 1 vol. 1.
   "Berceuse," AM 2 vol. 1.
   "Barcarolle," AM 3 vol. 1.
   "Lullabies for Sleepyheads," RCA CAS 1003(e).

For study

Like phrases
Chant rhythm and sing with syllables (See pp. 277-278)

left-hand piano

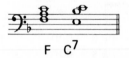

F   C^7

bells

F = F A C
C^7 = C E G B♭

Autoharp

F, C^7

ukulele

Tune: G C E A (key of F tuning)

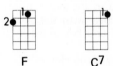

F   C^7

30. ALL THE PRETTY LITTLE HORSES

American folk song

Level: U and L
Key of d minor: start D (la)

From Dorothy Scarborough, *On the Trail of Negro Folk Songs,* © 1925 by Harvard University Press, Cambridge, Mass.: reprinted by permission of the publisher.

The action (See p. 59)

For study
Like phrases
Minor (See Major and Minor, and Minor Scales) *la-mi* skip characteristic of minor mode

Note major feeling beginning on third phrase, then return to minor feeling on "horses" (meas. 12)
Chant rhythm pattern, then sing with syllables (See pp. 277-278)

bells
d min = D F A
g min = G B♭ D
C7 = C E G B♭
B♭ = B♭ D F
F = F A C

31. JINGLE AT THE WINDOWS
Singing game

Level: U and L
Key of D: start F   (mi)

Pass one win-dow, ti - de - o, Pass two win-dows, ti - de - o,

Pass three win-dows, ti - de - o, Jin-gle at the win-dows, ti - de - o.

Ti - de - o, ti - de - o, Jin-gle at the win - dows, ti - de - o.

From *Exploring Music* series (teachers' ed.), Book 1 ©1966, by special permission of the publisher, Holt, Rinehart and Winston.

The action

1. When the song has been learned well, add these movements:
   a. make a single circle of partners (if there are girls and boys, the girl should be to the right of the boy)
   b. face clockwise. Each child places his left hand on the right shoulder of the one in front of him. March around (clockwise) in a circle, in time to the music in measures 1 to 8
   c. in measures 9 to 12 hook right elbow with partner and swing in place
   d. in repeat of measures 9 to 12, hook the left elbow with your partner and swing in place

   Repeat (a) through (d) as desired. Partners may be changed by having girls step one boy to the left at the end of the dance each time.

2. Add rhythm instruments as desired or as follows:

   measure 1: sticks play four times

   measure 2: finger cymbals play three times

   measure 3: sticks
               and
               woodblocks

measure 4: finger cymbals as in measure 2

measure 5: sticks
            and
            woodblocks
            and
            tambourine
                               R S R S

measure 6: finger cymbals as in measure 2
measure 7: shake tambourine and/or bells throughout
measure 8: finger cymbals as in measure 2
measure 9-10: triangle and finger cymbals

measure 11: see measure 7 above
measure 12: triangle and finger cymbals

3. Add harmony by having half the class sing the root syllable of the given chord, while the other half sings the melody of the song. (See p. 228.)

Related activities and materials

1. Listening:
   "Children's Dance" from "Merry Mount Suite," Hanson, AM 5 vol. 1.
   "Children's Symphony," 1st movement, McDonald, AM 3 vol. 2.

2. Learn other singing games.
   "Singing Games," RCA Basic Record Library.
   "Play Party Games," albums 1 and 2, BOL.

For study

Like phrases
Even rhythm pattern
Repeat sign :‖
Chant rhythm and sing with syllables (See pp. 277-278)
Transpose to key of C and accompany with Autoharp (See Transposing)
Conduct in 2-bt. pattern (See p 269)

left-hand piano

D   A7

bells

D = D F♯ A
A7 = A C♯ E G

ukulele

Tune: A D F♯ B (key of G tuning)

32. IF RABBIT WAS BIGGER

Level: U and L
Key of C: start G (sol)

Quickly

If rab-bit was big-ger And fat-ter and strong-er, Or big-ger than Tig-ger, If Tig-ger was smal-ler, Then Tig-ger's bad hab-it Of bounc-ing at Rab-bit Would mat-ter No long-er, If Rab-bit was tal-ler,

From A. A. Milne and Fraser-Simpson *The Pooh Song Book* E. P. Dutton. Reprinted by permission of Curtis Brown Ltd., London

The action:

1. Dramatize the song, with the children taking the parts of Rabbit and Tigger—becoming "smaller" and "taller" as these words occur in the song.
2. Find out what other creatures jump or hop in order to move (kangaroo, cricket, frog, etc.) and imitate their movement.
3. Do the "bunny hop," as follows: (Note: this dance is not meant to fit this music, thus it will be necessary to create a song for it or to find some appropriate recorded music in either $\frac{2}{4}$ or $\frac{4}{4}$ time).

Formation: single line with hands on the waist of the person in front

a. kick L foot out to the left and hop on R foot at the same time. Do this movement *twice*

b. repeat (a) with the right foot (kick right foot out to the right and hop on left foot at the same time); do twice

c. jump forward on both feet

d. jump backward on both feet

e. three jumps forward on both feet

Accompany dance with selected rhythm instruments if desired.

Related activities and materials

1. Dramatize some selected stories from *Winnie The Pooh* or *The House at Pooh Corner.*
2. Listening:
   "Of Brer Rabbit," L3 RCA Basic Record Library.
   "The Hare and the Tortoise," BOL #52.
   "Winnie the Pooh Stories," RCA CAS-1008(e).
3. For another Pooh song, see "Isn't It Funny?" no. 33.

Note: "Isn't It Funny" and "If Rabbit Was Bigger," as well as many other songs of Pooh, may be found in "The Pooh Song Book," published by E. P. Dutton and Co., New York. The illustrations by E. H. Shepard are delightful. If you feel that your children are too young to learn these songs, you might consider singing them for the children to hear.

For study

$\frac{6}{8}$ (compound) meter. Conduct in 2-bt. pattern (See p. 269)
Chromatic tone (meas. 14)
Tempo terms: rit. a tempo (See Glossary)
Even rhythm pattern

33. ISN'T IT FUNNY?

Level: U and L
Key of G: start E (la)

Isn't it fun-ny How a bear likes hon-ey? Buzz! Buzz! Buzz! I

won-der why he does? It's a ve-ry fun-ny thought that if Bears were Bees, they'd

build their nests at the bot-tom of trees. And that be-ing so (if the Bees were Bears) We

should-n't have to climb— up — all these stairs. —

From A. A. Milne and Fraser-Simpson *The Pooh Song Book* E. P. Dutton. Reprinted by permission of Curtis Brown Ltd., London

The action

1. Add sound effects with rhythm instruments.
2. Make up a dance such as Pooh might do to the music.
3. Write a poem about a favorite teddy bear, then put a tune to it. Use resonator bells or piano to improvise the tune, if desired.
4. Explore the following, then create a song about one or more, as desired:
   a. favorite foods of bears
   b. how honey is made
   c. the look, taste, and feel of honey

Related activities and materials

1. Illustrate the song with some art media.
2. Dramatize some selected stories from *Winnie the Pooh* or *The House at Pooh Corner.*
3. Listening:
   "Tame Bears," L2 RCA Basic Record Library.
   "Flight of the Bumblebee," EIM record album and BOL #52.
   "The Bee," Bol #64.
   "Bear Dance," Bartok, AM 3 vol. 2.
4. See another Pooh song, "If Rabbit Was Bigger," no. 32.

For study

Triplet
Rhythm patterns

Sixteenth rest

Tie on "stairs"
Conduct in 2-bt. pattern (See p. 269)

34. THE NOBLE DUKE OF YORK

English folk song (added verses by Mary Dutre)

Level: U and L
Key of A♭ : start C (mi)

Briskly

1. Oh, the no-ble Duke of York, He had ten thou-sand men, He marched them up to the top of the hill, And he marched them down a-gain.
2. Oh, when they were up they were up, When they were down they were down, But when they were on-ly half-way — up, They were nei-ther up nor down.

3. Oh, the noble Duke of York
   Saluted all his men,
   Saluted with his left and right,
   And saluted them again.

4. Oh, the noble Duke of York
   Rode a noble mount, of course,
   But he fell on his head and thought he was dead
   Till he got back on his horse.

From Wilson, Ehret, Knuth, Hermann, and Renna, *Growing with Music*, Book 1, Related Arts Edition, © 1970 by Prentice-Hall, Inc., Englewood Cliffs, N.J.; reprinted by permission.

The action

1. When the song is well learned, add the following action:
   verses 1 and 2: on word "up," stand
       on word "down," sit
       on words "half way up," assume position halfway between up and down
   verse 3: salute as indicated
   verse 4: on words "fell on his head," put head on desk
       on words "got back on his horse," resume sitting position
2. Without singing, the teacher claps the melody rhythm of the first line and the class claps the second. Alternate lines throughout the song.
3. Select a rhythm instrument to sound for each action, for example, cymbals for "up," drum for "down," tambourine shaken for "halfway," etc.
4. Play a listening game, as follows:
   The teacher first specifies the verse, then plays a portion of the melody from any place in the song. The class must identify the section by responding in movement with the appropriate action.

5. Using the same tune, sing the following words:

   Oh, a-hunting we will go, a-hunting we will go
   We'll catch a fox and put him in a box
   And then we'll let him go.

6. Using the words in number 5, try the following traditional dance:

Formation: two lines with partners facing each other
measures 1-4: head couple join both hands and take eight slides down the center, the length of the lines
measures 5-8: head couple take eight slides back to position
repeat of measures 1-4: head couple separate and lead off down the outside of each line, with the line following behind
repeat of measures 5-8: as head couple meet at the foot of the line, they form an arch under which all other couples pass, leaving a new head couple at the top ready to repeat the figure. While the head couple slide down and back, others should clap in time.

Related activities and materials

1. Discuss the meaning of "Duke." Find out about other titles, for example "Earl" and their origin.

2. For other singing games and dances, see the following albums:
   "Let's Square Dance," RCA Album No. 1.
   "Singing Games," RCA.

For study

Hold ⌢
Transpose to key of G and play on autoharp (See Transposing p. 273)
Note how tonal directions in measures 5 through 8 reflect the words
Conduct in 2-bt. pattern (See p. 269)

35. SOLDIER, SOLDIER

American folk song

Level: U
Key of G: start D (low sol)

She: O sol - dier, sol - dier, won't you mar-ry me, With your mus-ket, fife and

drum? He: O no, sweet maid, I can - not mar - ry thee, For I

have no coat[1] to put on. All: Then up she went to her
(fifth time) a wife of my own.

Fine *p* Faster

grand - fa-ther's chest, And got him a coat[1] of the ver-y ver-y best She

got him a coat[1] of the ver-y ver-y best, And the sol - dier put it — on

f *rit.*   *D.C. al Fine*

[2]hat [3]gloves [4]boots

From *Making Music Your Own,* Book 5, © 1971 General Learning Corporation; reprinted by permission.

The action

1. When the song is well learned, dramatize it. The soldier and maid may sing solo parts, with the chorus singing the narrative sections, or if desired, the chorus may sing the entire song with the soldier and maid pantomiming the action. On the last line "... a wife of my own," the maid might convey a feeling of hopelessness by holding her head in a gesture of "oh no, not that!" and exit dejectedly, or stamp her foot, fold her arms, toss her head and walk off with a haughty air.

2. Use a different rhythm instrument to represent each article of clothing as it occurs in the song, as well as sound effects such as walking upstairs or opening a chest. When the word "wife" occurs, it would add to the humor if some unusual sound could be made. Let the children explore the possibilities with "found" instruments, as well as with traditional instruments. If there is a drummer in the class, let him play a short drum roll at the word "soldier" every time it occurs in the song.

3. Divide the class into groups. Let each group work out its own interpretation of the ideas expressed in the words. Suggest that phrases which repeat be interpreted with movements which repeat.

Related activities and materials

1. The words "musket," and "fife" are a clue to the period of this song and may need further explanation. Perhaps some of the children may have such articles at home, or pictures may be available. In this connection, have the class listen to some of the various drum calls used as signals during that period*:

"Wood call" (telling men to go chop the wood for fires)

"Call to arms" (signal to assemble and wait for orders)

The drum call for "cease firing" was also accompanied by the fife:

Drum

If drumsticks are available, the children might wish to try some of these calls or to make up some of their own.

2. See "Deaf Woman's Courtship," no. 36.
3. Listening:
   "Drum Beats Around the World," Keyboard Publications, New Haven, Conn.
   "America: Its History Through Music," Keyboard Publications, New Haven, Conn.
   "Chester," from "New England Triptych," W. Schuman, EM 5 record album, Holt, Rinehart and Winston.
   "Our American Heritage of Folk Music" (FS and record), SVE.
   "Folk Songs in American History: The Revolutionary War" (FS and record).
4. Film: "Discovering American Folk Music," Film Associates.

*From *Drums Call the Patriots,* Keyboard Publications, New Haven, Conn.; used by permission. Recorded sounds of these drum calls, plus others from around the world, may be found in "Drum Beats Around the World," published by Keyboard Publications, New Haven, Conn.

For study

Dynamics and tempo: f, rit., cres. p
D.C. *al Fine*
Like phrases
Dialogue song

36. DEAF WOMAN'S COURTSHIP

American folk song

Program song
Level: U
Key of D: start A (sol)

With humor

1. Old wom-an, old wom-an, Are you fond of card - ing?
2. Old wom-an, old wom-an, Are you fond of spin - ning?

Old wom-an, old wom-an, Are you fond of card-ing?
Old wom-an, old wom-an, Are you fond of spin-ning?

Speak a lit - tle loud - er, sir! I'm ver - y hard of hear - ing.
Speak a lit - tle loud - er, sir! I'm ver - y hard of hear - ing.

3. Old woman, old woman, Will you darn my stocking? (*2 times*)
   Speak a little louder, sir! I'm very hard of hearing.

4. Old woman, old woman, Will you let me court you? (*2 times*)
   Speak a little louder, sir! I just begin to hear you.

5. Old woman, old woman, Don't you want to marry me? (*2 times*)
   Oh, my goodness gracious me! I think that now I hear you!

From *Exploring Music* Series (teacher's edition), Book 3, © 1966 by Holt, Rinehart and Winston; by special permission of the publisher.

The action

1. Sing as a dialogue song, using two groups or two solo voices. Add humor by having the boys sing very softly on verse 4 and even more softly on verse 5.
2. Dramatize as desired.
3. Use rhythm instruments adapted to the dynamics of the voices in each of the verses, as well as to word content.
4. Create a dance in the style of the early American folk dance. If the song is used as part of a program, sing the verses first, then perform the dance while the tune alone is played on a recorder or other melody instrument or sung by a chorus on *la*. Accompany with autoharp. (Transpose to key of C; see Transposing.) Add rhythm instruments as suggested in number 3.

2. See "Soldier, Soldier," no. 35. For other dialogue songs and American folk songs, see Index.
3. Listening:
   "America: Its History Through Music," Keyboard Publications, New Haven, Conn.
   "American Folk Songs for Children," Folkways Records 60101.

For study

Like phrases
Even rhythm
Recurrence of tonic chord in melody
Chant rhythm and sing with syllables (See pp. 277-278)
Transpose to key of C for use with autoharp (See Transposing)
Dialogue song

Related activities and materials

1. Learn about the meaning of "carding," as well as other processes in wool production.

37. POP GOES THE WEASEL

Traditional

Level: U and L
Key of E♭ : start E♭ (do)

All a-round the cob-bler's bench the mon-key chased the wea - sel The mon-key thought 'twas

all — in fun. Pop   goes the   wea - sel, A pen - ny for   a spool   of thread, a

pen-ny for a nee - dle, That's the way the mon - ey goes Pop   goes the wea - sel.

The action

Explain the meaning of "pop" and "weasel." (Tailors in early times were known to "pop" (pawn) their "weasel" (iron) when they needed money.)

1. Let the class suggest several different sounds that might be substituted for the word *pop* when it occurs in the song, then execute.
2. Substitute silence for the word *pop* and come in on time on the remaining words.
3. Start in a crouching position, then gradually come to an upright position in short, rhythmical bounces. On the word *pop*, everyone jumps as high as he can.
4. Add rhythm instruments to play throughout the song, sounding a different one each time *pop* occurs.
5. Clap the rhythm of the melody while tapping the basic 1-2 meter with the feet.

6. Try the following dance to the music:

Formation: Double circle with any even number of couples. Girls on boys' right. Each couple faces another couple, with all dancers in groups of four around the circle.

measures 1-4: Each group of four joins hands and circles to the left clockwise for eight steps (eight counts).

measures 5-8: With hands still joined, reverse directions and circle right (counterclockwise) for eight steps, ending in original starting position (eight counts).

measures 9-10: All take four short steps toward center, raising joined hands high at the same time (four counts).

measures 11-12: All take four short steps backward, lowering joined hands (four counts).

measures 13-16: All couples facing clockwise raise hands high. Other couples who are facing counterclockwise "pop" through under the raised hands arch and move on to next set (eight counts). New couples join hands in a new set and repeat as many times as desired.

Related activities and materials

1. Try other American square and round dances (see "Let's Square Dance" series and "World of Folk Dances" series, RCA).
2. Sing other American folk songs.

3. Listening:
   "Hoedown" from "Rodeo," Copland, AM 5 vol. 2 and EIM record album.
   Variations on "Pop Goes the Weasel," AM 4 vol. 1.
   "Arkansas Traveler," BOL #56.

For study

$\frac{6}{8}$ (compound) meter, conduct in **2-bt.** pattern (See p. 269)
Hold ⌒
Uneven rhythm pattern

38. WHEN JOHNNY COMES MARCHING HOME

Level: U and L
Key of g minor: start G (la)

Words and music by Louis Lambert

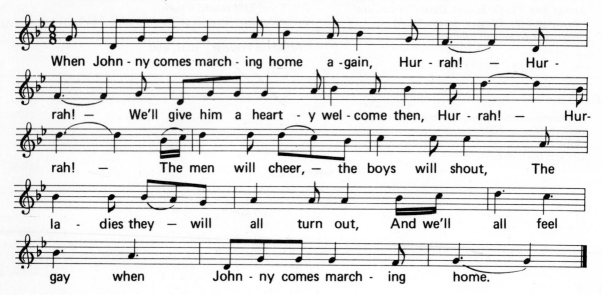

When John - ny comes march - ing home a - gain, Hur - rah! — Hur -
rah! — We'll give him a heart - y wel - come then, Hur - rah! — Hurrah! — The men will cheer, — the boys will shout, The
la - dies they — will all turn out, And we'll all feel
gay when John - ny comes march - ing home.

2. The old church bell will peal with joy, Hurrah! Hurrah!
   To welcome home our darling boy, Hurrah! Hurrah!
   The village lads and lassies say
   With roses they will strew the way
   And we'll all feel gay when Johnny comes marching home.

3. Get ready for the jubilee, Hurrah! Hurrah!
   We'll give the hero three times three, Hurrah! Hurrah!
   The laurel wreath is ready now
   To place upon his loyal brow
   And we'll all feel gay when Johnny comes marching home.

The action

1. Dramatize the verses as they are sung, with selected children taking the parts of the returning soldiers, others representing the crowd. Interest may be heightened by having the children make their own Civil War hats and small drums out of boxes covered with blue paper.

2. Add rhythm instruments in any of the following ways or as desired:
   a. Woodblock beats the rhythm of the melody while drums and sticks beat the basic meter (two beats per measure)
   b. Select other instruments for keeping the march rhythm. Change instruments as the content of each verse changes.
   c. If the children have learned to use drumsticks, have them beat the following drum pattern **throughout**:

   ♪♩ = flam

   X = use both sticks

3. Tap the basic meter (2) with the feet while clapping the melody rhythm, or divide into two groups, letting one clap while the other taps.

4. Try a simple grand march. See patterns used in the flag drill for "There Are Many Flags in Many Lands," no. 101. Let children suggest other figures to execute.

5. Try a "reel" with the music. Modify as desired, leaving out or adding steps.

> Formation: two lines facing
> meas. 1-4: forward and back (walk to center, bow or bob curtsy, return), four steps forward, four back
> meas. 5-8: forward and right hands around, four steps return to place, four steps
> meas. 9-12: forward and turn left hands around as above
> meas. 13-16: forward and turn both hands around as above
> meas. 1-4: do-si-do (meet partner in center, pass to left back to back without turning around), eight steps
> meas. 5-8: lead couple slides down the center between the two lines and returns, four slides down, four slides back
> meas. 9-12: first couple turns right hands in the center, then turns left hands with the next person in the opposite line
> meas. 13-16: swing partner by right hands in center again, then swing each person in turn by the left hand down the line; return to partner and swing right hands in between the turns of the others; head couple slides down and back again, then each leads his own line around the outside in a march, makes an arch at foot of line, others pass through; repeat as desired with new head couple.

Related activities and materials

1. Sing other war songs, service songs, and patriotic songs. Find songs that depict different facets of a soldier's life, for example, homesickness, humor, complaints, longing for loved ones, etc.

2. See suggested activities under "Soldier, Soldier," no. 35.

3. Listening:
   "American Salute," AM 4 vol. 1 (variations on this tune).
   "Songs of the Civil War" (FS and record), Bowmar.
   "This Is My Country," RCA 2662.
   "Stories and Songs of the Civil War," RCA CAL 1032.
   "Marches," BOL #54. (This album contains many different kinds of marches, e.g., "March of the Siamese Children" and "Stars and Stripes Forever.")
   "Decoration Day," Charles Ives, EIM record album.
   "Bugle Calls of the Army," parts 1 and 2, RCA 447-0158, 447-0159.

For study

Minor mode (See Major and Minor and Minor Scales)

$\frac{6}{8}$ (compound) meter, conduct in 2-bt. pattern (See p. 269)

left-hand piano

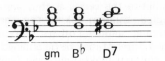

gm   Bb   D7

bells

gm = G Bb D
D7 = D F# A C
Bb = Bb D F

39. THE BEAR WENT OVER THE MOUNTAIN

Popular song

Level: U and L
Key of F: start F (do)

From *Sharing Music,* Music for Young Americans series, © 1966, by the American Book Company, by permission of the American Book Company.

The action

1. Sing well-known words to the same tune:
   a. We won't get home until morning, etc.
      We won't get home at all
   b. For he's a jolly good fellow, etc.
      Which nobody can deny.
2. Try "The Wiggle Song," * using the same tune:
   a. My thumbs are starting to wiggle, my thumbs are starting to wiggle,
      My thumbs are starting to wiggle around, around, around.
   b. My thumbs and fingers are wiggling, etc.
   c. My hand is starting to wiggle, etc.
   d. My arms are starting to wiggle, etc.
   e. My head is starting to wiggle, etc.
   f. Now all of me is a-wiggling, etc.
3. Create new verses for this tune.
4. Try the following simple dance to the music:

Formation: Two long lines facing (one girls, one boys, if desired)
   meas. 1-4: walk forward three steps, bow (curtsy), three counts walk backward three steps, bow (or curtsy), three counts
   meas. 4-8: lines walk toward each other, eight steps, with one line passing under raised arms of other line, eight counts
Lines face
   meas. 9-10: clap three times, hold
   meas. 11-12: clap three times, hold
   meas. 13-16: hook right elbows with partner in opposite line and swing or walk around eight steps (eight counts)
   meas. 17-20: hook left elbows and swing or walk around eight steps as before, only ending in opposite positions
Repeat whole dance from the beginning, ending in original positions.

Related activities and materials

1. Research the living habits and origins of various kinds of bears, then create some new verses about them, for example, "The grizzly lives in Alaska" or "The polar bear likes the cold weather."

2. Go on a "Bear Hunt," no. 39A.
3. Listening:
   "Bear Symphony," Haydn, *Enjoying Music,* NDM Series, American Book Company.
   "Three Bears," Coates, BOL #67.
4. See "Isn't It Funny," no. 33.

For study

$\frac{6}{8}$ (compound) meter, conduct in 2-bt. pattern (See p. 269)
Like phrases
Hold
Tie
Chant rhythm, then sing with syllables (See pp. 277-278)

left-hand piano

F   B♭   C7

bells

F = F A C
B♭ = B♭ D F
C7 = C E G B♭

Autoharp

F, B♭, C7

chord root syllables

F = *do*
B♭ = *fa*
C7 = *sol*

ukulele

Tune: G C E A (key of F tuning)

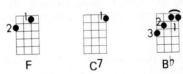

F   C7   B♭

* From *Sharing Music,* Music for Young Americans series, © 1966, by the American Book Company; by permission of the American Book Company.

39A. BEAR HUNT

After introducing the activity, narrate the adventure one line at a time. The children repeat each line. The narration is accompanied by a steady "walking" pattern (patting each thigh alternately). Between the sections of narration, time is allowed to act out in rhythm the motion indicated. When the "bear" is seen, the actions are reversed double-quick, with a very fast "walking" pattern, as if running away from the "bear."

Let's go on a bear hunt. Repeat after me everything I say, and do all the movements I do.	
I see a wheat field. Can't go over.	*Walking pattern*
Can't go under. Let's go through.	*Brush palms together back and forth several times.*
I see a bridge. Can't go around. Can't go under Let's go over.	*Walking pattern*
Scared? Not much.	*Thump chest with fists.*
I see some mud. Can't go over.	*Walking pattern*
Can't go under. Let's go through.	*Hand-walk through sticky mud, making "shloo, shloo" sound with mouth.*
I see a lake. Can't go over. Can't go under. Let's go through.	*Walking pattern* *Imitate overarm swim stroke. Shake self as if wet.*
I see a tree. Can't go over. Can't go under. Let's go up.	*Walking pattern* *Imitate climbing a tree. Shade eyes with one hand, looking all around.*
I don't see any bears!	*Imitate coming down a tree.*
I see a cave. Can't go over. Can't go under. Let's go in. I see two eyes. I see a nose. It's a bear!	*Walking pattern begins to slow up.* *Voice becomes quieter.* *Voice becomes almost a whisper.* *Whisper* *A real whisper* *Reach out one hand, feeling fur.* *Voice shouts.*

Now reverse all movements—climbing a tree, swimming a lake, walking through sticky mud, crossing the bridge, going through the wheat field—using the "running" pattern instead of a "walking" pattern.

At the very end, thrust hand forward as if slamming a door with a loud *bang*. Sit back and heave a sigh of relief.

From Edna Doll and Mary Jarman Nelson, *Rhythms Today,* © 1965 by Silver Burdett Co.; reprinted by permission of the General Learning Corporation.

40. HILL AN' GULLY
Calypso from Jamaica (English words by Margaret Marks)

Program song
Level: U
Key of F: start C (high sol)

From *Making Music Your Own* (teacher's ed.), Book 5, © 1971 by the General Learning Corporation; reprinted by permission.

The action

1. When the song has been learned, add bongo drums and maracas as indicated.
2. Assign the solo on the Verse part, with the chorus joining in on "hill and gully" and on the Refrain.
3. Create new verses for the melody.
4. Add a dance,* as follows:

> Formation: No set formation, no partners; a five-measure pattern is repeated throughout; each movement equals a quarter note
>
> (a) step sideways on right foot, cross left foot in back and step; step right, clap hands
> (b) step sideways on left foot, cross right foot in back and step; step left, clap hands
> (c) step in place, swiveling on the ball of the foot—right, left, right, *rest*
> (d) step forward on left foot, kick right leg and snap fingers; step forward on the right foot, kick left leg and snap fingers
> (e) step backward on the left foot, step backward on right foot, step backward on left foot; turn to the right to change direction.
>
> *From *Making Music Your Own* (teacher's ed.), Book 5, © 1971 by the General Learning Corporation; reprinted by permission.

Related activities and materials

1. Read about the islands of the Caribbean and find out why the music has so many different "flavors" (reflecting many nationalities).
2. Listen to the sound of music made by steel bands. Try constructing a simple steel drum.
3. Sing other calypso songs, for example:
   "Tinga Layo," *Expressing Music,* NDM American Book Co.
   "Song Games of Trinidad and Tobago," Cooperative Recreation Service.
   "Music of the West Indies," *Exploring Music,* Book 6, Holt, Rinehart and Winston.
   "Banana Boat Loader's Song," MMYO 6, Silver Burdett.
4. Listening:
   "A Visit to the Caribbean," Keyboard Publications.
   "Songs of the Caribbean," from "Songs of Many Cultures" album, Silver Burdett.
   "Children's Jamaican Songs and Games," Folkways Records #7250.
   "Jamaican Rhumba," BOL #56 and record album of *Expressing Music,* NDM, American Book Co.

For study

Syncopation

Note: in measures 1 and 3 the accents occur in the expected places—<u>hill</u> and <u>gully</u>. In measures 2, 4, 6, and 8, however, the accents occur in the expected places. It is the location of the tie, resulting in a long tone sounding between two shorter tones, that gives the effect of "displacing" the accent; thus "<u>hill</u> and <u>gully</u>" becomes "hill <u>and</u> gully."

Like phrases

Cut time

Rhythmic development of verse:

left-hand piano

F   B♭

bells

F = F A C
B♭ = B♭ D F

Autoharp

F, B♭

guitar

F

B♭

ukulele

Tune: G C E A (key of F tuning)

F

B♭

41. THE TRAIN IS A-COMING

American folk song

Level: U and L
Key of E♭: start D (ti)

Steady, pulsing rhythm

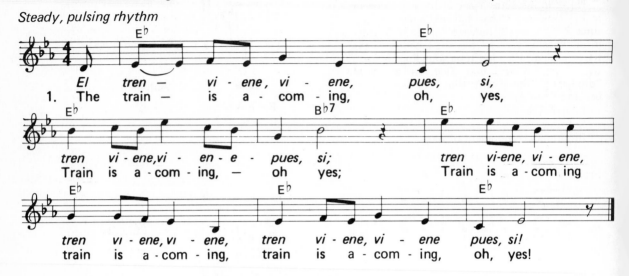

El   tren —   vi - ene, vi - ene,   pues,   si,
1.   The   train —   is   a - com - ing,   oh,   yes,

tren   vi - ene,vi - en - e - pues,   si;   tren   vi-ene, vi - ene,
Train   is a - com - ing, —   oh   yes;   Train is   a - com ing

tren   vi - ene,vi - ene,   tren   vi - ene, vi - ene   pues, si!
train   is   a - com - ing,   train   is   a - com - ing,   oh, yes!

2. Better get your ticket, oh, yes.
3. Train is a-leaving, oh, yes.

From Choate, Berg, Kjelson, and Troth. *Music for Early Childhood,* New Dimensions in Music Series, © 1970 by the American Book Company, New York.

The action

1. Assign the solo in "The Train Is A-Coming." The class answers "oh, yes."
2. Have a child or the teacher clap the melody rhythm of "The Train Is A-Coming" with the class answering by clapping the melody rhythm of "oh, yes." At measures 5-7 alternative between solo and class.
3. *Think* the sound of "The Train Is A-Coming," but do not sing aloud. Come in on "oh yes" at the proper time, singing aloud. Try this throughout the song.
4. Sing the song in Spanish, as shown. Assign several solos for repeats of "The Train Is A-Coming."
5. If a member of the class or the teacher speaks another language, translate the words into that language and sing.
6. Make up some new verses in English.

Related activities and materials

1. Make a "living" train.
2. Listen to ways in which the sounds of trains have been portrayed in music by different composers (see Listening under "New River Train," no. 47).
3. Imitate some train sounds, using instruments at hand (harmonica, sand blocks, etc.).
4. See Related Activities for other train songs. Nos. 42, 47, 77.

For study

Like phrases
Syncopation
Transpose to key of F and play on autoharp
Conduct in 4-bt. pattern (See p. 269)

left-hand piano

E^b B^b7

bells
$E^b = E^b$ G B^b
$B^b7 = B^b$ D F A^b

42. GET ON BOARD

Spiritual

Level: U and L
Key of A♭: start C (m

Here comes the train:

Chooka-chooka-chooka-chooka   Toot, toot   toot, toot.

Refrain

Get   on   board,   lit - tle   child - ren   Get   on

board,   lit - tle   child - ren,   Get   on   board,   lit - tle
End here   *verse*

child - ren, There's room for many- a   more   1. The   gos - pel train's a -
2. I   hear   the   train   a -

com - ing   I   hear   it,   just   at   hand, —   I
com - ing,   She's   com - ing   round   the   curve, —   She's
Go back to beginning

hear   the   car - wheels   rumb - ling   And   roll - ing   through the   land. So
loosen'd all   her   steam   and brakes, And   strain-ing   ev' - ry   nerve, Oh

From *Music Now and Long Ago,* © 1956 and 1962 by the Silver Burdett Co.; reprinted by permission of the General Learning Corporation.

The action

1. Have one child sing the solo part, with the class joining in on "little children" and/or assign the solo to the verse part of the song, with the class coming in on the chorus or portions of the chorus.
2. Create some train sounds with rhythm instruments, hands, mouth, feet, harmonica, recorder, etc., and insert them in appropriate places in the song.
3. Create a rhythm pattern for each of the sounds and write (for example, a whistle might be two long sounds such as o o or ♩ ♩, or line notation may be preferred: ———— ————).
4. Sound out the name of the local (or nearest) railroad and write in notation, for example, Pennsylvania railroad

5. Sound out some terms used in connection with trains and write in notation, for example:

station master   ♫ ♫

railroad   ♩ ♩

tracks   𝅗𝅥

6. Combine the rhythms in 4 and 5 into rhythm patterns. Add a tune and create a song about trains.

Related activities and materials

1. Sing other train songs and spirituals.
2. Listening:
   See Listening under "New River Train" for selections portraying train sounds in music by different composers.
3. See Spirituals (p. 283).

For study

Syncopation
Substitute a musical phrase for the words "go back to the beginning" that will mean the same thing
Like phrases
Conduct in 2-bt. pattern (See p. 269)

43. THIS LITTLE LIGHT OF MINE

Spiritual

Level: U and L
Key of G: start D (low sol)

This lit-tle light of mine, I'm gon-na let it shine.
This lit-tle light of mine, I'm gon-na let it shine.
This lit-tle light of mine, I'm gon-na let it shine, let it
shine, let it shine, let it shine. —

The action

1. Create new verses, with action, using different parts of the body, for example:
   a. these little hands of mine, I'm gonna let them clap
   b. these little feet of mine, I'm gonna let them tap
2. Choose four different actions to do four times each in order to the basic beat of the music; for example:

   clap clap clap clap
   march march march march
   snap snap snap snap
   nod nod nod nod

Repeat as many as needed to complete the music. For variation, add other actions to the four suggested above to complete the music in place of repeating the first four.

3. Choose a different rhythm instrument to play on each verse *or* select one to sound on the object (hands) and another on the action (clap), *or* create an original percussion score for the entire song.
4. In the upper grades, create a simple descant as a harmony part. Harmony may also be added through the use of *mi-fa* or chord root syllables, as well as three-part vocal chording. Find the appropriate accompaniment chords by ear on the autoharp.
5. Find the syncopation (displaced accent) within the various measures of this song. Find other songs that contain syncopation, (Nos. 44, 47, 48) then create rhythm patterns which contain syncopation.

Related activities and materials
1. See the suggested activities under Spirituals.
2. Listening:
   "America: A Singing Nation," Keyboard

Publications (FS, record, teacher's guide, students' booklets).
For additional listening suggestions, see Spirituals.

For study
   Syncopation
   Like phrases
   Spirituals

left-hand piano

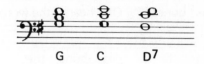

G   C   D^7

bells   Autoharp

G = G B D   G, C, D^7
C = C E G
C^7 = D F♯ A C

guitar

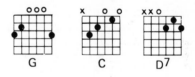

G   C   D^7

ukulele
Tune: A D F♯ B (G tuning, see p. 240)

G   C   D^7

44. DRY BONES
Traditional

Program song
Level: U
Key of F: start F (do)

Rhythmically

E - ze - kiel cried, "Them dry — bones!" E - ze - kiel cried "Them

dry bones!" Oh, hear the word of the Lord. The foot bone con-

nect - ed to the leg bone, the leg bone con-nect-ed to the knee bone,

The knee bone con-nect - ed to the thigh bone

The thigh bone con-nect - ed to the back bone

The back bone con-nect-ed to the neck bone, the neck bone con-nect-ed

to the head bone, Oh, hear the word of the Lord!

them bones. them bones gon- na walk a-roun' them bones, them bones

gon - na walk a-roun', Oh hear the word of the Lord! The

head bone con-nect - ed to the neck bone, the neck bone con-

nect - ed to the back bone, The back bone con-nect- ed to the

thigh bone, the thigh bone con-nect-ed to the knee bone, The

From Wilson, Ehret, Knuth, Hermann, and Renna, *Growing with Music,* Book 6 (Related Arts ed.), © 1970 by Prentice-Hall, Inc., Englewood Cliffs, N.J.; reprinted by permission.

knee bone con-nect-ed to the leg bone, the leg bone con-nect-ed
to the foot bone, Oh, hear the word of the Lord! —

The action:

1. When the song has been learned, assign the solo part ("Ezekiel cried"), with the chorus coming in at "them dry bones," and the solo again at "Oh, hear the word of the Lord."
2. Assign a different rhythm instrument for each bone as it is mentioned in the song, with all playing at "them bones, them bones gonna walk around."
3. Tap the foot on accented beats and clap on unaccented beats:

tap   clap   tap   clap, etc.

4. Create some movement for the song.
5. For variation, start in a sitting position. As each bone is mentioned, gradually work up to a standing position. Possibilities are kneeling, standing with torso bent over, torso erect with head bowed, and finally, straight, standing position with the hands on the head for "head bone." Reverse as bones descend, if desired.
6. Write out an original percussion score to be used with rhythm instruments as accompaniment throughout the song.

Related activities and materials

1. Sing other spirituals. (See Spirituals, Nos. 42, 43, 78.) Note suggested activities also.
2. Listening:

"Dry Bones," from "Deep River and Other Spirituals," Robert Shaw Chorale, RCA LSC 2247.
For additional suggestions, see Spirituals.

For study

Chromatic tones
Syncopation
First and second endings
Uneven rhythm pattern
Conduct in 4-bt. pattern (See p. 269)

45. THE ANGEL BAND
South Carolina folk song

Level: U and L
Key of G: start D (low sol)

From Carl Diton, *36 South Carolina Spirituals,* © 1930, 1957; by permission of G. Schirmer.

The action

1. Assign individual children solos on each angel number—for example, "There was one," "There were two," as it occurs in the song.
2. Strike a different rhythm instrument for each number as it is sung, selecting them so that as they progress numerically, they also increase dynamically, climaxing on "ten." All may play together on the refrain in the following pattern or as desired:

sticks,
woodblock
tambourine   ♩ ♩ |♩ ♩ |♩ ♩ etc.

drum   ♩ |♩ |♩ etc.

cymbals,
gong   ♩ | ▬ |♩ etc.

3. As an alternative to number 2, use a body sound for each angel (clap, snap, tap, hit knees, brush sides of knees with palms of hands, clap cupped hands, etc.).

4. Substitute a different "found" sound with objects in the environment for each angel number (see Found Instruments).
5. This song contains only the tones of the pentatonic scale (*do re mi sol la*); thus it is easy to play using only the black keys. Begin on D^b and find the tune by ear on resonator bells or the piano.
6. Using selected tones of the pentatonic scale, create an ostinato to play on bells or the piano while class sings the melody.
7. Create a new song, using tones of the pentatonic scale.
8. Introduce the children to the instruments found in an orchestra and in a band, and point out the differences between the two. (See Listening below.) Have each child choose an instrument he would like to "play," then all march in time to the music, pantomiming the playing of the chosen instruments.

Related activities and materials

1. Make some instruments. (For unusual ideas see "Whistles and Strings," published by the Elementary Science Study of Education Development Center, Inc., 55 Chapel St., Newton, Mass. 02160.)
2. Sing other songs about bands and orchestras, for example:
   "German Band," MNAF, Silver Burdett.
   "I Am a Musician," EIM, McGraw-Hill.
   "Instrument Song," GWM 5, Prentice-Hall.
3. Listening:
   "Instruments of the Orchestra," Keyboard Publications (record, overhead transparency masters, teacher's guide, and student booklets).
   "Meet the Instruments," Bowmar (FS and record).
   "Pan and Piper," "Tubby the Tuba," "Peter and the Wolf," Columbia.
   "Sparky's Magic Piano," Capitol.
   Symphony No. 3 for Band," 4th movement, Exploring Music 5 record album.
   "Toy Symphony, Haydn, EIM, record album.
   "Young Person's Guide to the Orchestra," Britten, EIM record album.

For study

Pentatonic scale
Syncopation
Like phrases
Instruments of the orchestra and band
Conduct in 2-bt. pattern; note upbeat at the
beginning (See p. 269)

left-hand piano

G   D^7

bells   Autoharp

G = G B D
D^7 = D F$^\sharp$ A C   G, D^7

ukulele
Tune: A D F$^\sharp$ B (key of G tuning)

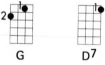

G   D^7

46. MARY ANN
Ardith Ries Shelley

Level: U and L
Key of F: start C (high sol)

1. Will you come and dance with me, Ma-ry Ann? — Will you come and dance with me Ma-ry Ann? Will you come and dance with me, Ma-ry Ann? — Ma-ry Ann, Ma-ry Ann, Ma-ry Ann.

2. Will you clap your hands with me, *etc.*
3. Will you take a walk with me, *etc.*

The action

1. When the song has been learned, add new verses with other activities, for example, "Will you bend and touch your toes," etc. Other names may be substituted.
2. Tap the basic meter with the feet while clapping the rhythm pattern of the melody, or have one group tap while another claps.
3. Walk in time to the music, indicating the beginning of each new phrase by changing direction of the walk—for example, forward on the first phrase, backward on the second, forward again on the third (because it sounds the same as the first), then in a circle on the fourth phrase. Vary by changing your walk to a skip. This will require a change in rhythm pattern from even to uneven:

and/or a change of meter, if preferred:

4. Add different actions to each phrase:

phrase 1 clap hands eight counts
phrase 2 snap fingers eight counts
phrase 3 tap foot eight counts
phrase 4 slap knees eight counts

or add different actions to each *measure,* doing each action for four counts and repeating the whole series to complete the song. Have the children suggest different actions.

5. Select a different rhythm instrument to accompany each action or create an original percussion score to play throughout the song.
6. Sound the rhythms of the names of different children in the class. Translate them into line notation by using long lines for long sounds and short lines for short sounds; then write in the music notation.
7. Add the following descant or let the class discover by ear where the changes from *mi* to *fa* should occur; then have them create their own descant:

Related activities and materials

1. Play "what's in a name," as follows, or vary as desired:

Question: What's in a name? (asked by group)

Answer: A sound (answered by individual doing the sounding)

Question: What sound?

Answer: The sound of (define category here so that class will know whether they are to listen for the word syllables of a poem, a familiar song, a name, etc.). Individuals then clap or beat on an instrument the word syllable sounds of the song, poem, name or whatever they have chosen, to see if the class can identify the name of the song, poem, child, or object.

Note: If desired, go one step further and place the sounds in line notation or music notation on the chalkboard after identification has been made. This should be done by the child making the identification.

For study
  Like phrases
  Syncopation
  Cut time
  Conduct in 4-bt. pattern (See p. 269)

left-hand piano

   F   B♭ C⁷

bells   Autoharp

F = F A C   F, B♭, C⁷
B♭ = B♭ D F
C⁷= C E G B♭

ukulele
Tune: G C E A (key of F tuning)

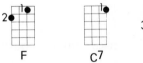

    F   C⁷   B♭

47. NEW RIVER TRAIN

American folk song

Level: U and L
Key of F: start F (do)

Rhythmically

1. I'm rid-in' that New Riv-er Train, — I'm rid-in' that New Riv-er Train; — Same old train that — brought me here, Gon-na take me back home a-gain. —
2. Oh, dar-lin, you can't love — one, — Oh, dar-lin', you can't love — one, — You can't love one and have any fun, Oh, — dar-lin' you can't love one. —

From Wilson, Ehret, Knuth, Hermann, and Renna, *Growing with Music* (Related Arts ed.), Book 2, © 1970 by Prentice-Hall, Inc., Englewood Cliffs, N.J.; reprinted by permission.

The action

1. Add new verses with more numbers, for example, "Darlin', you can't love two."
2. Add rhythm instruments (sticks and sand blocks), as indicated, or use others of choice.
3. Make some train sounds, using only the hands, mouth, and feet.
4. Add harmony, using any of the following devices:
   a. have one group sing the root syllable of the given chord while the other group sings the melody of the song. (See p. 228)
   b. create a simple descant by ear, choosing between *mi* and *fa* as the possible harmony notes in each measure. Substitute an instrument such as bells or recorder for the singing on the harmony notes, if preferred.
   c. accompany with three-part vocal chording or bottles. (See p. 299.)

Related activities and materials
1. Listening:
   "Departure," AM 2, vol. 1.
   "Little Train of the Caipira," EIM.

"Pacific 231," Keyboard Publications (recorded train sounds also on this recording).
"Little Train," BOL #52.
2. For other train and folk songs, see Classified Index.

For study

    Tonic chord beginning
    Syncopation
    Cut time
    Tie
    Chant rhythm and sing with syllables (See pp. 277-278)
    Conduct in 2-bt. pattern in fast tempo (See p. 269)

left-hand piano

F   B♭   C7

bells   Autoharp

F = F A C   F, B♭, C7
B♭ = B♭ D F
C7 = C E G B♭

guitar

F   C7   B♭

ukulele
Tune: G C E A (key of F tuning)

F   C7   B♭

48. I LIVE IN A CITY

Words and music by Malvina Reynolds

Level: U and L
Key of G: start D (low sol)

I live in a ci-ty yes I do, I live in a ci-ty yes I do, I live in a ci-ty yes I do, — Made by hu-man hands.

Black hands, white hands, yel-low and brown, all to-geth-er built this town, black hands, white hands, yellow and brown, all to-geth-er make the wheel go round.

2. Brown hands, yellow hands, white and black
   Mined the coal and built the stack
   Brown hands, yellow hands, white and black
   Built the engine and laid the track.

3. Black hands, brown hands, yellow and white
   Built the buildings tall and bright
   Black hands, brown hands, yellow and white
   Filled them all with shining light.

4. Black hands, white hands, brown and tan
   Milled the flour and cleaned the pan
   Black hands, white hands, brown and tan
   The working woman and the working man.

The action

1. Take a "sound walk" noting the many different sounds heard. Categorize the sounds as to whether they are high or low, soft or loud, long or short, rhythmical or nonrhythmical. Try to reproduce them in the classroom with rhythm instruments and other objects at hand.
2. Draw a scene of your choice after the walk. Choose suitable instruments to depict the "sound" of the scene.
3. Try to discover objects that reflect the city environment, on which sounds may be reproduced and bring them to class as "found" instruments (see Found Instruments). Create some sound compositions, working in groups with the instruments.
4. Discuss occupations frequently found in a city. Imitate the movement of these occupations. Find the rhythm of the movement, then create a song about the occupation, using the basic rhythm of the movement.
5. Create some new verses about life in the city, using the tune of "I Live in a City."
6. Help the children discover that a city has shape as well as sound. Draw the shapes found in a city skyline, find other shapes in the city, then compose a song about these "shapes."

Related activities and materials

1. Create a story using the sounds of the city. (Use rhythm instruments, "found" instruments, and other devices for creating sounds.)
2. Explore the sounds of other cities around the world through recordings, tapes, sound films, etc.
3. Relate ear training in the early grades to the city environment through the use of visuals, for example:

    Construct an elevator out of paper or on a flannel board.

    Play a short melody that goes either up or down. Have the child identify the direction of the melody by moving the elevator either up or down. Use the same type of activity for high and low, using buildings of different heights.
4. Listening:

    "A Walk in the City," *Enjoying Music,* New Dimensions in Music series, American Book Co.

    "The Sounds of My City," Tony Schwartz, Folkways record #7341.

    "Iron Foundry," Mossolov

    "An American in Paris," Gershwin, RCA, LSC 2367.

    "London Suite" (selections), Coates.

For study

Syncopation
D.C. *al Fine*
Conduct in 4-bt. pattern (See p. 269)

bells

$G = G\ B\ D$
$C = C\ E\ G$
$D^7 = D\ F\sharp\ A\ C$

Autoharp

$G,\ C,\ D^7$

left-hand piano

G   C   D⁷

ukulele

Tune: A D F♯ B (key of G tuning)

G   D⁷   C

49. WHISTLE, DAUGHTER
American folk song

Level: U
Key of G: start B (mi)

Group I

1. "Whis - tle, daugh - ter, whis - tle, and you shall have a cow."
2. "Whis - tle, daugh - ter, whis - tle, and you shall have a pig."

Group 2

" I can't whis - tle, moth - er, be - cause I don't know how."
" I can't whis - tle, moth - er, be - cause I am too big."

3. Whistle, daughter, whistle, and you shall have a man.
(WHISTLE) _____ I just found out I can.

The action

(Although "Whistle, Daughter, Whistle" and "Yoma" (page 104) are from different parts of the world, they share common thoughts.)

1. Sing each as a dialogue song, using either groups or solos or both in combination, for example, the group asks the question and an individual answers. "Whistle, Daughter" may be accompanied by the autoharp.
2. Select an appropriate rhythm instrument for each of the objects (cow, dress, bowl, etc.), and strike it when the object occurs in the song.
3. Select one rhythm instrument to play when the father (or mother) is speaking and a different one when the daughter is answering.
4. Add new verses, using different objects.

5. Note that "Yoma" is in a minor key, while "Whistle, Daughter" is in a major key. Try changing the key signature of "Whistle, Daughter" to:

and sing in a minor key (g minor)

Change "Yoma" to:

and sing in a major key (E major)

Discuss the effects of each change on the mood of the song.

Related activities and materials

1. Create some dance movements for each of the songs after researching American folk dancing and eastern European folk dancing.
2. Sing other dialogue songs. Compare "Yoma," no. 50, and "Minka," no. 60.

For study

Syncopation (meas. 2 and 6)
Like phrases
Sing with syllables (See pp. 277-278)
Conduct in 4-bt. pattern (see p. 269)

bells

G = G B D
D⁷= D F♯ A C

Autoharp

G, D⁷

left-hand piano

D⁷   G

ukulele

Tune: A D F♯ B (key of G tuning)

G   D⁷

50. YOMA

Eastern European folk song

Level: U
Key of e minor: start B (mi)

Moderately fast

Father 1. Yo-ma, Yo-ma sing me a song and tell me what you de-sire!
2. Yo-ma, Yo-ma sing me a song and tell me what you — wish!
3. Yo-ma, Yo-ma sing me a song and please don't make the guess!

Would you like a new red dress with ti-ny shoes the col-or of fire?
Would you like a Chi-na bowl or would you like a gold-en-fish?
Would you like a nice young man to court you? Daugh-ter, ans-wer yes!

Daughter

1-2. No, Pa-pa, no! You do not un-der-stand! You do not un-der-stand!
3. Yes, Pa-pa, yes! At last you un-der-stand! At last you un-der-stand!

From *Music for Young Americans*, Book 4, © 1963 by the American Book Company, New York.

The action (See p. 103)

For study

Minor (See Minor Scales and Major and Minor)
Chant rhythm pattern and sing with syllables (See pp. 277-278)
Conduct in 4-bt. pattern (see p. 269)

bells
e min. = E G B
B7 = B D♯ F♯ A

51. O MAMA, HURRY

Brazilian folk song

Level: U and L
Key of C: start G (sol)

O ma-ma, hur-ry   O ma-ma, hur-ry,   O ma-ma,
hur-ry give the bot-tle to the ba-by,   To stop the cry-ing,   To stop the
cry-ing,   To stop the cry-ing bring the ba-by's bot-tle now. —

From the *Exploring Music Series* (teacher's ed.), Book 1, © 1966; by special permission of the publisher, Holt, Rinehart and Winston.

The action

1. When the song has been learned, add the following rhythm instruments for a Latin American flavor:

maracas:  throughout
L R L R L R L R

claves: ♩ ♫ ♪ ♪♩ throughout

bongo drum: ♩ ♩♩ ♩ ♩♩ throughout
L R R L R R

2. Discuss some of the ways in which one might comfort a baby to stop crying, then create some new verses about these.
3. Vary the tempo when appropriate to fit the new verses.

Related activities and materials

1. Discuss the effects of the influence of other cultures on Brazilian music (African, Portuguese, Indian).
2. View some of the folk instruments of Brazil and listen to them, then try to find American counterparts or construct replicas of some. (Villa-Lobos used folk instruments in many of his works; see Listening below.)
3. Learn some dances done in Brazil, for example, the samba:
"Si Senor," "Fold Dances," #6, BOL (Latin American dances).
"Fado Blanquito," "Folk Dances," #6, BOL.
4. Sing songs from other South American countries: "Rique Ran" (Games and Songs of South American Children), Cooperative Recreation Service.
5. Create a dance to accompany this song.
6. Listening:
"Man and His Music: Brazil" (FS, record, teacher's guide, and childrens' booklets), Keyboard Publications.
"Songs and Dances of Brazil," Folkways Records #6953.
"Brazilian Impressions," AM 5, vol. 2.
"Brazilian Dance," Guarnieri, AM 6, vol. 2.
"Folk Instruments of the World," Follett.
"Little Train of the Caipira," Villa-Lobos.
7. Film: "Brazil—'Estados Unidos Do Brasil," Denoyer-Geppert AV.
8. Book: *Enchantment of South America, Brazil,* Allan Carpenter, Children's Press, Chicago, 1968.

For study

Tonic chord
Tie (last measure)
Conduct in 4-bt. pattern, note upbeat (See p. 269)
Recurrence of rhythm pattern

left-hand piano

C   G⁷

bells   Autoharp

C = C E G   C, G⁷
G⁷ = G B D F

ukulele

Tune: G C E A (key of F tuning,)

C   G⁷

52. CABALLITO BLANCO

Level: U and L
Key of C: start E (mi)

Mexican folk song

1. Ca - bal - li - to   blan - co   sa - ca - me de a - qui —
   Lle - va - me a   mi   pueb - lo   don - de - yo   na - ci —

2. *Tengo, tengo, tengo, tu no tienes nada*
   Tengo tres borregas en una manada

3. *Una me da leche, otra me da lana*
   Y otra mantequilla para la semana

Spanish pronunciation ("Caballito Blanco")

Kah-bah-yee-to blahn-ko
Sah-ka-may day a-kee
Yay-bah-may ah mee pway-blow
Don-day yo nah-see
Teng-oh teng-oh teng-oh
Too no tee-en-es nah-dah
Teng-oh tres bor-ay-gahs
En oon-ah mahn-ah-dah.

Oon-ah may dah lay-chay
Ot-rah may dah lah-nah
Ee ot-rah mahn-tay-kee-yah
Pah-rah lah say-mahn-ah.

English translation

White horse take me away from here
Take me to the town where I was born
I have, I have, I have,
You don't have anything
I have three lambs in a flock
One gives me milk, the other gives me wool
And the third one gives me butter
     for the whole week.

Through the courtesy of Aida Barrera Close, director, Bilingual Project, and Michael Hanson, executive producer, station KLRN-TV, Austin, Texas.

The action

1. Accompany with the sound of hooves, using coconut shells or a tone block in the following rhythm throughout:

2. Add harmony with the following descant, played on bells or other melody instrument or sung by a few selected voices, using words from the song or on "ah" or "oo."

3. Create some new verses in English or Spanish, using subject matter of choice.
4. Accompany with vocal chording, resonator bells in three parts, autoharp, or guitar.

Related activities and materials

1. Sing other Mexican singing games and folk-songs. (See Classified Index.)
2. Learn some Mexican folk dances.
3. See the resource material on Mexico. (See Classified Index.)

For study

Chant rhythm and sing with syllables (See pp. 277-278)
Conduct in 3-bt. pattern (See p. 269)
Tie
Slur

left-hand piano

C   F   G⁷

bells   Autoharp

C = C E G
F = F A C
G⁷ = G B D F

guitar

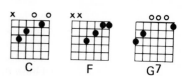

C   F   G⁷

53. SAN SERAFIN DEL MONTE
Words and music traditional

Level: U and L
Key of F: start F (do)

All: San Ser-a-fín del mon - te   San Ser-a-fín Cor - de - ro   (spoken)

eader: Yo co-mo buen Chris-tia - no   Me sen - ta - ré   All: Me sen-ta-ré?

(sing)

eader: Si, me sen-ta-ré!   All: Yo co-mo buen Cris - tia - no   Me sen - ta - ré

2. *Me dormiré* (substitute for *me sentaré*)
3. *Me pararé* (substitute for *me sentaré*)

Spanish pronunciation

Sahn sarah-feen del mon-tay
Sahn sarah-feen core-day-row
Yō cōmō bwain crees-te-ahn-o
May sayn-tah-ray.
2. May dor-meer-ray
3. May pahr-rah-ray

English translation

1. Saint Seraphin of the mountains Saint Sera-
   phin, the shepherd
   I'm a good Christian
   I will sit down.
2. [repeat first three lines of verse 1]
   I will go to sleep
3. [repeat as before]
   I will stand up

Through the courtesy of Aida Barrera Close, director, Bilingual Project, and Michael Hanson, executive producer, station KLRN-TV, Austin, Texas.

The action

1. Sing with actions as indicated. The leader does the action first and the chorus imitates on the repeat.
   (Note the spoken question and sung answer.)
   Circle formation.
2. Add rhythm instruments as desired or try the following:

Substitute another instrument for the tambourine in the final measure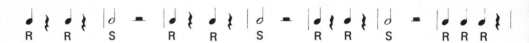

as the last line of each verse is sung. (Discuss the action to be done before choosing each instrument.)

3. Look up Spanish words for additional actions and write new verses.

tambourine:

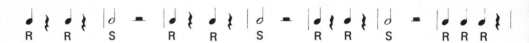

R   R   S   R   R   S   R   R   S   R   R   R

Related activities and materials

1. Accompany with autoharp or guitar.
2. Sing other Mexican singing games and folk-
   songs. (See Classified Index.)
3. Learn some Mexican folk dances.
4. See resource material on Mexico.

For study

Like phrases
Chant rhythm and sing with syllables (See pp. 277-278)
Repeat sign :
Conduct in 4-bt. pattern (See p. 269)
Music of Mexico

left-hand piano

F   C7

bells

F = F A C
C7 = C E G B♭

Autoharp

F, C7

guitar

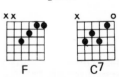

F   C7

54. CHIAPENECAS
Mexican dance song

Level: U
Key of E♭: start E♭ (do)

Gaily (one beat to a measure)

Sing, *Chia-pe - ne -cas,* O - lé!   O - lé!   Dance, *Chia-pe - ne-cas,* O-
clap clap   *Fine*

lé!   O - lé!   Sing,   Sing,   Sing, *Chia - pe - ne - cas,*

Dance,   dance,   dance, *Chia pe - ne - cas,*   Swing   your   part - ner now,
                                                                  D.C.al Fine

As   you   sing, *Chia - pe - ne - cas,*   and   clap!   O - le!

From Choate, Berg, Kjelson, and Troth, *Enjoying Music,* New Dimensions in Music series, © 1970 by the American Book Company, New York.

The action

1. Clap twice at the end of each of the phrases (on "ole!" where indicated).
2. Add rhythm instruments:

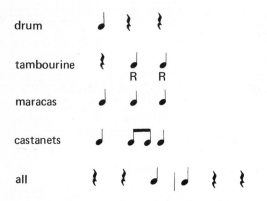

drum	on each measure throughout
tambourine	on each measure throughout
maracas	on each measure throughout
castanets	on each measure throughout
all	on "ole!"

3. As an alternate to number 2, play one instrument on the first beat of each measure and others on the second and third beats (throughout).
4. Increase the tempo and beat *one* beat to each measure, selecting instruments as desired. Accompany with guitar.
5. Add the following descant on the first eight measures or given a choice of *mi* or *fa*, let the children choose the one appropriate for each measure:

Related activities and materials

1. Learn some Mexican folk dances, for example, "Jarabe Tapatio," "La Raspa," "World of Folk Dances," RCA.
2. Create a new dance to the song.

3. Sing other Mexican folk songs. (See nos. 52, 53, 99.)
4. See resource material on Mexico. (See p. 285.)

For study

D.C. *al Fine* Repeat sign :‖
Chant rhythm and sing with syllables (See pp. 277-278)
See "Caballito Blanco," no. 52, which is also in $\frac{3}{4}$ meter. Compare the mood and character of the two songs as a basis for conducting *one* beat to a measure in "Chiapenecas" and three beats in "Caballito Blanco"
Transpose to key of C (see Transposing), then determine appropriate chords for autoharp, bells, and guitar

55. PETER AND PAUL

Hungarian folk song

Level: U and L
Key of D: start D (do)

Haj - má si Pé - ter, Haj - má-si Pál, Haj - má-si Pé - ter, Haj - má - si Pál,

Haj - má-si Pé - ter, Haj-má - si Pál, Haj-má-si Pé - ter, Haj-má- si Pál.

2. Off went our Péter, home stayed our Pál.
   Hajmási (silent) Hajmási Pál. (3)

3. Off went our Péter, off went our Pál.
   Hajmási (silent) Hajmási (silent). (3)

4. Back came our Péter, but not our Pál.
   Hajmási Peter, Hajmási (silent). (3)

5. Back came our Péter, back came our Pál.
   Hajmási Péter, Hajmási Pál. (3)

From "Merry Hours," © 1957; used by permission of Cooperative Recreation Service, Delaware, Ohio.

The action

1. Sing in English and in Hungarian as shown. Hajmasi is pronounced High-mah-shi. In Hungary, this is a family name; it always precedes the first name. Péter (Pay-ter) and Pál (Pahl) are the first names of two brothers. In verses 2, 3, and 4 of this game song, one of the brothers is going away. Whenever this occurs in the song, the singers remain silent on his name.

2. Select one rhythm instrument to sound when the name Peter is mentioned, and another for Pál.

3. Divide the class into two groups. Clap alternate measures of the melody rhythm and/or have one group clap the melody rhythm while the other group taps the basic meter with their feet.

Related activities and materials

1. View some Hungarian folk instruments and listen to their sound, for example, cimbalom (see Listening below).

2. Listen to some Hungarian gypsy folk music in which rapid changes of tempo occur. Characteristic of Hungarian gypsy music is the slow *lassu* accelerating to the fast *frisca* (see Listening below).

3. After several listening experiences, as suggested in number 2, create some dance steps which seem to fit the music, then learn some Hungarian folk dances. Compare the original dance steps with the authentic Hungarian dance steps. (See *Czardas* and *Cshebogar*, Hungarian dances in the RCA *World of Folk Dances* series.)

4. Listen to the music of and get acquainted with:

    Bela Bartok—Hungarian composer who collected Hungarian folk music, much of which is woven into his own compositions.

    Zoltan Kodaly—whose musical influence has been felt in many schools of the United States as well as in other countries. Stem

notation

(chanted "ta" on long sounds, "tee" on short sounds) and abundant use of folk melodies built on the pentatonic scale are frequently associated with the Kodaly system of teaching music.

5. Listen to the music of some composers who were influenced by Hungarian gypsy music, for example, Brahms and Liszt (see Listening below).

6. Learn other Hungarian folksongs. (See "Hungarian Round" in *Exploring Music*, Book 6, Holt, Rinehart and Winston. See also "Merry Hours," a collection of Hungarian songs published by Cooperative Recreation Service, Delaware, Ohio.)

7. Listening:
    "Music of Hungary" (record, overhead transparencies, teacher's guide, and children's booklets), Keyboard Publications.
    "Hungarian Dance No. 6, Brahms, BOL #62.
    "Bear Dance," Bartok, AM 3, vol. 2.
    "Hary Janos Suite," Kodaly, AM 4, vol. 2, also AM 2, vol. 1, Keyboard Publications.

For study

Transpose to key of C to play on autoharp (See Transposing)
Recurring rhythm patterns
Chant rhythm pattern, then sing with syllables (See pp. 277-278)
Conduct in 4-bt. pattern (See p. 269)
Lassu-frisca
Kodaly influence in America
Music of Hungary

left-hand piano

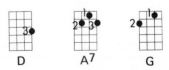

D   G   A⁷

bells

D = D F♯ A
A⁷ = A C♯ E G
G = G B D

ukulele

Tune: A D F♯ B (key of G tuning)

D   A⁷   G

56. MOS MOS

Hopi Indian

Level: U and L

Key: pentatonic: start G

Mos   Mos   Ngai -ti La
Pronun.(Mōs   Mōs   Nigh - tee - Lah)   Mos   Mos   Ngai -ti La

Kan- I - per- kye Ngai- ti La
(Kahn-Ith - purr-kay   nigh - tee - lah)   Kan -I per -kye Ngai- ti La

(spoken sharply)   Nyah Nayh etc.
Mos -   ah   Mos - - ah   (High cat sounds)

The action

This Hopi Indian children's song tells of a cat stealing a sheepskin. The final "ah" of each "mosa" on the last line should be spoken sharply and very staccato, in contrast to the long-drawn-out "mos" that precedes it.

1. When the song has been learned, divide the class into two groups. The first group sings the first two measures and the second group sings the third and fourth measures. They alternate throughout the song, with everyone making the high, cat sounds at the end.

2. Accompany with drum-beating the basic meter of the measure. Add other instruments such as rattles, if desired.

3. Dramatize in rhythmic movement.

Related activities and materials

1. Research the role of music and art in the life of the American Indian (see Listening below).

2. Secure permission to visit one of the national dig sites, if nearby.

3. Attend an Indian ceremony if held nearby.

4. Make some Indian instruments and Indian masks, using Indian designs.

5. Listening:
   "Man and His Music: The American Indian" (FS, record, teacher's guide, students' booklets), Keyboard Publications.
   "North American Indian Songs," (FS and record), Bowmar.
   "Hopi Tales," Folkways Records.
   See resource material on the American Indian (p. 283).

For study

Pentatonic scale
Quarter rest
Like phrases

57. JAPANESE RAIN SONG
Japanese folk tune (words by Roberta McLaughlin)

Level: U and L
Key of C: start C (do)

Lightly

1. Pit-ter pat-ter fall-ing, fall-ing, rain is fall-ing down; Moth-er come to bring umbrel-la,
2. Un-der-neath the droop-ing wil-low stands a lit-tle child, No um-brel-la child is weep-ing,
3. A-me, a-me fu-re, fu-re, ka-a-san — ga, Ja-no me de o mu kae —

Rain is fall-ing down.
Rain is fall-ing down. Pi-chi, Pi-chi cha-pu, cha-pu ran ran ran.
U-re-shi-na.

From Wilson, Ehret, Knuth, Hermann, and Renna, *Growing with Music* (Related Arts ed.), Book 1, ©
1970 by Prentice-Hall, Inc., Englewood Cliffs, N.J.; reprinted by permission.

The action

1. Sing in Japanese.
   pronunciation: a = ah; e = ay; i = ee; o = oh; u = oo; ran = lahn; pichi = pee-chee; chapu = cha-poo
2. Play ostinato on bells, piano, or pluck on autoharp strings to give "koto" flavor. (A koto is a 13-string instrument used in Japan.)
3. Strike tone block on "pichi pichi" (♪ ♪), sticks on "chapu chapu" (♪ ♪) triangle or finger cymbals on "ran ran ran" (♩ ♩ ♩).
4. Dramatize words.
5. Create a short dance or series of movements similar to those which characterize the Japanese dances. (See dance movement for "Cherry Bloom," no. 60.)
6. Compose some new verses about things connected with rain, for example the puddles it makes, the ponds and lakes filling, streams rising, patterns made by the drops on windows, what to wear in the rain, things we like about rain, why we need rain, etc.
7. This tune, like many from Japan, is based on the tones of the pentatonic scale (*do re mi sol la*), which may be sounded by playing all of the black keys, beginning with G♭. Compose some poems about rain and set them to tunes based on the pentatonic scale. Let the children explore possibilities for their own tunes individually, then sing or play them for the class.
8. Set some verses of Haiku poetry to pentatonic melodies. See Related Activities under "Cherry Bloom."

Related activities and materials

1. Explore the sound possibilities of objects in the classroom. Then try to make sounds like rain falling on different things, for example, the pavement, ground, windows, tent, roof, etc. Have the class divide into groups and each perform a sound of rain falling on some object, which the rest of the class must guess.

2. Experiment with sounds of different kinds of rain—a cloudburst; a soft, summer shower; big rain drops; little rain drops; etc.

3. Play the Japanese game of Jan Kem Po, which is similar to the traditional "scissors-rock-paper."

   Make a fist, strike it in the palm of the other hand three times, chanting "Jan Kem Po," then extend the hand in one of three positions—either as "scissors" with two fingers extended, or as a "rock" (a fist), or as "paper," with the hand in an open position. When two people play, the scissors win over the paper, the paper over the rock, and the rock over the scissors. It is a good counting-out game.

4. Try some origami (the art of folding paper).

5. Make some *bozu* dolls out of paper and hang in the room. In Japan these dolls, when hung on trees, are said to keep the rain away.

6. Have a Japanese tea ceremony with rice cakes.

7. Make a Japanese flower arrangement.

8. Learn a few Japanese words, for example, *moshi* (hello), *sayonara* (goodbye), *arigato* (thank you).

9. Try some Japanese writing, following a discussion of how it is derived from original symbols or figures, for example:

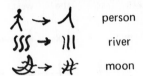

person

river

moon

10. Listening:
    "Music of Japan," Keyboard Publications.
    "Favorite Songs of Japanese Children" (FS and record), Bowmar.
    See Listening under "Cherry Bloom," no. 60.

11. Film: "Discovering the Music of Japan," color, 21 min., Film Associates.
    Filmstrip: "Children of Japan," McGraw-Hill.
    See resource material for Japan (p. 287).

For study

Pentatonic scale

Uneven rhythm

Conduct in 2-bt. pattern (See p. 269)
Music of Japan

58. SAIL SILVER MOON BOAT
Chinese melody

Level: U
Key: pentatonic: start A (la)

1. See the sil-ver moon in the sky gent-ly float Near the shin-ing stars, see the moon like a boat;
2. Shine on sil-ver moon in the clouds so — white, Shine on sil-ver moon with your smile so — bright;

Sail, sil-ver moon boat to the west, Sail, sil-ver moon boat while I rest.
Sail, sil-ver moon boat to the west, Sail, sil-ver moon boat while I rest.

Finger Cymbal

Triangle

Wood Block

From Choate, Berg, Kjelson, and Troth, *Enjoying Music,* New Dimensions in Music series, © 1970 by the American Book Company, New York.

The action

1. When the song has been learned, add the finger cymbals, triangles, and woodblock for accompaniment, as shown.
2. The song contains only three tones (*do sol la*) of the five-tone pentatonic scale (*do re mi sol la*); thus it is easy to play on any melody instrument such as a recorder or resonator bells. As a variation, play only the first note of each measure while the song is being sung.
3. Have one child play the song in reverse, from end to beginning, while another plays from beginning to end—simultaneously.
4. Create a new melody, using tones of the pentatonic scale, to be played while the song is being sung.
5. Set a Chinese poem or a saying of a Chinese philosopher to a melody, using tones of the pentatonic scale.
6. Learn the Chinese Ribbon Dance, no. 58A.

Related activities and materials

1. Play the Chinese stick game, as follows:

    Holding a long stick, players stand facing each other, right foot and right hand forward. Each strikes his stick on the ground, then against the stick of his opponent *high,* then against the stick of his opponent *low.* Do this in rhythm.

    Improvise a melody to accompany the stick game, using selected tones of the pentatonic scale.
2. Make a Chinese kite and try to fly it.
3. See "Yangtze Boatmen's Chantey," no. 59, for further activities.
4. Listening:
    "Ancient and Oriental Music," The History of Music in Sound, RCA.

    "The Challenge of China" (FS, record, teacher's guide, students' booklets), Keyboard Publications.

    "Ancient Chinese Music," Exploring Music, Book 6 record album, Holt, Rinehart and Winston.

    "Chinese Dance," from "The Nutcracker Suite," Tschaikovsky.

    "Folk Instruments of the World," Follett Publishing Co.

    "Laideronette, Empress of the Pagodas," Ravel, BOL #57.
5. See resource material on China (p. 287).

For study

Pentatonic
Like phrases
Sing with syllables (See pp. 277-278); try singing from end to beginning
Conduct in 4-bt. pattern (See p. 269)
Music of China

58A. CHINESE RIBBON DANCE

From Edna Doll and Mary Jarman Nelson, *Rhythms Today!* © 1965 by the Silver Burdett Company; reprinted by permission of the General Learning Corporation.

Accompany with woodblock, cymbals, gong, sticks. Crash cymbals on (crash).

Each dancer carries a stick three feet long, one inch in diameter, to which is tacked a ribbon two inches wide and 15 feet long. The ribbons should be of different colors.

Any number of participants, each with a ribbon-stick held high, run in to form a circle or rows.

Circle the ribbon-stick overhead (Crash!)

Circle the stick to front, as shown in Fig. 1 (Crash!)

Circle the stick to right (Crash!)

Change hands and circle the stick to left (Crash!)

Change hands and do a vertical figure 8 in front, as shown in Fig. 2 (Crash!)

Holding the stick high, start a figure 8 gradually lowering it (Fig. 3), bending the body until ribbon almost touches the ground. Rise up (Crash!)

Circle the ribbon alternately front and back (Crash!)

Circle the ribbon several times horizontally in front to the floor, keeping the arm straight (Crash!)

Each boy twirls his own ribbon continuously in a large, vertical loop as he jumps through once (Fig. 4), falls to the floor, drops stick, rises, clasps hands, bows three times, and runs off stage.

The dancers should experiment with ribbon figures, selecting ones for the dance that they can do best.

The dance may also be done as a cowboy version, using lariats instead or ribbon-sticks.

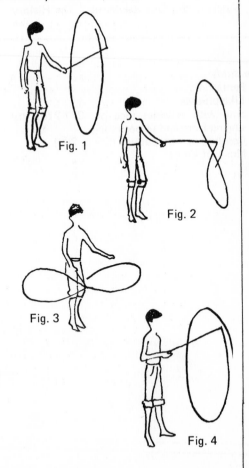

Fig. 1

Fig. 2

Fig. 3

Fig. 4

59. YANGTZE BOATMEN'S CHANTEY

Chinese chantey (English by Bliss Wiant)

Key: Pentatonic
Start G (la)

YAH HOO YAH HOO HEY! YAH HOO, YAH HOO HEY!

YAI YAI YAI HAI YAI YAI YAH HOO YAH HOO HEY!

From *All Asia Sings,* © 1967; used by permission of Cooperative Recreation Service, Delaware, Ohio.

The action

1. Discover what movements Chinese boatmen use to pull their boats upstream against the current. Discuss how the rhythm of the song may have evolved from the movements the men did. Have one group perform the movements in rhythm while another group sings the song. Compare the "Yangtze Boatmen's Chantey" with the Russian "Volga Boatman" (below) as to tempo, mood, rhythm, etc. (Try singing them together.)

Compare with river chanteys from the United States.

2. Add selected rhythm instruments for accompaniment, for example, finger cymbals, triangles, woodblock.

3. Let one child play the song or bells or recorder from beginning to end, while another child plays in reverse, from end to beginning.

4. Note that the song uses only four tones of the five-tone pentatonic scale, thus it is easy to play on any melody instrument.

5. Find a Chinese poem or a saying of Confucius and set it to a melody, using only the tones of the pentatonic scale. This may be done by ear by playing the black keys on the piano or bells:

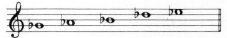

6. Create some new melodies, using only tones of the pentatonic scale (*do re mi sol la*).

7. Discover some familiar songs built on the pentatonic scale tones, for example, "Old MacDonald" no. 24, "The Farmer in the Dell" no. 13, and "Auld Lang Syne."

Related activities and materials
1. Make a Chinese gong, using the metal lid from a large paper packing carton.
2. Learn the Chinese Ribbon Dance, no. 58A.
3. Sing other Chinese songs, for example, "Sail, Silver Moon Boat, no. 58 (note the related suggestions). "The Pagoda" (a collection of songs), Cooperative Recreation Service. Selections from basic song series "Exploring Music," "New Dimensions in Music," "Making Music Your Own."
4. Listening: See Listening under "Sail, Silver Moon Boat," no. 58.
5. Film: "Children of China," 10 min., black and white, Encyclopedia Britannica, 1150 Wilmette Ave., Wilmette, Ill.
6. See resource material on China.

For study
Pentatonic
Like phrases
Sing with syllables (See pp. 277-278)
Conduct in 4-bt. pattern (See p. 269)
Music of China

60. CHERRY BLOOM (SAKURA)

Japanese folk song (words adapted)

Level: U
Key of c minor: start C (la)

Gently

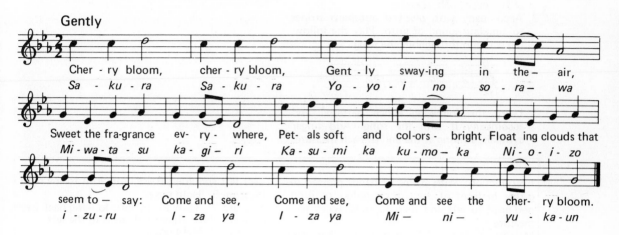

Cher - ry bloom,   cher - ry bloom,   Gent - ly   sway-ing   in   the - air,
Sa - ku - ra   Sa - ku - ra   Yo - yo - i   no   so - ra - wa

Sweet the fra-grance   ev- ry - where,   Pet- als soft   and   col-ors-   bright, Float ing clouds that
Mi - wa - ta - su   ka - gi - ri   Ka - su - mi   ka   ku - mo - ka   Ni - o - i - zo

seem to — say: Come and see,   Come and see,   Come and see   the   cher - ry bloom.
i - zu - ru   I - za   ya   I - za   ya   Mi —   ni —   yu - ka - un

From *Exploring Music Series* (teacher's ed.), Book 3, © 1966; by special permission of the publisher, Holt, Rinehart and Winston.

The action

1. Sing in Japanese. Pronounce as follows: a = ah; i = ee; o = oh; u = oo.
2. Accompany with *plucked* autoharp strings to simulate sound of koto. Play the following ostinato throughout the song:

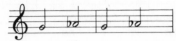

3. Learn the following dance pattern* and accompany it with the song: Add finger cymbals, striking at the end of each measure.

Introduction: With palms of hands pressed together in front of chest in prayerlike position, nod head to left and then to right twice to a measure.
Measure 1: Move right arm across chest and over head in a graceful arc. Take a small step to the right at the same time
Measure 2: Move left arm across chest and over head in a graceful arc. Take a small step to the left at the same time.
Measures 3-4: Repeat measures 1-2.
Measure 5: Turn to the right, looking back over left shoulder. Raise both arms to the right.
Measure 6: Hold pose.
Measure 7: Turn to the left, looking back over right shoulder. Raise both arms to the left.
Measure 8: Hold pose.
Measure 9: Face forward, spreading arms in a wide arc above head (as if holding a large balloon).
Measure 10: Bring hands together in front of chest; bow head.
Measures 11-14: Repeat actions for measures 1-4.

Point out to the children that, unlike American square dances Japanese dances occupy little floor space, use small steps, and are done without partners. Arm and head movements are also used more extensively.

4. After learning the dance pattern above and discussing the characteristics of Japanese dance, have children create some of their own movements in Japanese tradition.
5. Although this song is in the Oriental mode, much of the Chinese and Japanese music is based on the pentatonic mode. To sound a pentatonic scale, start on any *do* and sing *do re mi sol la*. On bells or the piano, start on G$\flat$ and play all the black keys in order:

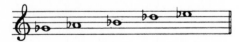

6. Create a tune, using only the tones of the pentatonic scale.

*From *Exploring Music Series* (Teacher's ed.), Book 3, © 1966; by special permission of the publisher, Holt, Rinehart and Winston.

Related activities and materials

1. Set selected verses of Haiku poetry to original pentatonic melodies. Haiku is traditionally a 17-syllable poem of three lines—five syllables in the first line, seven in the second, and five in the third—usually dealing with nature. Although simply stated, its thoughts frequently inspire the reader to contemplate its deeper meaning.
2. Write some original Haiku and set it to an original pentatonic melody.
3. See "Japanese Rain Song," no. 57 for further suggestions.
4. Listening:
   "Variations on *Sakura*," Exploring Music, Book 4 (album), Holt, Rinehart and Winston.
   "Oriental Scenes," BOL #66.
5. See resource material on Japan.

For study

$\frac{2}{2}$ meter
Minor: see Major and Minor and Minor Scales
Sing with syllables (See pp. 277-278)
Like phrases
Conduct in 2-bt. pattern in appropriate tempo (See p. 269)
Music of Japan

61.   TINIKLING

Philippine dance song (collected by Francisca Reyes
Aquino — English words by Margaret Marks)

Level: U
Key of G: start D (low sol)

1. Ev-'ry bod- y   dance like the   bird Tin -   i - Kling,
   fas - ter and fas - ter, — don't   stop.

As — he — jumps in and   out, out — and in. Hop-ping o - ver
Left, right, left, right, you step and — you hop. Bet - ter keep the

branch - es   so grace - ful and   light,   Keep— in — step and you'll
pace up, jump in and jump   out   Or — the— bam-boo will

dance this dance—right,   2. Now the dance goes
get you, watch—

out.   Care-ful that the

clip   and the clap   of the bam-boo   Come be-tween the tip - ping
tap-ping   toes!   Care - ful when the poles come to - geth - er, clip
                    May - be there are some who can   still jump and

clap,   That — your— feet are not caught in   their — trap!
         But— you— can - not be blamed if you —

Care-ful that the   stop!   Ev-'ry bod-y drop out and stop!

From *Making Music Your Own,* Book 6, © 1971 by the General Learning Corporation; reprinted by permission.

The action
This is primarily a dance song done in the Philippines, the movements of which are intended to imitate the long-legged tikling bird walking between long stem grasses and over fallen tree limbs. An interesting rhythmic accompaniment is provided by the click of two bamboo poles used to "trap" the dancer representing the bird.

Materials needed: 2 bamboo poles 6 to 9 feet long; 2 pieces of board 30 inches long and 2 inches thick

Position: set poles side by side about 12 inches apart, resting on the pieces of wood, with a player at each end, seated on the floor holding the ends of the poles, as shown:

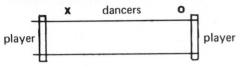

The players slide the poles together on the first beat of each measure, then hit the boards on which they rest on the second and third beats of each measure:

hit poles together   strike poles on boards

Players holding the poles should practice executing this movement in rhythm before the dancers attempt their steps.

Basic dance step*: stand outside the pole so that the poles are to the dancers' right.

measure 1: on beat 1, hop on left foot *outside* the left pole
on beat 2, hop on right foot *between* the poles
on beat 3, hop on left foot *between* the poles

measure 2: on beat 1, hop on right foot *outside* the right pole
on beat 2, hop on left foot *between* the poles
on beat 3, hop on right foot *between* the poles

Continue throughout the song, alternating right and left sides. Dancers should always plan to have both feet outside the poles on the first beat of each measure, for that is when the poles click together.

Variations: the children may choose partners, stand one in back of the other and dance the Tinikling step at the same time or in turn in Section A of the song. In section B, partners may stand across from each other, facing, so that the poles are to each dancer's left. As the Tinikling step is danced, the partners move toward each other and change sides with each measure of the music.

*Dance directions from *Making Music Your Own,* Book 6, © 1971 by the General Learning Corporation; reprinted by permission.

Related activities and materials
1. Have the children create their own variations of the basic Tinikling step.
2. Try other folk dances from the Philippines, for example, "Carinosa" (RCA World of Folk Dances series).
3. Sing other folk songs from the Philippines:

"Tayo'y Umawit" (a collection of Philippine folk songs), Cooperative Recreation Service. Selections from basic music series.
4. Listening:
   Folk Songs of the Philippines, Folkways Records.

For study

Chromatic tones
Endings 1, 2, and 3
D.S.

𝄊

Conduct in 3-bt. pattern (See p. 269)
Music of the Philippines

62. ALEKOKI

Hawaiian chant
(English version by Aura Kantra)

Program song
Level: U
Key of C: start G (sol)

A - o - le i, pi - li - wi i - a,
Ho-o - Ko - hu ka u - a i u - ka,

Ka - hi wa - i a - o A - le - ko - ki.
No - ho ma - i la - i Nu - u - a - nu.

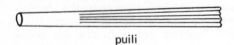

puili

"Nuuanu" is the break in the Koolau Mountain range on the island of Oahu. "Alekoki" is a pool of falls hidden by heavy tropical foliage in the valley of Nuuanu.

Strike the *puili* on the:

P̄alm

F̄loor

B̄ack of Hand

S̄houlder

P P P

Palm—moving the hands from left to right

B↗

Back of hand—away from body

B↓

Back of hand—close to body

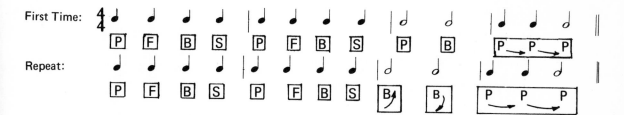

First Time:

Repeat:

The action

1. Sing in Hawaiian. Vowel pronunciation is as follows: a = ah; e = ay; i = ee; o = ō; u - oo.
2. Make some *puili* (fringed bamboo sticks) out of bamboo, and fringe the ends. In place of bamboo, newspaper may be rolled and fringed. The *puili* should be about 12 inches long.
3. Do the dance as follows:

   Position: kneel, then sit back on heels, holding the solid end of the stick in the right hand. This may be done in a partner formation, if desired.

   Movement: for practice, strike the fringed end on the following places:

palm of left hand	1 beat
floor	1 beat
back of hand	1 beat
shoulder	1 beat

   Repeat this pattern a number of times to get the feel of the *puili,* then study the movement directions and try the dance above.
4. Accompany with ukulele, autoharp, or resonator bells.

5. Sing the scale in Hawaiian:

   pa ko li ha no la mi pa

   The syllables *no pa li la* are the four scale tones used for tuning the ukulele. For the key of G tuning.

NO	PA	LI	LA
A	D	F♯	B

   For the key of F tuning:

NO	PA	LI	LA
G	C	E	A

6. Select some of the Hawaiian scale syllables at random and write a tune.

Related activities and materials

1. For simple costumes when this song is used as a program song; make some leis out of facial tissues. Wear on wrist, neck, ankles, and in the hair. The girls may wear brightly colored skirts with halters or blouses, while the boys wear white pants, colored shorts, or white shirts with colored sashes.
2. Make a Hawaiian instrument such as *uli-uli* (a gourd with brilliant feathers added) and slap it with the open hand for rhythm to accompany singing.
3. Learn some Hawaiian dances and hand movements, then create a song using the movements to tell the story of the song.
   "He-eia," from "Rhythms Today," Edna Doll, published by Silver Burdett.

   "Kiuia," from NMH, Book 5, Silver Burdett. Dances of Hawaii, Bowmar Sing other Hawaiian songs (see "Hawaiian Rainbows," EIM, McGraw-Hill).
4. Wish someone a "Merry Christmas" in Hawaiian—*Mele Kalikimaka* (*May*lay Kah-lee-kee-*mah*-kah).
5. Listening:
   "Music of Hawaii," Keyboard Publications. "Hawaiian Chant, Hula and Music," Folkways Records. "Na Mele Ohana," Hula Records, P.O. Box 2135, Honolulu, Hawaii. "Folk Songs of our Pacific Neighbors," Bowmar.
6. See resource material on Hawaii.

For study

Even rhythm
Repeat sign :‖
Chant rhythm and sing with syllables (See pp. 277-278)
Conduct in 4-bt. pattern (See p. 269)

left-hand piano

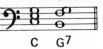

    C   G⁷

bells   Autoharp

C = C E G   C, G⁷
G⁷ = G B D F

ukulele

Tune: G C E A (key of F tuning)

   C   G⁷

63. TITI—TORIA

Maori folk song of New Zealand
(Leone Holbrook, English by Max Exner)

Program song
Level: U
Key of F: start A (mi)

E pa-pa—wai-a-ri ta-ku nei—ma—hi,
Smile o my—fa-ther but nev-er de-ny—me,

Ta-ku nei—ma-hi he tu-ku ro—ma-ta ta-ku roi-
Nev-er de—ny me the pleas-ure of—dream-ing, pleas-ure of

ma-ta E-au-e ka ma-te-au. — E-hi—ne*
dream-ing Way a-way, my love is a-way. E-hi-ne
*Girl of mine.

ho-ki i-ho ra. — — ra. Ma-ku e kau-te o
come a-gain to me! — me! Cold is the path-way that

hi—koi tang-a Ma-ku e kau-te o hi-koi tang-a.
led her from me, Warm will the path be that brings her to me.

From *All Asia Sings,* published by Cooperative Recreation Service, Delaware, Ohio.

The action

1. Learn the song in the Maori language. The
   vowel pronunciation is:

   A—*ar* as in lark
   E—*ea* as in bread
   I—*ee* as in feed
   O—*or* as in fork
   U—*oo* as in moon

   In the consonants, *ng* has a nasal sound.
   Sound spelling for the first line of the song
   is:

   Eh pah pah wah-hee-ah-ree
   tak-koo neh-ee mah-hee

2. When the song has been learned, play the following stick game to the rhythm of the song:

Formation: two players face each other in a kneeling position, sitting back on their heels.

Equipment: each player has a pair of sticks 14 or 15 inches long and 1 inch in diameter. Each stick may be painted in two colors, for example, half red and half black.

Movements: grasp each stick between thumb and fingertips at the center, holding it in a vertical position. (The sticks should remain in a vertical position at all times, even when thrown.) Perform one movement to each beat of the measure. A few of the possible movements are:

Hit

(a) hitting own sticks together
(b) hitting own sticks on floor
(c) hitting partner's sticks with own sticks

Flip

Tossing the sticks in the air so they revolve end over end (one half a full turn) and catching them

Throw

Throwing the sticks gently to the partner, using either a straight across or slightly upward motion to avoid dropping

Note: in this movement each player should concentrate on *catching* the stick coming toward him rather than on the one he's throwing.

The game is played using a combination of different movements:

Part A

Measure 1: *hit* floor, *hit* together, *throw* right stick only to partner

Measure 2: *hit* floor, *hit* together, *throw* left stick only to partner _
(repeat movements for measures 1 and 2 throughout Part A)

Part B

hit floor, *hit* together, *hit* both sticks of the partner
(repeat these movements throughout Part B)

Part C

hit floor, *hit* together, *throw* both sticks to partner
(Note: one player should hold his sticks apart so that he may throw his set outside while the other player throws his set inside. This enables one set of sticks to pass between the other.)

---

3. Make up some figures as desired.
4. Sing a harmony part a third above the melody on Part A.

Related activities and materials

1. Make a replica of a *poi* ball out of available materials such as paper; for example: roll a four-inch (diameter) ball and cover with a lightweight material such as cotton. Sew securely at the top and attach a 9-12 inch string with a fair size knot on the holding end. The string should be fairly thick. Fishing cord works well if the thick size is used. Swing the *poi* ball to the rhythm of the music by holding the string between the thumb and index finger of one hand and keeping the knot in the palm of the same hand. Change the direction of the swing when desired by patting the ball lightly with the other hand as it swings.

2. Sing other Maori songs (see Listening and Song Collections below).

3. Accompany with Autoharp, ukulele, and/or resonator bells in three parts.

4. Listening:
"Maori Songs of New Zealand," Folkways Records.
"Koia Ano," Kiwi Records, Wellington, New Zealand.
"Folk Songs of Our Pacific Neighbors," Bowmar.

5. Books:
   Music of the Maori, Barrow, Seven Seas Publishing Co., Willington, N.Z.
   The New Zealand Maori in Colour, Kenneth Nad, Jean Bigwood, Charles Tuttle Co., Rutland, Vermont.

6. Song Collections:
   "Maori Games and Hakas," Alan Armstrong and A. W. Reed, Auckland, N.Z.
   "Maori Action Songs," Armstrong and Ngata and A. W. Reed, Auckland, N.Z.

For study
Chromatic tone
𝄋
First and Second endings
D.S.
Da Capo
Fine
Conduct in 3-bt pattern (See p. 269)

left-hand piano

F   B♭   C⁷

bells
F = F A C
B♭ = B♭ D F
C⁷ = C E G B♭

Autoharp
F, B♭, C⁷

ukulele
Tune: G C E A (key of F tuning)

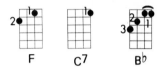

F   C⁷   B♭

64. AMONG THE PINES

Folk song of Assam sung by Kim Singh
(English by Max Exner)

Level: U
Key of d minor: start A (mi)

Slowly, Softly

A-mong the pines that bend their fra-grant boughs, The forest winds their whis-pered tales un-
Ah, Tiew-la - run, my own be - lov - ed flow'r, To you a-lone, my heart is ev - er

fold; The splen - did stars like jew - els light the sky, And now the moon has turned the wa-ters
drawn, By day and night my eyes see you a - lone, You are my day, my night, my ris-ing

gold. Ah, Tiew - la - run.* be - lov - ed flow'r of mine, When will you
dawn.

come? I ask the si - lent pine Ah, Tiew-la - run, Ah, Tiew - la - run.

*Girl's name pronounced Taû'-lä-roon'.

From *All Asia Sings,* © 1956 by the Cooperative Recreation Service, Delaware, Ohio; used by permission.

The action

1. Compare these two folk songs (Nos 64 and 65) from different sections of India in terms of mood and mode. Each contains something known all over the world—humor in tall tales and longing for a loved one. Explore with the class the other "universals"— Things common to all the world's peoples— then have the children try to find songs from other nations which reflect these characteristics.

2. Discuss what a "tall tale" is. Make up some tall tales and tell them. Choose one or two and create some music for them.

3. Select rhythm instruments to accompnay each of the songs. Selection should be based on timbre and dynamics appropriate to the contrasting moods of the songs.

Related activities and materials

1. Listen to the sound of instruments of India and look at some pictures of them, for example, a sitar and a tambura (see *Folk Instruments of the World*, Follett Co.).

2. Research the meaning of quarter tones (microtones) found in Indian music, and the chanting of the rhythmic drum patterns.

3. See sections on Music of India, in *Investigating Music, Mastering Music,* and *Experiencing Music*—all NDM series, American Book Co.

4. Listening:
   "Sounds of India," Ravi Shankar, Col. CS 9296.
   "Folk Music of India," Folkways Records.
   "Folk Instruments of the World," Follett Publishing Co.

5. Film: "Discovering the Music of India," Film Associates.

For study

Like phrases
Alternate measures of varying meter signature (see "Dipidu," no. 68)
Signs: mf, hold ($\frown$), p, crescendo, mp
Ornamentation over word "pine"
Use of *si* (C$\sharp$) denotes harmonic minor

65. GUP!—TALL TALE

Indian

Level: U
Key of E♭ : start E♭ (do)

Chorus

Gup su-no Bha-i, Gup! Gup su-no Bha-i, Gup!
I'll tell a tall tale Gup! I'll tell a tall tale Gup!

Gup su-no Bha-i, Gup! su-no gap-pi me-ra nam —
I'll tell a tall tale, Don-key— climbed up a palm tree,

FINE

charh-i charh-i, Kha-joor per aur Kha-ne la-gi a-nar!
There he did sit and eat pome—gran ates, Hap-py as he could be.

Chun-ti mar-ri — pa-har par Khin-chan cha le cha-
Out on the hill-a poor ant died, Bold cob-bler skinned her at
Chick-en would vis-it her in-laws, Paint-ed and pow-dered well
This is the tall-est tale of all - Our well, it caught on —

mar, Khin-chan cha-le-cha-mar
once, Bold cob-bler skinned her at once,
well, Paint-ed and pow-derred — well,
fire, Our well, it caught on — fire,

D.C.

Do sau jo-re ju-te, ba-na-e Mash ken—kai ha-zar
They made shoes, two hun-dred full pairs and five thou-sand skin bags too.
Comb and brush she held in her hand, she primped as she walked a-long.
Mud and wa-ter in flames they van-ished; fish-es all flew a-way.

From *All Asia Sings*, © 1956 by the Cooperative Recreation Service, Delaware, Ohio; used by permission.

Pronunciation:

gup suno bhai gup (u as in "cup" soo-no bye-ee)

gappi mera nam (gah-pee mare-nah nahm)

gadhi charhi khajoor per aur (gahd-dee je-rah-hee kha-jure pahr awr)

khane lagi anar (kah-nay laggee anahr)

chinti mari pahar par (jun-tee mar-ee pah-ar par)

khinchan chale chamar (keen-chahn cha-lay cha-mahr)

do sau jore jute banae (do so jor-ay-ju-tee banahee)

mash ken kai hazar (mahsh ken ky-ee hah-zahr)

For study

Like phrases
Frequent use of slur
Chromatic tone (meas. 8)
Signs: D.C. Repeat :‖
Note solo and chorus

66. MINKA

Russian folk song (English words by Margaret Marke)

Level: U

Key of g minor: start G (la)

1. Said the Cos - sack to the maid - en "Love my heart is heav-y lad - en,
2. Off the Cos - sack went to bat - tle All a - lone poor Mink-a sat e-

Du - ty calls so I'm a - fraid, en - chant-ress we must part.
lev - en years and she grew fat, al - though her heart was true.

I be - seech you fair - est Mink-a, Wait for me, I hate to think An -
When at last her Cos - sack lov - er Came back home and looked her o - ver,

oth - er man might come and tink - er With your faith — ful heart.
He be - gan to court an - oth - er, Broke her heart — in — two!

From *Making Music Your Own*, Book 6, © 1971 by the General Learning Corporation; reprinted by permission.

The action

1. Assign the solo on the Cossack part, with the chorus singing the narrative parts.
2. Assign two children to dramatize the Cossack and maiden parts in pantomime, while the chorus sings the entire song.
3. Choose appropriate rhythm instruments to accompany the Cossack sections and con-

trasting instruments for the maiden sections.
4. Create a new verse which the maiden might sing in answer to verse 1 by the Cossack.
5. Compare "Minka" (no. 66) with "Yoma" (no. 50) as to mode, rhythm patterns, melody, etc.

6. Dance the *troika* ("troika" means a three-horse sleigh; this is a vigorous Russian dance representing the team of three horses). The tempo should be adapted to the ability of the dancers to keep up the pace of *one* step to *each eighth note* (this means *run*!).

Formation: sets of threes, facing counterclockwise in a circle, with the middle person holding hands with the person on each side at shoulder height.

meas. 1: run four steps diagonally *right*
meas. 2: run four steps diagonally *left*
meas. 3-4: run eight steps forward
meas. 5-6: the middle and left persons raise their hands to make an arch, while the person on the right runs under the arch, still holding the hands of the middle person (middle person turns in place). Eight steps.
meas. 7-8: repeat as in meas. 5-6, with the person on the left running under the arch

made by the middle and right persons. Eight steps.
meas. 9-12: make a circle of three persons, hold hands, run 12 steps counterclockwise, then stamp three times quickly

♪   ♪   ♪   ↷

stamp   stamp   stamp

meas. 13-16: repeat as in meas. 9-12, running in a clockwise direction and ending with three quick stamps, as before.

Related activities and materials

1. Explore the possible influence of climate on the music and dance of various people in different parts of the world.
2. View and listen to the sound of some Russian folk instruments, for example, the balalaika. See Listening below.
3. Learn other Russian folk songs and folk dances. (See "Korobushka," MMYO 6, Silver Burdett.)
4. Listening:
   "Music of Russia" (record, visual masters, teacher's guide, students' booklets), Keyboard Publications.

"Three Horse Sleigh," Tchaikovsky.
"Troika" from "Lieutenant Kije," AM 2, vol. 2.
"Osipov Balalaika Orchestra, USSR Melodyia (Angel Records).
"Folk Instruments of the World," Follett Publishing Co.
"Meadowland and other Favorites," Don Cossack Chorus, Decca Records.
"Russian Sailor's Dance," from "Red Poppy Suite," Gliére.
"Russian Dance," from "Petrouchka," AM 1, vol. 2.

For study

Harmonic minor indicated by presence of "si" (F♯); see Minor Scales and Major and Minor

Sequence

Sing with syllables, chant rhythm first (See pp. 277-278)

Descending melody characteristic of Russian songs

Conduct in 2-bt. pattern (See p. 269)

Music of Russia

left-hand-piano

gm   D⁷   B♭

bells

g min = G B♭ D
D⁷ = D F♯ A C
B♭ = B♭ D F

Autoharp

g min, D⁷, B♭

67. HAVAH NAGILA

Palestinian folk dance—adapted words

Lively

Program song
Level: U
Key of g minor: start D (mi)

Out in   the mead-ow mu-sic   is play-ing: Peo-ple   are danc-ing, They cir-cle a-bout.

Arms linked with one an - oth-er   they dance the ho - ra   and while they dance mer - ri -ly shout:

"Come, do the ho-ra now, Watch, and we'll show you how; Step, hop, and once a-gain. See how it is done

Hear how   we keep the beat,   Step-ping with   live -ly feet;   Come, join   our cir-cle now;

Come,   dance with your friends!   Now   that   we're   to - geth - er,

Ev'-ry one steps a lit-tle fast -er, Ev'-ry one hops a lit- tle   fast-er See how the cir-cle's turn-ing fast-er;

See how the cir-cle's turn-ing fast-er! Now it is done? rest ev-'ry one. We've danced the ho-ra joy-ful -ly!

From *Studying Music,* Music for Young Americans series, © 1966; by permission of the American Book Company.

The action

1. Note tempo markings:

   accelerando (meas. 19)

   ritard (meas. 23)

   a tempo (meas. 24)

   These should be observed as much as possible in order to retain the spirit of the song.

2. When song has been learned, add rhythm instruments as desired or as follows:

   meas. 1-16: use the following rhythm pattern throughout these measures:

   tambourine   R   R R R   R R

   drum

   finger cymbals

   meas. 17:

   tambourine   S   S

   meas. 18:

   tambourine   R   R   R   R

   meas. 19-23:

   tambourine   R   R   S   S

   drum

   meas. 24:

   tambourine   R   R   R   R

   drum

   finger cymbals

   R = Rap
   S = Shake

3. Learn the *hora.* Let one group dance while another sings:

   Formation: circle with arms extended and resting on each other's shoulders.

   Step right on the left foot; put the left foot behind the right and place weight on it.

   Step sideways on the right foot and place weight on it.

   Kick the left foot across in front of the right while hopping on the right at the same time.

   Step on the left foot, place weight on it, kick the right foot across in front of the left, and hop on the left foot at the same time.

   May be chanted while learning: "side, back, side, kick, side, kick." There are six even counts to each complete pattern.

   The pattern is repeated throughout the dance. Start it slowly and gradually increase in tempo, as indicated by the tempo markings.

Related activities and materials

1. Learn some other folk dances from Israel, for example, "Cherkassiya" and "Shiboleth Bas-adeh" (RCA World of Folk Dance series).

2. Sing other Israeli folk songs.

3. Listening:

   See resource materials for Israel, p. 286.

For study

Triplet
Minor (presence of *si* [F♯] indicates harmonic form)
Syncopation
Accelerando
Ritard
A tempo
Recurrence of rhythm pattern
Hold ⌒
Music of Israel

bells

D7 = D F♯ A C
g min = G B♭ D
c min = C E♭ G
D = D F♯ A

68. DIPIDU

Uganda

Level: U
Key of F: start C (high sol)

Rather slowly

From *Sing a Tune*; used by permission of Cooperative Recreation Service, Delaware, Ohio.

The action

This song is sung by guides in Uganda.

1. When the song has been learned, let one child sing the solo part as the leader, with the class as the chorus. (This type of "call and response" singing characterizes much of the music of Africa.)

2. Clap on the off beats, where indicated in the music.

3. Add drums and rattles, as desired, for accompaniment.

4. Create some new verses substituting other names for "Guidee."

5. Note the change of meter from triple to duple. In the triple ($\frac{3}{4}$) section, have the class choose one action to execute on the first beat of each measure and a different action on the second and third beats of each measure, for example slap sides, clap, clap, etc. Do the same for the duple ($\frac{2}{4}$) section, with one action on the first beat and a different one on the second.

6. In number 5, try the movements in alternating measures of triple and duple meter, first one in three, then one in two, then another in three, followed by one in two, and so on.

7. Try the rhythm pattern on p. 143 with the suggested instruments. This pattern is not meant to accompany this song; rather it is simply to get the feel of the intricate interweaving of rhythm patterns characteristic of the music of Africa.

Related activities and materials

1. Make some African masks, using some form of art media.
2. After viewing some African instruments, make some replicas and play them.
3. Communicate some messages through the drums, as African drummers do, for example, station the students around the room to represent villages. Through the use of certain combinations of drum beats and drums, send a message from the first drummer to the second, who in turn relays it to the third, and so forth.
4. Sing other African folk songs:
   "Sing Noel," no. 71.
   "African Songs," Cooperative Recreation Service, Delaware, Ohio.

See New Dimensions in Music series, American Book Co. (sections on Africa in the following titles: *Expressing Music, Enjoying Music, Mastering Music, Investigating Music*).
5. Listening:
   "The Sounds of Africa" (FS, records, teacher's guide, students' booklets), Keyboard Publications.
   "Afrikaans Children's Folk Songs," Folkways Records.
   See Listening under "Sing Noel."
6. Films:
   "Discovering the Music of Africa," 28 min., color, Film Associates.
   "Masks," 12 min., color, McGraw-Hill text films.
   See resource material on Africa, p. 287.

For study

Change of meter within song from $\frac{3}{4}$ to $\frac{2}{4}$
Syncopation
Tonic chord (meas. 1 and 3)
Repeat sign :‖
Conduct in 3-bt. pattern, then in 2-bt. pattern (See p. 269)
Music of Africa

The number patterns for the following rhythm are included below the rhythm pattern. Players should play on the numbers and rest on each "x." Return from the last beat immediately to the first beat without hesitating in between. Count slowly and aloud at first, then increase the tempo.

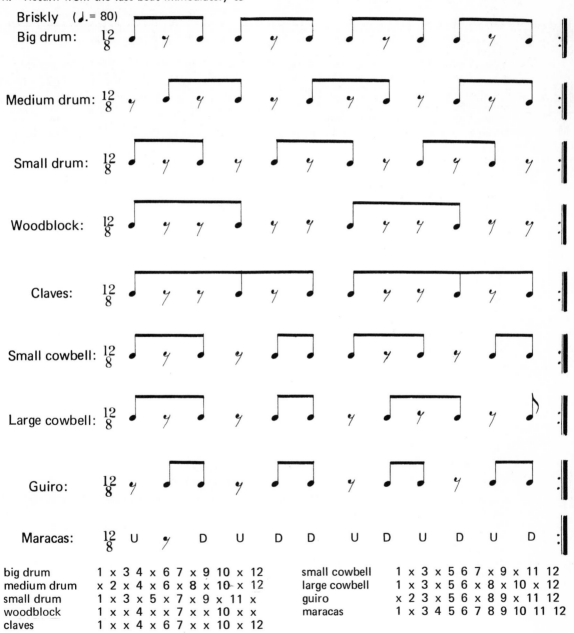

big drum	1 x 3 4 x 6 7 x 9 10 x 12	small cowbell	1 x 3 x 5 6 7 x 9 x 11 12
medium drum	x 2 x 4 x 6 x 8 x 10 x 12	large cowbell	1 x 3 x 5 6 x 8 x 10 x 12
small drum	1 x 3 x 5 x 7 x 9 x 11 x	guiro	x 2 3 x 5 6 x 8 9 x 11 12
woodblock	1 x x 4 x x 7 x x 10 x x	maracas	1 x 3 4 5 6 7 8 9 10 11 12
claves	1 x x 4 x 6 7 x x 10 x 12		

Rhythm patterns and number pattern from Robert Choate, Richard Berg, Lee Kjelson, and Eugene Troth, *Mastering Music,* New Dimensions in Music series, © 1970, American Book Company, New York.

69. ARE YOU SLEEPING?
(Frere Jacques)
Round

Level: U and L
Key of F: start F (do)

Are you sleep - ing,   Are   you   sleep - ing, Broth - er John?   Broth-er John?

Morn-ing bells are ring-ing, Morn-ing bells are ring-ing,   Ding ding dong.   Ding ding dong.

The action

1. After the song has been learned, sing as a three-part round.
2. Assign an action to each part, for example:
   measures 1-2: clap hands
   measures 3-4: slap knees
   measures 5-6: snap fingers
   measures 7-8: tap feet

   and sing through in unison and then in three-part round form.
3. Originate other actions, using percussive sounds on the body.
4. Select a rhythm instrument to play in each section.
5. Create some interpretive body movement for each section, then sing as a three-part round with the movement in round form also.
6. Change the key signature to four flats and play in f minor:

      etc.

   Discuss the effect of the change of key on the mood of the song. Create some new verses to sing in the minor key.
7. Sing as a partner song with "Three Blind Mice," "The Farmer in the Dell," or "Row, Row, Row Your Boat." All four may be sung together or in any grouping of two. Just be sure they're in the same key.

8. Use tune as a tone-matching game, for example (T = teacher, C = child)

   (T) Where is _____ (child's name)
   (C) Here is _____
   (T) Where is_____ (another child)
   (C) Here is _____
   (T) Where is _____ (1st and last name)
   (C) Here is _____
   (T) Glad you're here
   Class: Glad you're here

9. Use the same tune for a familiar finger-play song:
   a. Where is Thumbkin, Where is Thumbkin?
      Here I am here I am
      How are you today, sir
      Very well, I thank you,
      Run away run away.
   b. Where is pointer
   c. Where is long man
   d. Where is ring man
   e. Where is little man
   f. Where are all men

10. Create some new verses to fit an occasion or need:
    Sit up straighter, sit up straighter
    Never slump, never slump
    Or you'll be a camel,
    Yes, you'll be a camel
    With a hump, with a hump.

11. Add a simple ostinato to be sung or played on recorder or bells:

or

12. Sing the song in other languages:

Frere Jacques, Frere Jacques
Dormez vous, dormez vous?
Sonnez les matines, sonnez les matines
Din din don, din din don.

13. Using the same tune, sing new words in another language:

Buenos dias, buenos dias
¿Como estan, como estan?
Estamos muy bienes,
    estamos muy bienes,
Muchas gracias, muchas gracias.

Pronunciation:

Bway-nos dee-ahs
Komo ess-tahn
Es-tah-mos moo-ee-bee-en-es
Moo-chahs grah-see-ahs

Translation:

Good day, how are you
I am fine, thank you.

Related activities and materials

Symphony #1, 3rd movement, Mahler, BOL #62 (the first theme of this movement is the tune of "Are You Sleeping?" in the minor mode, played at a very slow tempo).

For study

Even rhythm pattern
Like phrases
Chant rhythm and sing with syllables (See pp. 277-278)
Conduct in 4-bt. pattern (See p. 269)

left-hand piano

F   C⁷

bells   Autoharp
F = F A C   F, C⁷
C⁷ = C E G B♭

70. ROW, ROW, ROW YOUR BOAT

Level: U and L
Key of C: start middle C (do)

The action

1. Sing as a round. Try having each section hold one note on "merrily" until all four "merrilys" are sounding together in harmony (*do sol mi do*), then all sing "Life is but a dream." in unison.
2. Add ostinato on the bells or with voice. Harmony may also be added using chord root syllables.

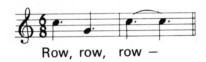

3. Create actions for each section and sing as a round with actions.
4. Choose a different rhythm instrument for each section to accompany the singing with. For variation, omit singing and play as a round.
5. Sing as a partner song with "Three Blind Mice," "Are You Sleeping?", or "Farmer in the Dell." All four may be sung together or in any combination (see Partner Songs).
6. Sing in Spanish:

   Ven ven ven aca, vamos a remar
   Rema que rema que rema que
   rema me tienes que a yudar *

   Pronounce: e as ā; a as ah; q as k; i as ēe; yu as you

7. Sing in minor key. Change the key signature to "3 flats" as shown:

8. Divide the class in half—half row and half sing. Or divide by boys and girls, if preferred. The rowing position may be a seated one, with legs outstretched or standing with one foot forward. For the rowing motion, make a circle with the hands—moving them up as they go forward and down as they go back—one forward and backward movement for eacn measure.
9. Assign a body sound such as tapping feet, clapping, snapping fingers, or slapping knees, to each section and accompany the song, for example, four claps, on "Row, row, row your boat," then four taps on "gently down the stream," followed by four of the sounds on each of the last two lines. Sing in round form.
10. Discuss other ways to move a boat and other kinds of water transportation. Show movements involved in moving various kinds of boats—sailing, paddling, etc. (Scarves may be used as sails by holding one corner high and attaching the other corner to the waist.) Find the rhythm involved in the movement of each as it is executed, then create a new song using the rhythm, with words about the kind of boat.

*From *Cantos*, © 1961; used by permission of Cooperative Recreation Service, Delaware, Ohio.

Related activities and materials

1. Play on the harmonica (see Playing the Harmonica).

    4 4 4 ④ 5
    5 ④ 5 ⑤ 6
    7 7 7 6 6 6 5 5 5 4 4 4
    6 ⑤ 5 ④ 4

2. Listening:
    "Boating on the Lake," Kullak, RCA Basic Record Library, R2.
    "En Bateau," BOL #53.
    "Harbor Vignettes," BOL #53.

For study

$\frac{6}{8}$ (compound) meter; conduct in 2-bt. pattern (See p. 269)
Tie (meas. 4 and 8)
Round form
Chant rhythm and sing with syllables (See pp. 277-278)

left-hand piano

C   G⁷

bells

C = C E G
G⁷ = G B D F

Autoharp
C, G⁷

bottles

C = *do mi sol*
G⁷ = *sol ti re fa*

71. SING NOEL
African round

Level: U and L
Key of D: start F♯ (mi)

Sing No-el, sing No-el, No-el, No- el — Sing No - el, sing No- el,
No-el, No- el. — Sing we all No - el, sing we all No - el.

From *Basic Goals in Music*, Book 5, © 1967 by McGraw-Hill Book Co. of Canada.

The action
This tune is derived from the Liberian folk song "Banuwa."

1. When the song has been learned, sing as a three-part round.
2. Add drums to play on the (1) part, rattles on the (2) part, and cowbell on the (3) part; thus when the third voice enters, all instruments will be sounding.
3. Create new verses, for example, "Hallelu, hallelu, hallelujah" or "Sing for joy."
4. Discuss the ways in which movement can communicate different emotions through changes in the level of the body, size of movement, direction, etc. Then create body movements that will express the joyous spirit of the song.
5. Strap small bells to ankles to sound while executing movements in number 4.
6. Try the rhythm pattern on p. 143, with the instruments indicated. This rhythm is not meant to accompany this song, but rather it is included for the purpose of getting the feel of the intricate interweaving of rhythms characteristic of African music.

Related activities and materials
1. See suggestions for "Dipidu," no. 68.
2. Listening:
   "Folk Songs of Africa" (FS and record), Bowmar.
   "Africa" (FS, record, teacher's guide, student booklets) Keyboard Publications.
   "Around Africa in Song," Silver Burdett.
3. Film:
   "Rhythm of Africa," 17 min. B/W, Radim Film Inc.
   See resource material on Africa.

For study
Round form
Syncopation
Repetitive rhythm patterns
Tie
Conduct in 2-bt. pattern (See p. 269)
Music of Africa

72. HALLELUJAH
Israeli folk song (three-part round)

Program Song
Level: U
Key of b minor: start B (la)

Moderato

Hal - le - lu - ia, — hal - le - lu - ia, — hal - le - lu - ia, hal-le - lu - ia.

Hal - le - lu - ia, Hal - le - lu - - ia, —

Hal - le - lu, hal - le - lu, hal - le - lu - ia. —

From Choate, Berg, Kjelson, and Troth, *Experiencing Music,* New Dimensions in Music series, © 1970, American Book Co., New York.

The action

1. Learn the song well, then sing as a three-part round.
2. Create some body movement for each of the sections, then execute in three-part round form as the song is sung.
3. Add a rhythm instrument each time a new voice enters, so that there will be three different rhythm instruments playing with the three voices, for example, the tam-bourine could accompany part 1 playing the melody rhythm of the part ov r and over throughout the song. The finger cymbals could play the melody rhythm of part 2 throughout and the drum could play the melody rhythm of part 3 throughout.
4. Discuss the word "hallelujah" and its use in music of other parts of the world.
5. Sing other songs containing the word "hal-lelujah" (or "alleluia"), no. 80.

Related activities and materials

1. Create a visual representation of the three-part round form, using an art media and showing the delayed entrance of voices and imitation of the pattern of the first voice.
2. Learn to dance the *hora* and other Israeli folk dances.
3. Sing other Israeli folk songs (nos. 67, 73, 74, 100)
4. Listening:

"Hallelujah Chorus," from "The Messiah," Handle, "Alleluia" Randall Thompson.
"Charles Matthew Hallelujah," Dave Brubeck.
"Israeli Songs for Children," Folkways Records.
"Voices from the Middle East," Keyboard Publications.
See resource material on Israel.

For study

Minor (See Major and Minor and Minor Scales)
$\frac{6}{8}$ (compound) meter, conduct in 2-bt. pattern (See p. 269)
Recurrence of *mi-la* interval, characteristic of minor
Round form
Music of Israel

73. HINEY MAH TOV
Israeli round

Program song
Level: U and L
Key of D minor: start D (la)

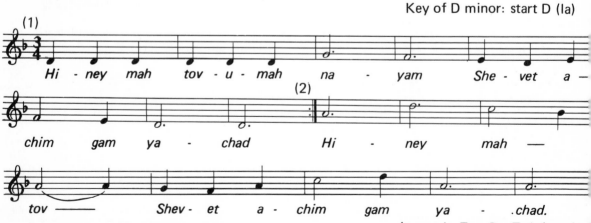

(as sung by Tova Ben-Tsvi, Jerusalem)

From *All Nations Sing,* used by permission of Cooperative Recreation Service, Delaware, Ohio.

The action

1. Learn the song well, then sing as a two-part round.
2. Whistle the parts instead of singing.
3. Use bells to play the melody in place of one of the voices; thus while the voice is carrying one part, the bells will be carrying the other.
4. Substitute whistling for the bells in number 3.
5. Accompany part 1 with the tambourine, as follows:

6. Create some new verses to the tune.
7. Find one action to do on the first beat of each measure and contrasting actions on the second and third beats, for example, sway, clap, clap; or stamp, clap, clap.
8. Create a body movement for each of the sections and execute in round form as the song is sung. Accompany with rhythm instruments, as suggested in number 5.

accompany part 2 with finger cymbals, as follows:

Related activities and materials

1. Using some form of art media, create a visual representation of the round form which will illustrate voice 2 entering after voice 1 and imitating the melody pattern of voice 1.
2. Learn to dance the *hora* and other Israeli folk dances (See p. 140.)
3. Sing other Israeli folk songs (nos. 67, 72, 74, 100)

4. Listening:
   "Folk Songs of Israel," Bowmar.
   "Voices from the Middle East" (FS, record, teacher's guide, and students' booklets), Keyboard Publications.
   "Israeli Songs for Children," Folkways Records.
   See resource material on Israel p. 286.

For study

Minor (See Minor Scales and Major and Minor)
Round form
Chant rhythm then sing with syllables (See pp. 277-278)
Conduct one beat per measure for free flow
Repeat sign :‖
Music of Israel

74. TZENA, TZENA*

Israeli folk song (English words by Phyllis Resnick)

Program song
Level: U
Key of C: start C (do)

Tze-na, tze-na, tze-na, tze-na   come in-to the fields and we'll be-gin —   to work the
Hoe-ing, sow-ing, new things growing, pi-o-neer-ing all to-geth-er, come —   and lend a

1. land.
2. hand.

Tze — na, Tze — na,

build-ing a new   na-tion,   toil — ing bus-i-ly all day, —

Soon we'll dance and have a cel-e-bra-tion,   But first   we'll work and then we'll play.

* *Tzena* is derived from the Hebrew verb meaning "to go forth" or "to go out."

From *Making Music Your Own*, Book 5, © 1971 by the General Learning Corporation; used by permission.

The action

1. Assign the solo part in the first section, with the chorus coming in on second section.
2. When the song has been learned well, divide the class into two groups and use the first and second sections together as partner songs—that is, one group sings measures 1 to 4 and repeats those measures, while another group sings measures 5 to 12 simultaneously.
3. Accompany with the tambourine, as shown. Add other rhythm instruments such as finger cymbals and drum in various measures where desired.
4. Dance the *hora* (p. 140). Learn other Israeli folk dances as desired.
5. Discuss what the "new things growing" mentioned in the song might be.

Related activities and materials

1. Learn about the occupations of ancient and modern Israel and recreate them in movement (see source material on Israel).
2. Research instruments mentioned in the Old Testament and note which ones are in use today.
3. Learn other Israeli folk songs.
4. Listening:
   See resource material on Israel p. 286.

For study

Syncopation
Slur on "day"
Tie
Tonic chord beginning
First and second endings
Music of Israel

75. THE MAN ON THE FLYING TRAPEZE

Traditional American song

Level: U and L
Key of G: start D (low sol

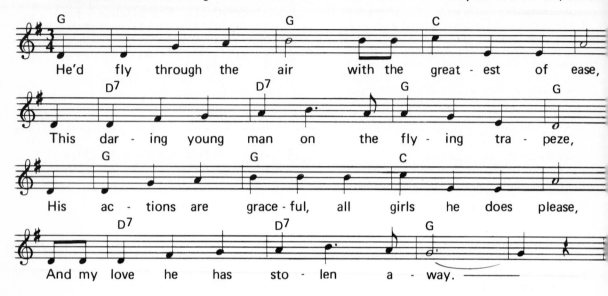

He'd fly through the air with the great - est of ease,

This dar - ing young man on the fly - ing tra - peze,

His ac - tions are grace - ful, all girls he does please,

And my love he has sto - len a - way.

The action

1. Reenforce the feeling for the three-beat meter by executing long swings from side to side (one for each measure, on the *first* beat) or by contrasting actions as in number 1, "Bicycle Built for Two," no. 26.
2. When the song has been learned well, add the "Calliope Song," no. 27, as a descant. (Transpose the "Calliope Song" to the key of G for use with this song; see pp. 273-274.)
3. Sing as a partner song with the chorus of "My Bonnie," beginning with words "bring back." Be sure they are both in the same key.
4. Sing with the following descant. Play or sing the descant through *twice.* (Note the repeat sign.) The descant may be whistled, hummed on "hn," sung on "oo," or with the words taken from the song, for example, "flying, flying, daring young man." (Use bells, recorder, or another melody instrument, if preferred.)

5. Using this tune, create some words about other circus subjects and/or create new tunes to the new words.

Related activities and materials

1. Accompany with bottles in oom-pah rhythm (see pp. 251-252).
2. Portray some circus scenes in movement (tightrope walking, clowns, etc.). Choose appropriate rhythm instruments for accompaniment or tape-record selected excerpts from recordings to accompany each "act." See Listening below.
3. Listening:
   "Under the Big Top," BOL #51.
   "Circus Polka," BOL #51.
   "Circus Music," from "Red Pony Suite," AM 3, vol. 1, RCA.
   "High Stepping Horses," Clowns, R1, RCA Basic Record Library.
   "The Circus Comes to Town" (early primary level), YPRC.

For study

Three-beat meter; conduct in the 3-bt. pattern (See p. 269)
Like phrases
Tie

left-hand piano

G   C   D7

bells

G = G B D
C = C E G
C7 = D F♯ A C

Autoharp

G, C, D7

ukulele

Tune: A D F♯ B (key of G tuning)

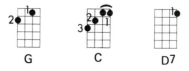

G   C   D7

76. GREENSLEEVES
Old English folk song

Program song
Level: U
Key of e minor: start E (la)

1. A - las! my love, — you do me wrong—To cast me off — dis-
2. Ah Green - sleeves, now — fare - well, a - dieu — To God I pray — to

cour - teous - ly; For I have loved you, oh, so long, — De - light - ing in—your
pros - per thee, For I am still thy sweet-heart true;—Come once—a - gain - to

com - pa - ny. Green-sleeves — was all my joy,—And oh, Green - sleeves—was my de-light,
meet — me.

Green - sleeves, — my heart of gold, — And all — for La - dy Green - sleeves.

This song is mentioned in Shakespeare's plays and was a favorite of Queen Elizabeth I. The title refers to the fact that the nobility were known by the color of silk they wore on their sleeves. Each house or family had a distinctive color.

Notice the change from minor in the third phrase. Such changes of mood are typical of music all over the British Isles.

From *Exploring Music* series (teacher's ed.), Book 6, © 1966; by special permission of the publisher, Holt, Rinehart and Winston.

The action

1. When the song has been learned, add the following descant, played on recorder, sung or plucked on autoharp strings.

In unison with melody here

2. Make up a stately dance to the music in keeping with the character of Elizabethan times, or learn the following dance.*

Formation: Large double circle, facing clockwise, girls on partners' right. Partners clasp hands at shoulder height, holding a small pine bough in their hands. In the dance two couples work as a group. Designate these groups before the dance begins.

meas. 1-4: All walk forward eight steps; begin on inside foot.

meas. 5-6: Two couples join hands to form a right-hand star; walk four steps clockwise.

meas. 7-8: Reverse direction and form a left-hand star; walk four steps counterclockwise.

meas. 9-10: With all couples again facing clockwise, the first couple of each group bends forward and walks backward four steps under the arched arms of the second couple, who meanwhile walk forward four steps.

* From *Exploring Music* series (teacher's ed.), Book 6, © 1966; by special permission of the publisher, Holt, Rinehart and Winston.

3. Sing with Christmas words:

What Child is this who laid to rest
On Mary's lap is sleeping
Whom angels greet with anthems sweet
While shepherds watch are keeping
This, this is Christ the King
Whom shepherds guard and angels sing
Haste, haste to bring Him laud
The Babe, the Son of Mary.

words by William C. Dix

Related activities and materials

1. Using art media of your choice, create a visual representation of the sweep and flow of this melody while listening to "Fantasia on Greensleeves" (see Listening below).

2. View some early instruments such as the viola da gamba, lute, and recorder, and listen to the sound. Some of these instruments are still in use today. If there is a small chamber group orchestra in the community, invite them to the classroom for a demonstration lecture and concert.

3. Research the English origin of many familiar American songs.

4. Sing other English folk songs and learn some English folk dances, for example, "Gathering Peascods," "Ribbon Dance," or "Maypole Dance" (RCA World of Folk Dances series).

5. Accompany with the guitar or autoharp.

6. Listening:
   "Fantasia on Greensleeves," Vaughan Williams, AM 6, vol. 2.
   "Folk Dances from Somerset" (English folk-song suite), Vaughan Williams, BOL #56.
   "London Suite," Coates, BOL #60.
   "English Dances," Arnold, AM 2, vol. 2 and AM 1, vol. 2.
   "Morris Dance," "Henry VIII Suite," AM 1, vol. 2.

7. Film:
   "Discovering the Music of the Middle Ages," 21 min., color, Film Associates.

For study

Minor (melodic form—note *fi* and *si*--D$^\sharp$ and C$^\sharp$).
See Minor Scales and Major and Minor
Note change to major feeling in third phrase
$\frac{6}{8}$ (compound) meter; conduct in 2-bt. pattern for smooth flow of melody as well as rhythm
Repeat uneven rhythm pattern
See "Silent Night," no. 96.

77. I'VE BEEN WORKING ON THE RAILROAD

Level: U and L
Key of G: start G (do)

Old American work song

I've been work-ing on the rail - road, All the live - long day;

I've been work -ing on the rail - road, Just to pass the time a - way.

Don't you hear the whis - tle blow - ing? Rise up so ear - ly in the morn.

Don't you hear the cap-tain shout - ing:— "Di - nah blow your horn!"

G   C   D7   G
Dinah won't you blow, Dinah won't you blow, Dinah won't you blow your horn?
G   C   D7   G
Dinah won't you blow, Dinah won't you blow, Dinah won't you blow your horn?
G   D7
Someone's in the kitchen with Dinah, Someone's in the kitchen, I know,
G   C   G   D7   G
Someone's in the kitchen with Dinah, Strummin' on the old banjo.
G   D7
Fee, Fie, Fiddle-ee IO, Fee, Fie, Fiddle-ee IO,
G   C   G   D7   G
Fee, Fie, Fiddle-ee IO, Strummin' on the old banjo.

From *Music Near and Far,* © 1956, 1962 by the Silver Burdett Company; reprinted by permission of the General Learning Corporation.

The action

1. Sing the section beginning "Someone's in the kitchen" as a partner song with "When the Saints Go Marching in" (no. 20) or with the verse part only of "Good Night Ladies" (see Partner Songs).
2. Tap the steady beat of the meter with the feet, while clapping the rhythm of the melody.
3. Play a musical "on and off" game for practice in "inner hearing," as follows:
   a. Decide on what signals will be used to designate "on" and "off."
   b. Start the song and have the class sing until the "off" signal is given by the teacher (or student leader), at which time the audible sound stops. But each singer should continue to "hear" the song continue inside through "inner hearing." When the "on" signal is given, the singers should have arrived at the same point in the song as they would have had they continued to sing it aloud.
   c. Alternate between "on" and "off" throughout the song.

   This same game may also be played with other songs of choice.
4. When the song has been learned, add the harmony part below.
5. Find the harmony by ear for "Someone's in the Kitchen," throughout to the end of the song.

— — — blow your horn *etc.*

Related activities and materials

1. Research early trains, the laying of the first railroad in America. Discuss the history of the railroads and possible reasons for their recent decline. Create some new verses about any of these topics.
2. Sing and note activities for other related train or railroad songs.
3. Accompany with ukulele.
4. Listening:
   "Famous American Railroad Songs," RCA, CAS 1056.
   "The Railroad in Folksong," RCA, LPV 532.
   "Working on the Railroad" (songs and narration), YPRC.
5. Filmstrip:
   "Music to Work by" (FS and record), Denoyer-Geppert AV.

For study

Chromatic tone (G♯); note the return to the scale tone through the use of ♮
Uneven rhythm pattern ♫ ♩ ♫
Slur
Conduct in 4-bt. pattern (See p. 269)

left-hand piano

G   C   D⁷   A⁷

bells

G = G B D
D⁷ = D F♯ A C
C = C E G
A⁷ = A C♯ E G

Autoharp

G, C, D⁷, A⁷

ukulele

Tune: A D F♯ B (key of G tuning)

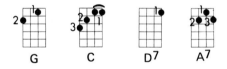

G   C   D⁷   A⁷

78. I'M GONNA SING

Spiritual

Level: U and L
Key of G: start D (low sol)

1. I'm gon-na sing when the spir-it says "Sing" — I'm gon-na sing when the spir-it says
2. I'm gon-na shout when the spir-it says "Shout" — I'm gon-na shout when the spir-it says

"Sing" — I'm gon-na sing when the spir-it says "Sing" — And be hap-py all the day long.—
"Shout" — I'm gon-na shout when the spir-it says "Shout"— And be hap-py all the day long.—

3. I'm gonna clap when the spirit says "Clap" *(three times)*
   And be happy all the day long.

4. I'm gonna run when the spirit says "Run" *(three times)*
   And be happy all the day long.

From Choate, Berg, Kjelson, and Troth, *Enjoying Music,* New Dimensions in Music series, © 1970, American Book Co., New York.

The action

1. Tap foot on the accented beats and clap on the unaccented beats:

   tap   clap   tap   clap

2. Add new verses, substituting other words for "sing"—for example,

   dance, snap, tap, run, hop, wiggle, walk.

3. In number 2, adapt the tempo to the movement. For variation, think of movements that would require a meter that moves in 3's, for example waltz or sway; then try singing the song in triple meter to fit the movement.

4. After the song has been learned, add harmony as follows:

   a. descant below
   b. chord root syllables
   c. three-part vocal chording or resonator bells

sing   sing   sing   sing   sing   sing oh sing sing sing

Related activities and materials

1. Sing other spirituals and discuss the difference in moods (nos. 87, 89).
2. Listening:
   "I'm Gonna Sing," Robert Shaw Chorale,

RCA, LSC 2580.
"Spirituals and Hymns," Songs of Many Cultures, Silver Burdett.
For additional suggestions, see Spirituals.

For study

   Syncopation
   Like phrases
   Slur
   Tie
   Conduct in 4-bt. pattern (See p. 269)

left-hand piano

bells

G = G B D
D⁷ = D F♯ A C

Autoharp
G, D⁷

ukulele

Tune: A D F♯ B (key of G tuning)

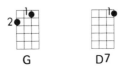

G   D7

79. THE WHITE HAWK
(EL QUELÉLE)
Folk song from Spanish California

Program song
Level: U
Key of F: start F(do)

Well accented

Pa - pá Que - lé - le has died, ay, ay, ay, ay, ay! Died as the morn-ing was
Spanish: El Que - lé - le se mu rió, ay, ay, ay, ay, ay! A las tres de la ma-

break - ing. Pa - pá Que - lé - le has died, ay, ay, ay, ay, ay!
ña - - na, El Que - lé - le se mu - rio,

Now to his grave he must go. — Three — dra - goons and a
Y lo lle - van á en - te - rrar — Tres — dra - go - nes y un

cor - pr'-al Tom-cat for sac - ris - tan too. And all the
ca - bo, ay, ay, ay, Yel ga - to de sa-cris - tán. — Y los Que —

ba - by, Que - le - les, ay, ay, ay Cry them to death in their woe. —
lé - les chi - quí-tos, ay, ay, ay Ya se mue - ren de llo - rar. —

From *Spanish Songs of Old California*, collected by C. F. Lummis and A. Farwell, © 1923 by G. Schirmer, Inc.; used by permission.

DESCANT

Pa - pá Que - lé - le has died — Died as the morn - ing was break-ing.

Pa - pá Que - lé - le has died. — Now to his grave he must go. —

Dra - goons, cor - po - ral, Tom-cat for sa - cris - tan too. —

Ba - by Que - lé - - les, Cry them to death in their woe. —

The action

1. In order that the proper mood and tempo may be established for this children's song about the death and burial of a white hawk, discuss the word content at the outset. Clarify the meaning of dragoon, corporal, and *quelele.*
2. Sing the song in Spanish.
3. Sing the song with the descant given or play the descant on recorder, flute, or bells.
4. Add the sound of a tambourine gently

rapped and shaken

R S S

and finger cymbals played throughout. Add other instruments as desired.

5. Accompany with guitar, autoharp, 3-part vocal chording, or chords on resonator bells.
6. Create some interpretive body movement that will communicate the true spirit of the song. See Interpretive Body Movement, p. 232.

Related activities and materials

1. See "Don Gato," Making Music Your Own, Book 4, Silver Burdett.
2. Listening:

"Funeral March of a Marionette," BOL #64.
"Doll's Burial," BOL #68.
"Dance of the Firebird," EIM record album.

For study

Triplet
Chant rhythm and sing with syllables (See pp. 277-278)
Conduct in 3-bt. pattern (See p. 269)

left-hand piano

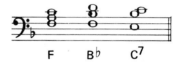

F   B♭   C⁷

bells

F = F A C
B♭ = B♭ D F
C⁷ = C E G B♭

Autoharp
F, B♭, C⁷

guitar

F   B♭   C⁷

80. ALL CREATURES OF OUR GOD AND KING

Thoughts to Teach By

Maintain the solemnity of a processional and the joyfulness of a song of praise. Keep the groups small, with approximately four or five in a group. Guide the children in the discovery of the form of the movement in relation to the canon form of the hymn.

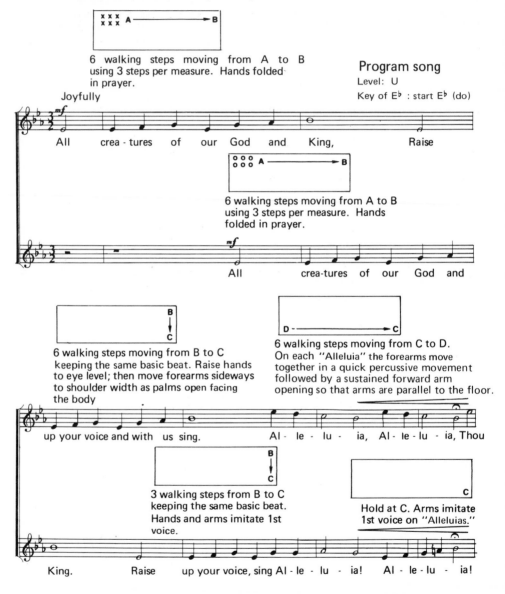

6 walking steps moving from A to B using 3 steps per measure. Hands folded in prayer.

Program song
Level: U
Key of E♭ : start E♭ (do)

6 walking steps moving from A to B using 3 steps per measure. Hands folded in prayer.

6 walking steps moving from B to C keeping the same basic beat. Raise hands to eye level; then move forearms sideways to shoulder width as palms open facing the body

6 walking steps moving from C to D. On each "Alleluia" the forearms move together in a quick percussive movement followed by a sustained forward arm opening so that arms are parallel to the floor.

3 walking steps from B to C keeping the same basic beat. Hands and arms imitate 1st voice.

Hold at C. Arms imitate 1st voice on "Alleluias."

All crea-tures of our God and King, Raise

All crea-tures of our God and

up your voice and with us sing. Al - le - lu - ia, Al - le - lu - ia, Thou

King. Raise up your voice, sing Al - le - lu - ia! Al - le - lu - ia!

From Sally Monsour, Marilyn Chambers Cohen, and Patricia Eckert Lindell, *Rhythm in Music and Dance for Children,* © 1966 by Wadsworth Publishing Company Inc., Belmont, California; reprinted by permission of the publisher.

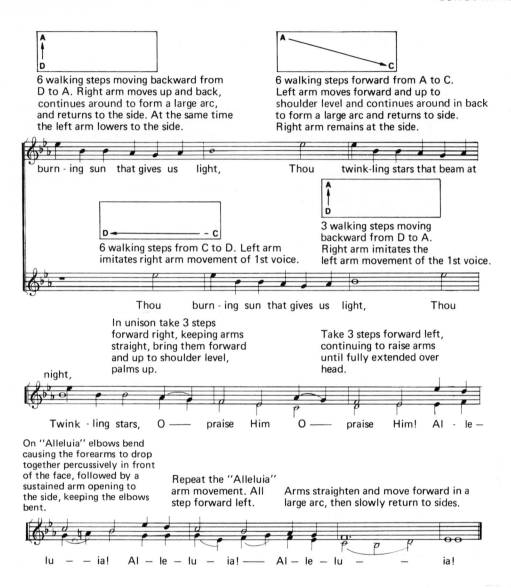

6 walking steps moving backward from
D to A. Right arm moves up and back,
continues around to form a large arc,
and returns to the side. At the same time
the left arm lowers to the side.

6 walking steps forward from A to C.
Left arm moves forward and up to
shoulder level and continues around in back
to form a large arc and returns to side.
Right arm remains at the side.

burn - ing sun   that gives us   light,   Thou   twink-ling stars that beam at

6 walking steps from C to D. Left arm
imitates right arm movement of 1st voice.

3 walking steps moving
backward from D to A.
Right arm imitates the
left arm movement of the 1st voice.

Thou   burn - ing sun that gives us   light,   Thou

In unison take 3 steps
forward right, keeping arms
straight, bring them forward
and up to shoulder level,
palms up.

Take 3 steps forward left,
continuing to raise arms
until fully extended over
head.

night,

Twink - ling stars, O —— praise Him   O —— praise Him! Al - le —

On "Alleluia" elbows bend
causing the forearms to drop
together percussively in front
of the face, followed by a
sustained arm opening to
the side, keeping the elbows
bent.

Repeat the "Alleluia"
arm movement. All
step forward left.

Arms straighten and move forward in a
large arc, then slowly return to sides.

lu — — ia! Al — le — lu — ia! —— Al — le — lu — — ia!

The action

1. Learn each part well, then sing it in canon form as indicated. This means that one voice begins, followed by a second voice entering and imitating the melody of the first voice—very much like a round. In a canon, however, the voices may end together because of slight changes within the framework of the song as it progresses.
2. Perform the movement as shown. Note that there is a group for each of the two parts; thus the movement will also be in canon form, with group 2 imitating the movement of group 1, except in selected unison parts.

3. Create some original interpretive body movement in keeping with the spirit of the song.
4. Have the class select a psalm, poem, or story they would like to interpret in movement. Let one group do a choral-speaking interpretation of the selection while another does the movement. Rhythm instruments (selected with discretion) may be used to heighten the dramatic effect. Let the class determine the climax of each section and build to it through gradually increasing dynamics in the instruments.
5. Introduce the fugue as another type of imitative musical form. See Listening below.

Related activities and materials

1. Using an art medium of choice, try to represent the canon form through a visual interpretation.
2. Learn other songs in the canon form and create movement for them.
3. Listening:
   "Round and Round" (a good beginning listening experience for introducing the fugue; explanation and musical examples are on the record), YPRC.
   "Cat's Fugue," Scarlatti, Keyboard Publications.
   "Pumpkin Eaters' Little Fugue," BOL #65.
   "Little Fugue in G Minor," Bach, AM 6, vol. 1 and EIM.
4. Film:
   "Canon," 9 min., color, National Film Board of Canada.

For study

Canon form
Chromatic tone (A♮)
Hold
$\frac{3}{2}$ meter
Sing with syllables (See pp. 277-278)
Conduct in 3-bt. pattern (See p. 269)

81. SING WE NOW OF CHRISTMAS

French folk song

Program song
Level: U
Key of F minor: start F (la)

Briskly
Finger Cymbals

1. Sing we now of Christ - mas No - el — sing we here!
2. An - gels call to shep - herds: Leave your flocks at rest,
3. In Beth - le - hem they found them, Jo - seph and Mar-y mild,
4. From the East-ern coun - try Came the — King a - far,
5. Then they of-fered gold and myrrh, Gifts of — great-est price;

1. Sing we now of Christ - mas, No - el — sing we
2. An-gels called to shep - herds: "Leave your—flock at
3. In Beth -le-hem they found them, Jo-seph and Ma-ry
4. From the east-ern coun -- try Came the kings a-
5. Then they of - fered gold and myrrh, Gifts of great - est

Hear our grate-ful prais – es To the — babe so dear.
Jour - ney forth to Beth - l'hem, Find the — lamb-kin blest.
Seat - ed by the man - ger, Watch-ing the ho-ly child.
Bear - ing gifts to Beth - l'hem, Guid-ed by a star
There was ne'er a sta – ble So like par – a - dise.

here! Hear our grate ful -prais – es To the—babe so
rest, Jour - ney forth to Beth - l'hem, Find the —lamb-kin
mild, Seat ed, by the Man - ger Watch-ing the ho - ly
far, Bear ing gifts to Beth - l'hem, Guid-ed - by a
price, There was ne'er a sta - ble So like par - a -

CHORUS

Sing we no - el, The King is born, no - el! no - el! ―

dear.
blest." The King is born, no - el !
child.
star.
dise.

The King is born, no - el !

Sing we no — el, The King is born, no - el!

Finger cymbals

Sing we now of Christ - mas, Sing we—here no - el !

Sing we now of Christ - mas Sing we—here no - el!

From Coleman and Jorgensen, *Christmas Carols from Many Countries,* © 1934, G. Schirmer, Inc.; used by permission.

The action

1. Sing each part in unison. Note that some of the sections imitate each other exactly and some do not.
2. Divide the class and sing in two parts as a canon.
3. Use finger cymbals on first verse. Vary dynamics on each verse according to the words.
4. Select other rhythm instruments, either singly or in combination, for other verses.
5. As an alternative to number 4, choose one instrument to play on the first four measures and a different one on the next four, or choose an instrument to play with the first voice and another to play with the second voice. When the voices are together, both instruments will be playing.
6. Dramatize each verse as it is sung.
7. Create some interpretive body movement and dance in canon form. The dancing should be imitative, just as the voices are imitative in canon form. Thus one group will dance one voice part and another group will dance the second. Where the tune of the first voice is imitated by the second voice, the movement by the group dancing the second voice will imitate the movement done by the group dancing the first voice. See movement directions for "All Creatures of Our God and King," no. 80, and Interpretive Body Movement (p. 232).

Related activities and materials

1. Using some kind of art medium, create a visual representation of each verse. Explore the possibilities of assembling this into a mural.
2. Create a visual representation of canon form. form.
3. Sing other Christmas songs of French origin, for example, "Il Est Né" or "March of the Three Kings."
4. Learn some Christmas songs in other languages.
5. Sing other songs in canon form.
6. Listening:
   "Farandole" (March of the Three Kings" melody), AM 6, vol. 1.
   See p. 209 for additional Christmas listening.
7. Film:
   "Canon," 9 min., color, National Film Board of Canada.

For study

Canon form
Melodic minor indicated by presence of D♮ and E♭ (See Minor Scales, Appendix, and Major and Minor)
Rhythm pattern
Note tie in the chorus. It is important to hold the full count in the first voice while the second voice moves
Conduct in 2-bt. pattern (See p. 269)

82. AIN'T GONNA GRIEVE MY LORD NO MORE

American folk song

Level: U and L
Key of F: start F (do)

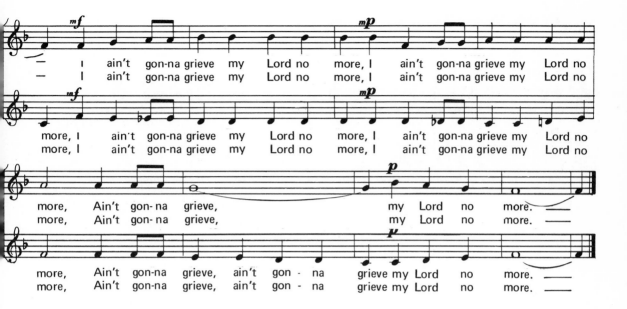

I ain't gon-na grieve my Lord no more, I ain't gon-na grieve my Lord no
I ain't gon-na grieve my Lord no more, I ain't gon-na grieve my Lord no

more, I ain't gon-na grieve my Lord no more, I ain't gon-na grieve my Lord no
more, I ain't gon-na grieve my Lord no more, I ain't gon-na grieve my Lord no

more, Ain't gon-na grieve, my Lord no more.
more, Ain't gon-na grieve, my Lord no more.

more, Ain't gon-na grieve, ain't gon - na grieve my Lord no more.
more, Ain't gon-na grieve, ain't gon - na grieve my Lord no more.

The action

1. In measures **1** through **8** choose a leader to sing the soprano part (upper staff), with the chorus singing the part written for the alto part (lower staff). The chorus simply repeats what the leader sings. (If preferred, divide the class in half, with half singing the leader's part and the other half singing the chorus.) In the remaining measures, sing in two parts, as written, or in unison if the class cannot carry parts.
2. Create some new verses to the tune.
3. Use rhythm instruments in any one of the following ways:
   a. Choose one instrument to play on "heaven" each time the word occurs in the song and a different instrument for each of the other objects in the verses, for example, roller skates, pearly gates, etc.
   b. Choose one or more instruments to play on the leader's part and another group to play when the chorus answers.
   c. Choose an instrument such as the tambourine to play general accompaniment throughout the song.
4. Tap foot on the accented beats, clap on the off beats:

   tap   clap   tap   clap, etc.

5. Express the ascending and descending scale patterns in the harmony part with body movement.

Related activities and materials
See Spirituals.

For study
Chromatic tones
Tie
2-part harmony
Dynamics symbols: f, mf, mp, p
Cut time

83. A LA VIBORA DE LA MAR

Words and music traditional

Level: U and L
Key of G: start D (low sol)

Through the courtesy of Aida Barrera Close, director, Bilingual Project, and Michael Hanson, executive producer, station KLRN-TV, Austin, Texas.

The action

1. This singing game, which Mexican children play, is very much like "London Bridge":

> Two children form an arch with their arms. One is supposed to represent an angel, the other the devil. However, since the term "devil" may not appeal to some children, it is suggested that they use the name of fruits such as watermelon and canteloupe. The remaining children form a line, holding on to the waist of the person in front, and pass under the arch singing. The last child to pass through is stopped and asked with whom he wants to go. He selects a side by indicating his favorite fruit (of the two) and goes behind that person. When all children have chosen sides, the game ends with a tug-of-war.

2. When the song has been learned, sing in two parts as indicated. Note that the harmony part follows the melody a third lower all the way through.
3. Add rhythm instruments such as tambourine, maracas, castanets, as desired, using different combinations for the contrasting sections of the song.
4. Create some new verses in English, using any desired subject matter.

Related activities and materials

1. Sing other Mexican folk songs (see pp. 107, 109, 111).
2. Learn some Mexican folk dances.
3. See resource material on Mexico.

English translation (A La Vibora De La Mar)

Sea serpent, sea serpent, sea serpent, you can pass through here
The ones in the front run a lot, the ones on the back will get behind
La, la la, la [clap]
There was a Mexican girl who sold plums, apricots, cantaloupes or watermelons [repeat]
Verbena, verbena, early morning garden
Verbena, verbena, early morning garden.
Little golden bell, let me go through with all my children
But the one on the back
La, la la, la [clap]
Will it be cantaloupe, will it be watermelon
Will it be the old lady I saw the other day
Day, day, day day.

Spanish pronunciation

Ah-lah be-borah beeborah day lah mahr
Por ah-kee pway-den pah-sahr
Los day ah-day-lahn-tay koren moo-cho
Ee los day ah-trahs say kay-dahr-an
trahs trahs trahs trahs
Oona Meh-hee-kahna kay frootos ben-dee-ah
Sir-way-lah cha-bah-kahn-o may-lon oh sahn-dee—ah
[repeat above two lines]
Kay pay-nah kay pay-nah
Har-deen day mah-tah-tay-nah
[repeat above two lines]
Kahm-pah-nee-tah day-oro, day-ha-may pah-sar sar
Kon to-dos mees ee-hos may-nos el day ah-trahs, trahs, trahs, trahs
Say-rah mel-on, say-rah sahn-dee-ah
Say-rah lah bee-ay-ha del o-tro dee-ah, dee-ah, dee-ah, dee-ah.

For study

Alternate measures of $\frac{2}{4}$ and $\frac{3}{4}$ meter
Syncopation
Repeat sign :‖
Change of key (modulation)
Music of Mexico

bells

G = G B D
D = D F♯ A
C = C E G
F = F A C
G⁷ = G B D F
d mi = D F A

Autoharp
G, D, C, F, G⁷,
d mi

guitar

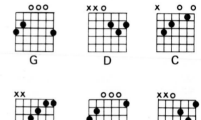

84. DU, DU, LIEGST MIR IM HERZEN

German folk song

Program song
Level: U
Key of E♭: start G(mi) and
E♭ (do)

Du, du, liegst mir in Her - zen, Du, du,
You, you, live in my You, dear, heart, you,

liegst mir im sinn. Du, du, machst mir viel schmer - zen
live in my mind, You, you make me feel sor - row,

Weisst nicht wie gut ich dir bin; ——— Ja, ja,
Do you not know I love you. ——— Ja, ja,

ja, ja, Weisst nicht wie gut ich dir bin.
ja, ja, Do you not know I love you?

From *Basic Goals in Music,* Book 3, © 1967 by McGraw-Hill Book Co. of Canada.

The action

1. Sing in German.
2. Sing in two parts as written, then add a third part through the use of root chording. While a portion of the class is singing the two parts, have the remainder of the class sing the root syllable of the indicated chords; for example:

   for every E♭ chord indicated, sing *do*
   for every B♭7 chord indicated, sing *sol*
   for every A♭ chord indicated, sing *fa*

3. Let a few voices sing the melody while others accompany with three-part vocal chording.
4. Provide a bottle-band accompaniment with an oom-pah-pah rhythm.
5. Play the harmony part on the resonator bells while the class sings the melody.
6. Reenforce the feeling for the waltz rhythm by doing one action on the first beat of the measure and a different action on the second and third beats of each measure (for example), *snap,* clap, clap or *leap,* run, run. ("Waltz" comes from the German *walzen,* meaning "to roll about." Originally, waltzes were much heavier and less graceful than they are today.)
7. Adapt rhythm instruments to number 6 by having selected instruments play on the first beat of each measure and other instruments play on the second and third beats of each measure.

Related activities and materials

1. Sing other songs in waltz meter.
2. Try a waltz step. Extend right foot forward, put weight on it, bring the left foot up to the right and place weight on left foot, extending right foot forward again. Repeat, starting with the left foot forward. Chant

   | 1 | 2 | 3 |
   "Step together step."

3. Sing other German folk songs. See "Seven Steps," GWM Book 3, Prentice Hall.
4. Learn some German folk dances. See "Hansel and Gretel" and "Come Let Us Be Joyful," in the RCA World of Folk Dances series.
5. Listening:
   "German Waltz," Paganini, BOL #53.
   "Selected Waltzes by Johann Strauss and Brahms
   Other waltzes:
      "Minute Waltz," EIM record album
      "Sleeping Beauty Waltz," BOL #67.
      "Skater's Waltz, BOL #55.
   "Children's Folk Songs of Germany," Folkways Records.
   Prelude to "Hansel and Gretel," EIM record album.
6. Filmstrip:
   "The Goose Girl," A Folk Tale of Germany, McGraw-Hill.

For study

Like phrases
Chant the rhythm and sing the syllables of each part (See pp. 277-278)
Conduct in 3-bt. pattern, with a strong accent on the first beat of each measure (See p. 269)

85. TUMBALALAIKA

Jewish folk song (English words by Margaret Fishback)

Program song
Level: U
Key of c minor: start G (mi)

1. Pac - ing, puz - zling all the night long, A young lad
2. "Maid - en, maid - en, can you ex - plain — What can
3. "I - dle lad, you're jok - ing I know A stone can

sang a haunt — ing song. "What shall I say to
grow with - out snow or rain? What can burn for
grow with - out rain or snow, Love — can blaze and

my love to - day, Oh, what shall I say to my love to - day?"
end - less years And what - can cry and shed — no tears?"
nev - er die, A heart - can weep and nev - er cry."

Refrain

Tum - ba - la, tum - ba - la, tum - ba - la lai - ka, Tum - ba - la,

tum - ba - la tum - ba - la - lai - ka, Tum - ba - la - lai - ka.

play ba - la - lai - ka, Tum - ba - la - lai - ka, laugh and be gay.

The action

1. Sing in two parts as written.
2. Divide appropriate verse parts between girls and boys or assign solo parts, with the chorus singing the narrative section of the verse and the complete refrain.
3. Add rhythm instruments as desired or as follows (R = rap):

   a. on *refrain,* play tambourine

   ♩♪♩
   R R

   on each measure throughout, except on measures 15-16 play

   ♩♩♩ | ♩♪♪

   b. on *refrain,* play finger cymbals

   ♩♪♪

   on each measure throughout, except on measures 15-16 play

   ♩♩♩ | ♩♪♪

4. Create some body movement which will reflect the musical climax in measures 9 to 12 and the anticlimax in measures 13 to 16. Repeat on the refrain. Execute to the melody played on an instrument or hummed by the chorus. See Interpretive Body Movement.
5. Reenforce the feeling for triple meter by doing one movement on the first beat of each measure and a contrasting movement for the second and third beats, for example, leap, walk, walk, etc.
6. Discuss the differences in sound between major and minor. (See Major and Minor.) Sing other songs in minor. Play major and minor chords on the Autoharp or piano for recognition.

Related activities and materials

1. Find pictures of a balalaika mentioned in the song and listen to some balalaika music either live or recorded. (See related materials for "Minka," no. 66, and "Folk Instruments of the World" album for picture and sound, (Follett Publishing Co.).
2. Try to construct a replica of a balalaika.
3. Sing an American folk song that contains similar riddle questions. (See "Riddle Song," Exploring Music, Book 4, Holt, Rinehart and Winston.)
4. Learn other Jewish folk songs.
5. Learn a Jewish folk dance.
6. See resource material on Israel.

For study

Minor (See Minor Scales and Major and Minor)

Note *sol* in melody, *si* in harmony part in the refrain

Conduct 1-bt. per measure for smoother flow (see p. 269) and "Chiapenecas," no. 54

Music of Israel

86. THE LORD IS MY SHEPHERD

Thomas Koschat

Program song
Level: U
Key of A♭: start E♭ (low sol)

1. The Lord is my shep-herd, no want shall I know, He leads me in,
2. A - bun-dance of glad - ness on me He be - stows, With boun - ti - ful

pas - tures where cool wa - ters flow.— `Be - side the still wa - ters in
bless - ing my cup o - ver - flows. With joy has He crowned me in

safe - ty, I rest — With love and pro - tec - tion my spir - it is
days that are past, — His good-ness and mer - cy for ev - er will

blessed, With love and pro - tec - tion my spir - it is blessed.
last, His good-ness and mer - cy for ev - er will last.

The action

1. Sing in two parts or sing one part and play harmonizing part on the recorder or resonator bells.
2. Assign solo on second verse with background humming by chorus in assigned parts. On the words "His goodness and mercy," have the chorus join the soloist in singing the words through to the end of the song.
3. Create movement to be done by one group while another group sings. (See "All Creatures of Our God and King," no. 80, and Interpretive Body Movement.)

Related activities and materials

1. Sing other settings of the Twenty-third Psalm. (See "Brother James Air," in "Music for Young Americans," Book 5, American Book Co.)
2. Using the Twenty-third Psalm or other psalms of your choice, let the class prepare them as choral-speaking presentations, using solos, low, medium, and high voices, variations in tempo and dynamics, and rhythm instruments wherever appropriate for added dramatic effects. Add movement also, if desired (see number 3 above).
3. Listening:
   "All the Favorite Music from Handel's "Messiah," RCA, VCS-7081.
   "Great Sacred Choruses," RCS' LM-1117.
   "Hallelujah Chorus" from "The Messiah" EIM record album.
   Other selections from musical settings of Biblical material as desired.

For study

Chromatic tones in the second part (G♭, A♮, B♮)
Conduct in 3-bt. pattern; contrast with the fast one beat per measure pattern of "Chiapenecas," no. 54, or "Man on the Flying Trapeze," no. 75
Slur

87. GOOD NEWS

Spiritual

Program song
Level: U
Key of C: start E (high mi)

From Wilson, Ehret, Knuth, Hermann, and Renna, *Growing with Music,* Book 6, © 1966 by Prentice-Hall Inc., Englewood Cliffs, N.J.; reprinted by permission.

The action

1. Sing in two parts as written. Note that beginning in measure 9, the melody is sung an octave lower and the word "news" becomes a  rather than as in the beginning.
2. Assign the solo on the first "good news" of each section, with the chorus coming in on the second "good news."
3. Tap your foot on the accented beats, clap or snap your fingers on the off beats:

tap   clap   tap   clap , etc.

4. Strike tambourine and cymbals each time "good news" is sung by the chorus.
5. Create some new verses about things that mean "good news" to the class. Explain the meaning of "chariot" as it is used in the song.
6. Discuss musical devices in the song that contribute to the "good news" mood (for example, quick tempo, major mode, exuberant spirit when singing). Then have the class discover how these might be altered (slow tempo, change to minor mode, subdue performance) to make the mood one of "bad news."
7. After trying number 6, sing the first phrase in a "good news" mood, then the second phrase in a "bad news" mood. Try alternating the phrases throughout the song for contrast.

Related activities and materials

1. Sing other spirituals (see nos. 42, 44, 78, 89 and note the suggested activities).
2. Research the origin of the spiritual and its place in American music. See additional suggestions and information in Spirituals.

For study

Syncopation
Cut time
Two-part harmony
Spirituals

8. WHEN SAMMY PUT THE PAPER
ON THE WALL

Level: U
Key of C: start G (sol)

Traditional

Briskly

When Sam-my put the pa-per on the wall, — He put the par-lor pa-per in the
When Sam-my put the pa-per on the wall, — He spilled a pot of glue upon us

When Sam-my put the pa-per on the wall, He
When Sam-my put the pa-per on the wall, He

hall, He — pa-per'd up the stairs, He pa-per'd all the chairs, He
all, Let us

put the par - lor pa - per in the hall, pa-per'd the stairs, paper'd the
spilled a pot of glue up-on us all,

e - ven put a bor - der on grand - ma's shawl, all stick to-geth-er, Like
chairs, bor-der on Grand-ma's shawl, all stick to

birds of a feath-er, Since Sam-my put the pa - per on the wall.
geth - er Since Sam-my put the pa - per on the wall.

From Wilson, Ehret, Knuth, Hermann, and Renna, *Growing with Music* (Related Arts ed.), Book 5, ©
1970 by Prentice-Hall Inc., Englewood Cliffs, N.J.; reprinted by permission.

The action

1. Learn the parts separately, then sing the song in two parts, as shown.
2. Dramatize, with the children taking the parts of the objects (chairs, stairs, etc.).
3. Select a rhythm instrument to sound for each of the objects mentioned in the song.
4. Call attention to the meter signature of $\frac{12}{8}$ and suggest that by using the dotted quarter note as the unit of beat, each measure may then fall into a basic count of four, which is more suitable for a fast tempo. Have half the class clap the basic 4-beat pattern while the other half claps the rhythm of the melody, and/or have the entire class foot-tap the 4-beat pattern while clapping the rhythm of the melody.
5. Find other songs in 6, 9, or 12 meter, whose suggested tempos would indicate that the basic count for each measure is either two, three, or four (depending on the upper figure of the meter signature), and tap-clap as in number 4.
6. The arrangement of the notes is such that the song has a boundy, uneven rhythm. Try singing it in an even rhythm:

and discuss the effect of the change on the humor of the song.
7. Have the children explore some of the elements that add humor to the song, then sing other humorous songs and explore their humorous elements.

Related activities and materials

1. Create a humorous musical composition, either vocal or instrumental using vocal or body sounds and traditional classroom or "found" instruments (see Found Instruments).
2. Some composers reflect a sense of humor in certain works. Listen to some of the recordings listed below to discover what musical devices are used to add humor. (See Listening below.)
3. Listening:
   Variations on "Pop Goes the Weasel," AM 4, vol. 1.
   "Tortoises," from "Carnival of the Animals," BOL #51 and EIM record album.
   "The Glow Worm Turns," "Family All Together" album, RCA.
   "Toy Symphony," Haydn, EIM record album.
   "Humor in Music," Leonard Bernstein, Col. 5625.
   "Afro-American Symphony," 3rd movement, Enjoying Music NDM series, American Book Co.

For study

Chromatic tones
$\frac{12}{8}$ (compound) meter; conduct in 4-bt. pattern (See p. 269)
1st and 2nd endings
Repeat signs :‖
𝄾 in second part

left-hand piano

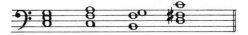

bells

C = C E G
F = F A C
G⁷ = G B D F
D⁷ = D F♯ A C

Autoharp

C, F, G⁷, D⁷

89. LET US BREAK BREAD TOGETHER

Spiritual (arranged by William S. Haynie)

Program song
Level: U
Key of F: start middle C (low sol)

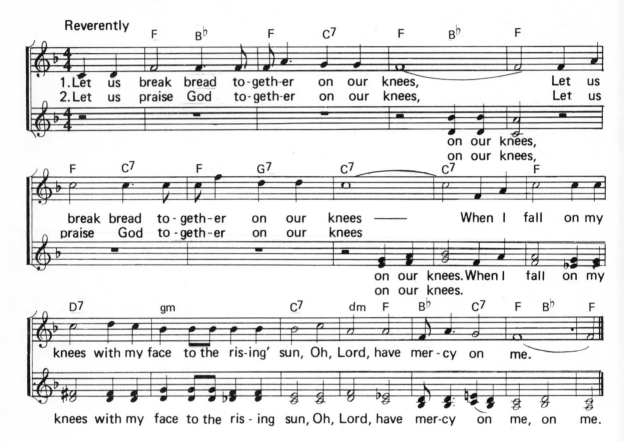

From *Exploring Music* series (teacher's ed.), Book 6, © 1966; by special permission of the publisher, Holt, Rinehart and Winston.

The action

1. Sing in three parts, as shown. Vary by assigning the solo voice to sing the first phrase, with the chorus coming in at "on our knees." Repeat with second phrase.
2. Create new verses, keeping the same spirit of the song, for example, "Let us give thanks together on our knees."
3. Contrast the mood of this spiritual with that of "Good News," no. 87.
4. Create interpretive body movement. (See "All Creatures of Our God and King," no. 80, and Interpretive Body Movement.) Help the children discover the climax of the song before attempting to create movement, so that the movement may reflect the musical climax as well as communicating the spirit of the song.

Related activities and materials
    See Spirituals (p. 283)

For study
    Descending *chromatic* progression in harmony
    Syncopation
    Tie
    Conduct in 4-bt. pattern (See p. 269)
    Spirituals

bells

F = F A C
B♭ = B♭ D F
C⁷ = C E G B♭
D⁷ = D F♯ A C
g mi = G B♭ D
d mi = D F A
G⁷ = G B D F

Autoharp
F, B♭, C⁷,
d mi
g mi,
D⁷

guitar

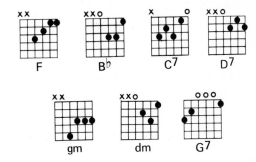

90. I SEE THE MOON

Words and music by Meredith Wilson

Program song
Level: U
Key of F: start middle C (low sol) and A (mi)

From Wilson, Ehret, Knuth, Hermann, and Renna, *Growing with Music*, Book 6 (Related Arts ed.), © 1970 by Prentice-Hall, Inc., Englewood Cliffs, N.J.; reprinted by permission.

The action

Note that the melody of the song is found on the lower staff and sung by the lower voice in the two-part section, while in the three-part section it begins in the middle voice (middle staff), then changes over to the higher voice (upper staff).

1. Sing the two and three parts as indicated.
2. If desired, assign the solo on the first eight measures, accompanied by the chorus humming the harmony part. Then everyone sings the words in parts in the last eight measures. Variations in tempo and dynamics in selected places throughout the song will greatly enhance its effect as a program number, as will simple costumes, props, and lighting wherever possible. In this connection, a simple suggestion might be to divide the class into two groups, one on each side of the stage (either boys and girls or mixed). While one group sings the first four measures (lighted), the other group remains in darkness. On the next four measures, the second group is lighted and sings while the first group remains in darkness. On the last eight measures both groups are lighted while they sing together.
3. Have the class create a simple set of movements (or dance routine), which would, in effect, dramatize the song, but would also be rhythmical, for example:

a. Facing the audience, step diagonally right on the right foot, bring the left foot up close to the right heel, tap the left toe but do not put weight on it.
b. Step back on the left foot, bring the right foot back close to the left toe, tap the right toe but do not place weight on it.
c. Repeat (a) and (b).
d. Beginning on right foot walk eight steps around to the right in a wide circle (if done in partners, the boy can pivot in place while holding the girl's hands as she walks around in the circle).
e. Repeat (a), (b), and (c), beginning on the left foot.
f. Repeat (d), beginning on the left foot and walking eight steps around to the left.

The simple steps suggested here can be done to an instrumental accompaniment at a slightly faster tempo and can precede the final singing of the song in parts. In other words, the movement can simply be an interlude for added interest.

Related activities and materials

1. Sing other songs by Meredith Wilson, for example, "Seventy-Six Trombones."
2. Select a few songs and scenes from "The Music Man" or another Broadway musical of choice and work them up for a program.
3. Research the history of American musical theatre and learn some selected songs from each period.

4. Listening:
   "Moon Legend," BOL #67.
   "The Planets," Keyboard Publications.
   "Clair de Lune," BOL #52 and EIM.
   "The Music Man" (original cast album) and other musicals of choice.

For study

Chromatic tones (E♭, F♯, G♯)
Uneven rhythm pattern
Two- and three-part harmony

91. JOE TURNER BLUES
American blues

Level: U
Key of C: start G (sol)

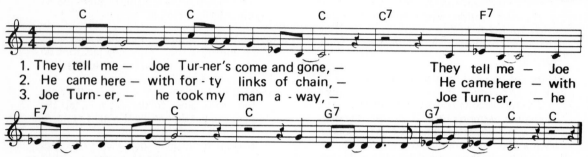

1. They tell me — Joe Tur-ner's come and gone, — They tell me — Joe
2. He came here — with for-ty links of chain, — He came here — with
3. Joe Turn-er, — he took my man a-way, — Joe Turn-er, — he

Tur-ner's-come and gone.— He left me-here to sing —this —song.
for-ty — links of chain.—
took my — man a-way.—

The action

Traditionally the structure of the blues has been a three-line verse (or three phrases), with the words of the first two phrases the same or very nearly so, and the third line or phrase, different. Since the spiritual (p. 283) and the blues are rooted in the same hearts, their African heritage is similarly evident in their rhythmic, as well as melodic, structure. Syncopation is fairly common, and some tones are sung slightly flatted (see number 3 below). This slight flatting results in a rather plaintive sound, befitting the subject matter of the song which, unlike the spiritual, deals with wordly things (often in very earthy terms).

Historically, spirituals were sung unaccompanied, while blues songs were frequently performed to the accompaniment of small instrumental groups. Blues is considered to be one of the stages in the evolution of *jazz,* the heart of which is *improvisation.* "Usually the blues singer's melody only fills the first three bars of each phrase; the last measure is filled with an instrumental improvisation on the vocal melody. These brief improvisations may well have been the germ from which the whole art of jazz improvisation grew."*

1. Research the origin of the blues in America and the kinds of things that might have

*From *Exploring Music,* (teacher's ed.), Book 6, p. 171, © 1966, Holt, Rinehart and Winston.

motivated early blues, such as lost love, working too hard, a need to be free, etc.
2. Compare this with the things people might sing the blues about today.
3. Note the three-phrase blues form and the word content. Listen to a blues scale, in which the third and seventh tones are sounded a half step lower:

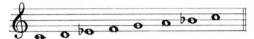

4. Listen to more blues songs, then create an original song in the blues form, using the tones of the blues scale, based on the following harmonic progression:

phrase 1	I (tonic chord)
phrase 2	IV I chords
phrase 3	V7 I chords

Note that the accompaniment remains in the major, while the melody uses the blues scale.
5. In "Joe Turner Blues" improvise on the given chords in the measures of rest, for example, add the sixth and ninth to the C7 chord. There are no words for the singer here; the time is meant to be used for improvisation, which is the essence of jazz.
6. Do some "talkin' blues." (See *Exploring Music,* Book 6, Holt, Rinehart and Winston.)

Related activities and materials

1. Listening:
"Joe Turner Blues," MMYO 6 record album, Silver Burdett.
"America: The Cradle of Jazz," Keyboard Publications.
"From Jazz to Rock." (FS and record), Keyboard Publications.
"W. C. Handy Blues," Folkways Records.
"Jazz, Vol. 2: The Blues," and "Jazz, Vol. 4: Jazz Singers," Folkways Records.

Selected larger works in which the jazz idiom is used:
"Rhapsody in Blue," Gershwin
"Creation of the World," Darius Milhaud
"Ragtime," Stravinsky
" 'Blues' from 'The Lenox Avenue Suite,' " Still.
"Golliwog's Cakewalk," Debussy
Film:
"Discovering Jazz," Film Associates.

For study
 Blues   form
 Blues   scale
 Syncopation
 Rests on final measure of each phrase, pro-
 viding for improvisation
 Evolution of jazz in America

guitar

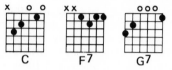

C   F7   G7

92. OVER THE RIVER

Traditional American song

Level: U and L
Key of D: start A (sol)

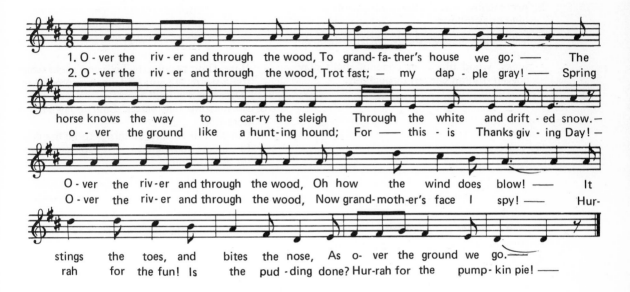

1. O-ver the riv-er and through the wood, To grand-fa-ther's house we go; —— The
2. O-ver the riv-er and through the wood, Trot fast; — my dap-ple gray! —— Spring

horse knows the way to car-ry the sleigh Through the white and drift-ed snow.—
o-ver the ground like a hunt-ing hound; For —— this-is Thanks giv-ing Day! —

O-ver the riv-er and through the wood, Oh how the wind does blow! —— It
O-ver the riv-er and through the wood, Now grand-moth-er's face I spy! —— Hur-

stings the toes, and bites the nose, As o-ver the ground we go.——
rah for the fun! Is the pud-ding done? Hur-rah for the pump-kin pie! ——

From Wilson, Ehret, Knuth, Hermann, and Renna, *Growing with Music* (Related Arts ed.), Book 2, ©
1970 by Prentice-Hall, Inc., Englewood Cliffs, N.J.; reprinted by permission.

The action

1. Show a picture of a horse-drawn sleigh as an early means of transportation.
2. Accompany with rhythm instruments as desired or as follows:

   bells, play steady pattern throughout

   sticks, wood block, or coconut shells play uneven rhythm pattern throughout:

Strike each of the following instruments *once* on the word specified as it occurs in the song:

"stings"	triangle
"toes"	woodblock
"bites"	rap tambourine
"nose"	cymbals

Note: Omit playing the bells and sticks when these words are sounded, then resume all on "Over the ground."

3. Create some new verses about today's transportation.
4. Out of a discussion of things to be thankful for, create some graces for Thanksgiving and set them to music.

Related activities and materials

1. Draw or paint the scene set by the song.
2. Dramatize the first Thanksgiving in movement.
3. Learn an Indian song. See No. 56.
4. Listening:
   "Sleigh Ride," Mozart.
   "Sleigh Ride," Leroy Anderson.
   "Three Horse Sleigh," Tchaikovsky.
   "Turkey in the Straw," Guion, RCA Basic Record Library R5
   "A Mighty Fortress" (Thanksgiving Hymns), RCA LSC2199.
   "Pumpkin Eater's Little Fugue," AM 2, and BOL #65.
   See Additional Listening for the Thanksgiving Season below. See resource material on the American Indian.

Additional Listening for the Thanksgiving Season

"Pop Goes the Weasel" (variations), AM 4, vol. 1.
"The Snow Is Dancing," AM 3, vol. 1.
"In Wartime," AM 5, vol. 1.
"Harvest Song," AM 1, vol. 2.
"Ballet of the Unhatched Chicks," AM 1, vol. 1.
"Little Indian Drum," YPRC.
"America the Beautiful," Robert Shaw Chorale, RCA.
"Wheat Dance," AM 4, vol. 1.
"Hoe-Down," AM 5, vol. 2.
"Chester," from New England Triptych, EM 5 and BOL #75.
"North American Indian Songs," Bowmar.
"Old American Songs," EM Kindergarten record album.
"Corn Grinding Song" and "Silversmith Song," EM 3, record album.

For study

$\frac{6}{8}$ (compound) meter; conduct in 2 (See p. 270)
Like phrases
Tie meas. 4, 12, 16
Slur meas. 8
For practice, transpose to key of C (See Transposing)

93. ADESTE FIDELIS (O COME, ALL YE FAITHFUL)

Traditional

Program song
Level: U
Key of G: start G (do)

1. O come, all ye faith-ful, Joy-ful and tri-um-phant, O come ye, O
1. A-des-te, fi-de-les, Lae-ti, tri-um-phan-tes, Ve-ni-te, ve,

Come — ye to Beth — — le -hem; Come and be-hold Him,
ni - te in Beth — — le -hem; Na-tum vi-de - te,

Refrain

Born the King of An-gels, O come, let us a-dore Him,   O come, let us a-
Re-gem an-ge-lo-rum: Ve-ni-te a-do-re-mus,   Ve-ni-te a-do-

dore him, O come let us a-dore Him, — Christ — the Lord.
re-mus, Ve-ni-te a-do-re-mus — Do — — mi-num.

2. Sing, choirs of angels,
   Sing in exultation,
   O sing, all ye citizens of heav'n above,
   Glory to God, in the highest.
   O come, etc.

The action

1. Sing in Latin. (It might be of interest to the class to know that this was originally a Portuguese folk tune.)
2. Add the following descant on the chorus part, using either voice or melody instrument such as recorder, resonator bells etc:

Ve - ni - - te, ve - ni - - te, ve - -ni - te a - do - re - mus - Do - mi - num.

3. Say the English words as a choral-speaking selection, to emphasize the importance of proper interpretation as a means of more effective communication.
4. Create some interpretive body movement, using the speaking chorus as accompaniment. See "All Creatures of Our God and King," no. 80.
5. Use rhythm instruments as accompaniment to heighten the dramatic effect of the chorus and movement combination:

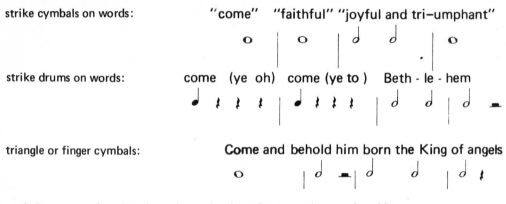

strike cymbals on words:　　　　"come"　"faithful" "joyful and tri—umphant"

strike drums on words:　　　come (ye oh) come (ye to) Beth - le - hem

triangle or finger cymbals:　　Come and behold him born the King of angels

shake one tambourine throughout the line: Oh come, let us adore him

shake two tambourines as above: Oh come, etc.

shake three tambourines as above: Oh come, etc.

drum and cymbals:

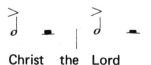

Christ   the   Lord

6. Sing in English, using body movement as before. Add the rhythm instruments suggested above or as desired. Evaluate with the class the worth of choral-speaking interpretation preceding the singing (as suggested in number 3 above), not only in terms of improved musical performance, but also as a factor in creating more effective movement.

Related activities and materials

1. Learn some Christmas songs in other languages. See Classified Index for the other Christmas songs.
2. In contrast to the mood of "Adeste Fidelis," yet still in keeping with the season, try the activities suggested for "The Twelve Days of Christmas," no. 97. The music is available in MYA Book 4, American Book Company.
3. See Christmas Listening.

For study

Slur

Feeling of fleeting change of key (modulation) on "Bethlehem"

Sing with syllables (See pp. 277-278)

Note dynamics possibilities in the refrain; for practice, put in appropriate markings to indicate a rise to the climax (See Glossary)

Conduct in 4-bt. pattern (See p. 269)

94. JOLLY OLD ST. NICHOLAS

Traditional tune

Level: U and L
Key of B♭: start D (mi)

1. Jol-ly old Saint Nich-o-las, lean your ear this way! Don't you tell a sin-gle soul what I'm going to say, Christ-mas Eve is com-ing soon, now, you dear old man, Whis-per what you'll bring to me, tell me if you can.

2. When the clock is strik-ing twelve, When I'm fast a-sleep, Down the chim-ney broad and black, with your pack you'll creep; All the stock-ings you will find hang-ing in a row, mine will be the short-est one, you'll be sure to know.

From Berg, Kjelson, Troth, Hooley, Wolverton, and Burns, *Meeting Music,* Music for Young Americans Series, © 1966, American Book Co., New York.

The action
1. When the song has been learned, dramatize it, with different children taking the parts of Saint Nicholas, the clock, child, chimney, stockings, etc.
2. As an alternative to number 1, simply add action pantomiming the words.

3. Add rhythm instruments to heighten the effect in selected places, for example, the clock (woodblock), chimney (shake tambourine), all stockings (ascending or descending notes on xylophone or bells).
4. Add more verses to include desired toys or other gifts.

Related activities and materials
1. Look up the origin of the name St. Nicholas.
2. Look up other names by which Santa Claus is known in other parts of the world, as well as Christmas and holiday customs.
3. Learn some different ways of saying "Merry Christmas," for example,

    Hawaiian   *Mele Kalikimaka*
    (May-lay Kah-lee-kee-mah-kah)
    Spanish   *Felices Navides*
    (Fay-lee-sayce Nah-vee-dahd-ayce)

    French   *Joyeux Noel*
    (Szhoy-ur Noh-el)
    Swedish   *Gud Jul* (Gude Yule)

4. See suggestions for other Christmas holiday songs.
5. Listening:
    Dance-A-Story, "The Toy Tree," RCA.
    "The Holiday Spirit," Keyboard Publications.
    See Christmas Listening.

For study

Chromatic tone in measure 7
Chant rhythm pattern then sing with syllables (See pp. 277-278)
Even rhythm
Like phrases
Conduct in 2-bt. pattern (see p. 269)

bells
Bb = Bb D F
D⁷ = D F♯ A C
g min = G Bb D
C⁷ = C E G Bb
Eb = E G Bb
F⁷ = F A C Eb

95. JINGLE BELLS

James Pierpont

Level: U and L
Key of G: start B (mi)

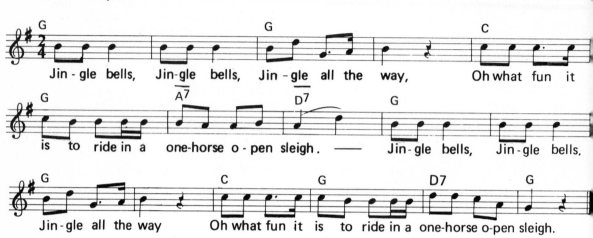

Jin - gle bells, Jin-gle bells, Jin - gle all the way, Oh what fun it

is to ride in a one-horse o - pen sleigh. —— Jin-gle bells, Jin - gle bells,

Jin - gle all the way Oh what fun it is to ride in a one-horse o-pen sleigh.

The action

1. Accompany with sleigh bells beating a steady eighth-note rhythm throughout ♫ ♫ and triangles beating two beats to each measure.
2. Sing in Spanish:

   Cascabel, cascabel, musica de amor
   Dulces horas, gratas horas
   Juventud en flor
   Cascabel, cascabel, tan sentimental
   No dejes cascabellito de repiquetear

3. Sing in French:

   Tintez cloches, tintez cloches tintez dans la nuit
   Père Noel et ses grands daims, arrivent tout de suite
   Tintez cloches tintez cloches tintez dans la nuit
   Père Noel et ses grands daims arrivent tout de suite

4. Create an original percussion score for rhythm instruments to accompany the singing, using resonator bells for the melody.

5. Create original movements to go with the song or try the following:

   Formation: double circle, partners facing, boys on inside

   a. "Jingle bells" clap knees 3 times ♫ ♩
   b. [repeat] clap hands 3 times ♫ ♩
   c. "Jingle all the way" swing partners (face partner, hook right elbows, and turn in place)
   d. "Oh what fun," etc., to "sleigh" 4 slides left, then four slides right
   e. [repeat (a), (b), and (c)]
   f. "Oh what fun it is to ride" walk four steps forward in counterclockwise motion
   g. "In a one-horse open sleigh" boys stand still, girls move counterclockwise on to new partners; face new partners and bow and curtsy

6. Add the following descant:

Bells, bells, jingle bells, oh fun   o-pen sleigh, Bells, bells, jingle bells, oh fun open sleigh.

Related activities and materials

1. Have the children discover the many different sounds made by various kinds of bells. Bring in any that can be carried and record the sounds of others. Discuss the function of bells throughout the world—past and present, calling people together, telling time, call to worship, locating objects by sound (cows, etc.), accompaniment and adornment for dancing (wrist and ankle bells), calling for an answer (telephone, doorbell), announcing activities (end of class, recess, lunch, etc.).
2. If a set of hand bells can be procured, have the children learn to play a simple tune on them. If not, invite some local bell ringers to play.
3. See the Classified Index for other Christmas and holiday songs.
4. Listening:
   "Bells," Hanson, AM 1, vol. 2.
   "This Is Rhythm," Ella Jenkins, Folkways Records,, FC 7652.
   "Children's Symphony," 3rd movement, AM 2, vol. 1.
   See additional Christmas listening, p. 209.
5. Reference:
   "The Book of Bells," Satis Coleman, John Day Co.

For study

Like phrases
Chant rhythm and sing with syllables (See pp.277-278)
Even and uneven rhythm patterns ♫ ♩. ♪
Conduct in 2-bt. pattern (See p. 269)

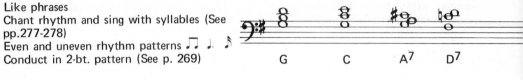

left-hand piano

G   C   A⁷   D⁷

bells

G = G B D
C = C E G
D⁷ = D F♯ A C
A⁷ = A C♯ E G

Autoharp
G, C, D⁷, A⁷

guitar

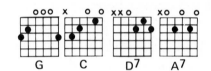

G   C   D⁷   A⁷

ukulele

Tune: A D F♯ B (G tuning)

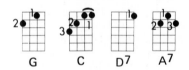

G   C   D⁷   A⁷

96. SILENT NIGHT

Joseph Mohr, Franz Gruber

Program song
Level: U and L
Key of C: **start G (sol)**

Si - lent night, Hol - ly night, All is calm, — all is bright, Round yon Vir - gin

Moth - er and Child, Ho - ly In - tant so ten - der and mild,

Sleep in heav - en - ly peace — Sleep — in heav - en ly peace. ——

Spanish

Noche de paz noche de amor
Todo duerme en derredor
Entre los astros que esparcen su luz
Bella anunciando al nino Jesus
Brilla la estrella de paz,
Brilla la estrella de paz

German

Stille Nacht, heilige Nacht
Alles schlaft einsam wacht
Nur das traute hoch heilige Paar
Holder Knabe im lokkigen Haar
Schlaf in himmlischer Ruh
Schlaf in himmlischer Ruh

The action

1. Sing in two languages as shown.
2. Add the following descant with the voice or a melody instrument such as a recorder or resonator bells, or find the harmony by ear, choosing between *mi* and *fa* as the harmonizing note for each measure.

3. Accompany with Autoharp, three-part vocal chording, or resonator bells. Since this song was originally sung to the accompaniment of the guitar, it would be most effective if guitar accompaniment could be provided.
4. Create some interpretive body movement to perform. See Interpretive Body Movement and "All Creatures of Our God and King," no. 80.

Descant:

Related activities and materials
1. See suggestions for other holiday songs.

2. Listening:
See Christmas listening, p. 209.

For study
$\frac{6}{8}$ (compound meter: contrast the conducting of this song, using 6-beat pattern (see p. 270) with the conducting of "Over the River," no. 92 or "When Johnny Comes Marching Home," no. 38, using the 2-beat pattern
Note the uneven rhythm ♩ ♪ ♩ throughout, except on "sleep"

left-hand piano

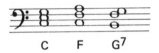

C   F   G⁷

bells

C = C E G
F = F A C
G⁷ = G B D F

guitar

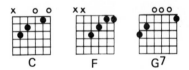

C   F   G⁷

Autoharp
C, F, G⁷

vocal chording
(See p. 299)

97. THE TWELVE DAYS OF CHRISTMAS

Program song
Level: U

Music available in MYA Book 4, American Book Company.

The action
1. After the song has been learned, let individual children take the solos on each of the gifts.
2. Create a movement for each of the objects and execute it each time the gift is mentioned in the song. Movements may be done by the soloist in number 1, by the entire class, or by small groups.
3. Select a rhythm instrument (or group of instruments) that sounds appropriate for each of the objects and play as each is mentioned.
4. Select *one* rhythm instrument to be sounded only on the word that indicates the days, for example, "first," "second."
5. Create some new verses, using other objects as gifts.

Related activities and materials
1. Discuss the similar custom of giving gifts in other countries, as well as the holiday seasons of those countries.
2. Discuss gifts one might be likely to receive in Hawaii, Alaska, Japan, Africa (and other parts of the world), and create new verses using these objects as gifts. In each group, substitute the appropriate native bird and tree for the partridge and the pear—for example, in Hawaii it might be a coconut or papaya tree and mynah bird.
3. See the Classified Index for other Christmas songs.
4. Listening:
See Christmas listening.
5. Film:
"The Twelve Days of Christmas," Weston Woods, Weston Conn.

98. JESU, JOY OF MAN'S DESIRING

Melody by Johann Schop, arranged by Johann Sebastian Bach

Program song

Level: U

Key of G: start B (mi)

A chorale is a choral hymn intended to be sung in unison by the congregation. In Bach's day organists found that the people often paused at the end of each phrase. This pause allowed time for the organist to improvise a brief interlude on the organ. Gradually, these interludes became more and more important and elaborate. The chorale was sometimes arranged in parts for the choir to sing, and the interludes were given to instruments of the orchestra.

Je - su, joy of man's de - sir - ing, Ho - ly wis - dom,
Drawn by Thee, our soul's as - pir - ing, Soar to un - cre-

love — most — bright. Word of God, our flesh that fash - ioned
a - ted — light.

With the fire of life im - pass - ioned. Striv - ing still to

truth un - known, Soar - ing, dy - ing round Thy — throne.

INTERLUDE

From *Exploring Music* series (teacher's ed.), Book 6, © 1966; by special permission of the publisher, Holt, Rinehart and Winston.

The action

1. When learning the song, give special attention to phrasing, dynamics, and general expression as a means of securing the best interpretation of the text.
2. Listen to a recording of this chorale (see Listening below), noting the instrumental interludes that occur between phrases.
3. If there is a student in the class who can play the instrumental interludes on a solo instrument, have him do so while the class sings the chorale (see interlude on song page 208).
4. As an outgrowth of number 2 and 3, explore the following:

a. Using an art medium of choice, make a visual representation of the chorale, interspersed with the interludes.
b. Create interpretive body movement that reflects the spirit of the chorale and of the interludes. See "All Creatures of Our God and King," no. 80, and Interpretive Body Movement.
c. Divide the class into groups. Have one group perform the movement for the chorale and another perform movements they have created for the instrumental interludes.

Related activities and materials

1. Listen to other chorales and compositions by Bach.
2. This chorale is often sung during the Christmas season. See Classified Index for other songs of Christmas.
3. Listening:
   "Jesu, Joy of Man's Desiring," EM, Book 6, record album, and AM 5, vol. 1.
   "A Mighty Fortress," Robert Shaw Chorale, RCA, LSC 2199.
   "Little Fugue in G Minor," Bach, AM 6, vol. 1, EIM record album.
   See other Christmas listening selections.
4. Additional listening for the Christmas Season
   "Jesu, Joy of Man's Desiring," AM 5, vol. 1.
   "Hallelujah Chorus," EIM record album.
   "Ceremony of Carols," Britten, Robert Shaw Chorale, RCA, LSC-2759.
   "Amahl and the Night Visitors," BOL #58.
   "Jack in the Box"' Mikrokosmos Suite No. 2, AM 2, vol. 1.
   "Fantastic Toy Shop," AM 2, vol. 1.

"March of the Toys," Herbert, AM 2, vol. 1.
"Toy Symphony," Haydn, EIM record album.
"Concerto for Toys and Orchestra," Bizet.
"Children's Symphony," 3rd movement, McDonald, AM 2, vol. 1.
"Nutcracker Suite," Tchaikovsky, "Beginning Music," NDM series ABC.
"The Holiday Spirit" (contains visual masters, record, teacher's guide, students' booklets), Keyboard Publications.
"Sleigh Ride," Leroy Anderson, "Pops Christmas Party," RCA, LSC 2329.
"Christmas Hymns and Carols," Robert Shaw Chorale, RCA, LSC 2139.
"Music at Christmas TIme," RCA, WE-88.
"Canciones de Navidad," RCA, MKS-1800.
Film:
"The Twelve Days of Christmas," Weston Woods, Weston, Conn.
Filmstrip:
"The Story of Handel's 'Messiah,'" FS and record), SVE.

For study

Chorale prelude
Slur (meas. 7 and 23)
Repeat sign :‖
Sing with syllables (See pp. 277-278)
Conduct in 3-bt. pattern (See p. 269)

99. THE PIÑATA

Mexican folk song (English words by Nona K. Duffy)

Level: U
Key of C: start G (sol)

Bril-liant lan-terns are light-ed, Our friends are in-vi-ted, In cho-rus u-nit-ed," ¡Pi-

ña-ta!" There's no need to re-mind us, With blindfolds they'll bind us, They'll

turn and they'll wind us, "¡Piñata!" *Ay, que bue-na, Ay, que buena, Ah, que*

bue-na, que bue-na, que bue-na. All the chil-dren will scram-ble for
All the chil-dren will grab for a

can-dy All the chil-dren will scram-ble and shout.
cook-y And the oth-er good things that spill out.

From *Making Music Your Own*, Book 3, © 1971 by the General Learning Corporation; reprinted by permission.

The action

1. When the song has been learned, let each of three children sing "Ay, que buena" as a solo.
2. Accompany with Autoharp or guitar. Add maracas, tambourine, castanets, or other rhythm instruments:

maracas

tambourine

castanets

3. Create a dance to the song.

Related activities and materials

1. A *piñata* is an earthenware bowl or paper bag made to look like a bird or an animal. Have the class construct a *piñata* and play the game as Mexican children do. Look up other Christmas customs of Mexico.
2. Sing other Mexican folksongs. See Classified Index.

3. Learn some Mexican folk dances:
   "El Jarabe Tapatio" ("Mexican Hat Dance"), "Special Folk Dances," RCA.
   "La Raspa," "All-Purpose Folk Dances," RCA.
4. Listening:
   See resource material on Mexico.

For study

$^6_8$ (compound) meter; conduct in 2-bt. pattern (See p. 269)
Like phrases
Repeat sign :‖

left-hand piano

C   G⁷

bells

C = C E G
G⁷ = G B D F

guitar

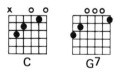

C   G⁷

Autoharp
C, G⁷

100. DREYDL SPIN

Israeli folk song (translated by E.W.T.)

Level: U and L
Key of f minor: start F (la)

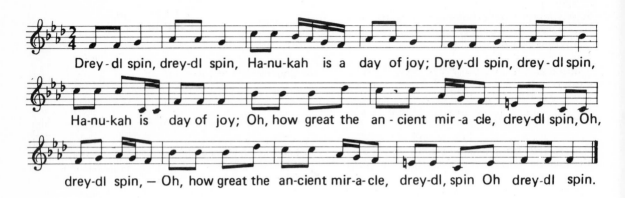

Drey-dl spin, drey-dl spin, Ha-nu-kah is a day of joy; Drey-dl spin, drey-dl spin,

Ha-nu-kah is day of joy; Oh, how great the an-cient mir-a-cle, drey-dl spin, Oh,

drey-dl spin, — Oh, how great the an-cient mir-a-cle, drey-dl, spin Oh drey-dl spin.

From Choate, Berg, Kjelson, and Troth, *Enjoying Music,* New Dimensions in Music series, © 1970, American Book Co., New York.

The action
Before learning the song, discuss the significance of Hanukah and the meaning of related words such as "ancient miracle" and "dreydl." Show a menorah, if possible, while the story is told:

Hanukah (sometimes spelled *Chanuka*) is a Jewish holiday observed in December. It joyously celebrates the victory of Judas Maccebeus and his group of brave men over King Aschasveras more than two thousand years ago. At that first celebration service in 165 B.C., it was suddenly discovered that there was oil enough for only one day in the Holy Lamp. The "ancient miracle" referred to in the song is that although no more oil was available, the Lamp kept burning for eight days and nights. The eight-branch Menorah (candelabra) holds the candles which are lighted one at a time during each night of Hanukah until on the last night all eight burn at once. Gifts may be exchanged during Hanukah and games played by the children. One such game uses a four-sided top with Hebrew letters on the sides indicating "win" or "lose," and is played very much like the regular spin-the-top game.

1. Clap the basic meter of each measure (two claps) while singing.
2. Use rhythm instruments as desired or as follows:

R = Rap
S = Shake

measures 1-4:

woodblock

finger cymbals

tambourine

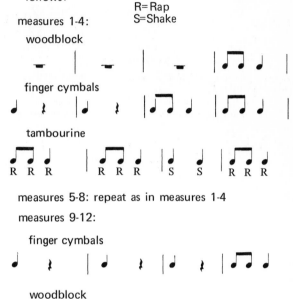

measures 5-8: repeat as in measures 1-4

measures 9-12:

finger cymbals

woodblock

tambourine

measures 13-16: repeat as in measures 9-12

3. Create some movement to the song:

Formation: circle
meas. 1-2: four slides to right
meas. 3-4: three claps (♫ ♩) then three stamps (♫ ♩)
meas. 5-6: four slides to the left
meas. 7-8: repeat as in meas. 3-4
meas. 9-10: walk four steps to the right turning in place
meas. 11-12: three claps and then three stamps as in meas. 3-4
meas. 13-14: walk four steps to the left, turning in place
meas. 15-16: repeat as in meas. 11-12

4. Dance the *hora.* Learn other folk dances of Israeli origin.
5. Note that the song is written in a minor key, as are many other Israeli folk songs. Try changing the key signature to one flat:

and sing in F major instead of f minor. **Discuss the effect of the change.**
6. Sing other Israeli folk songs. See Classified Index.

Related activities and materials
1. Construct a dreydl and compare it to a top, or draw a picture of a dreydl.
2. Spin a dreydl, then try to move as it moves. Depict other toys in movement.
3. Listening:

"The Top," BOL #53.
"The Ball," AM 1, vol. 1.
"Jack in the Box," AM 2 vol. 1.
"The Story of Toys" (FS and record), Denoyer-Geppert AV.
4. See additional source material on Israel.

For study
Harmonic minor indicated by presence of *si* (E ♮)
Rhythm patterns:

a. ♪♪♩   b. ♪♪♪♪   c. ♪♪♪

Moderato
Conduct in 2-bt. pattern (See p. 269)
Music of Israel

101. THERE ARE MANY FLAGS IN MANY LANDS

Program song
Level: U and L
Key of A♭: start C (mi)

Composer unknown (Words by M. H. Howliston)

In march time

There are man-y flags in man-y lands, There are flags of ev- ery hue;But there
is no flag, how-ev - er grand, Like our own Red, White and Blue. Then hurrah for the flag, our coun-try's flag, Its stripes and white stars, too, For there
is no flag in an - y land Like our own Red, White and Blue.

From *Exploring Music* series (teachers' ed.), Book 3 © 1966; by special permission of the publisher Holt, Rinehart and Winston.

The action

1. Perform a flag drill. Each child may carry a flag and march in time to the music, making various formations, for example:

(a) Enter by single line from *each* side of the rear of the stage or performing area. Each line marches diagonally to the opposite corner of the front of the stage. As the lines begin to meet, each child in one line crosses in front of a child in the other line:

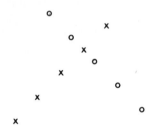

(b) As the lead child in each line reaches the front of the stage, he turns and marches around to the rear. At the rear both lines meet and walk forward in twos.

(c) As the couples reach the front of the stage, one couple goes left, the next right, etc., alternating down the line.

(d) As couples meet at the rear, they walk forward in fours to the center of the stage or performing area. End people pivot in place as each line marches around in a circle to the left, to form equidistant lines moving like spokes of a wheel.

(e) Close up to make four lines again, marching in place, then march forward. At the front, one set of four goes left, one goes right, alternating down the line. At rear, the fours meet to form lines of eight and march forward. If desired, children may stand in this formation to sing another song or medley of patriotic songs.

(f) The group may leave the stage by the front line exiting left, followed by the second line exiting right, etc., or half of the front line may exit left and the other half right, followed by each half of the remaining lines.

Note: It may be necessary to repeat the whole song in order to complete the figures, depending on the amount of space and the number of children taking part.

2. Whistle the whole song or whistle the first eight measures, then sing the words on the last eight measures.

3. Beat the basic meter with the feet while clapping the rhythm of the melody, or divide class into two groups--one clapping, the other beating the meter.

4. March in place in time to the music. At the end of each phrase, face a different direction.

Related activities and materials

1. Study the history of the United States flag.

2. Look up the flags of other countries and note the colors used. Make some copies of flags, using some form of art media.

3. Look up state flags and other types of flags frequently flown.

4. Look up the meaning of the language of the flag, e.g., when flown upside down, at half mast, etc.

5. Sing other flag and patriotic songs, for example, "You're a Grand Old Flag,"* See Classified Index for others.

6. Listening:
"Stars and Stripes Forever," AM 3, vol. 2.
"Fourth of July," Ives.
"America the Beautiful," Robert Shaw Chorale, RCA, LSC 2662.

7. Filmstrips:
"The Story of Our Flag," Denoyer- Geppert AV, 66046.
"What Our Flag Means to You," Denoyer-Geppert AV, 66048.

*R. P. Gelineau, *Experiences in Music,* New York: McGraw-Hill, 1970, p. 31.

For study
Syncopation
Transpose to key of G and accompany on
   Autoharp
Like phrases
Conduct in 4-bt. pattern (See p. 269)

bells
$A\flat = A\flat\ C\ E\flat$
$D\flat = D\flat\ F\ A\flat$
$E\flat 7 = E\flat\ G\ B\flat\ D\flat$

102. AMERICA

Words by Samuel F. Smith, music by Henry Carey

Level: U and L
Key of F: start F (do)

The action

1. Discuss the meaning of the words in the song for improved interpretation, then create some interpretive body movement for all three verses.
2. Sing in the English version:

"God Save the Queen"

God save our gracious Queen
Long live our noble Queen
God save the Queen
Send her victorious
Happy and glorious
Long to reign over us
God save the Queen.

3. Since this is such a familiar tune, try the following by way of simple ear training (see Ear Training).

Play the first four measures of the song as written. Play the same four measures, but alter them in some way, either by changing the key, the melody, or the meter (changes in the rhythm pattern, tempo, and dynamics should also be listened for). Have the class identify the nature of the change, using the appropriate musical term.

4. Create an original descant to accompany the melody.

Related activities and materials

1. Sing other songs about "America," such as "America the Beautiful" and "God Bless America."
2. See Classified Index for other patriotic songs.
3. Listening:
   "America the Beautiful," Robert Shaw Chorale, RCA, LSC 2662.
   "Variations on 'America,' " Charles Ives.

Listen to some patriotic songs and national anthems of other countries ("National Anthems," Folkways Records).
See source material on other countries.

4. Film:
   "What Does Our Flag Mean?", 11 min., BW/Col., Coronet.
5. Filmstrips:
   "Stories of Great Americans" series, SVE.
   "Our Flag" series, McGraw-Hill.

For study

Recurring rhythm pattern
Chant rhythm and sing with syllables (See pp. 277-278)
Conduct in 3-bt. pattern (See p. 269)

left-hand piano

F   B♭ C⁷

bells

F = F A C
B♭ = B♭ D F
C⁷ = C E G, B♭

Autoharp
F, B♭, C⁷

103. EV'RYBODY SAY "PEACE"

Lyrics by Fred Tobias, music by Stan Lebowsky

Program song
Level: U
Key of E♭: start E♭ (do)

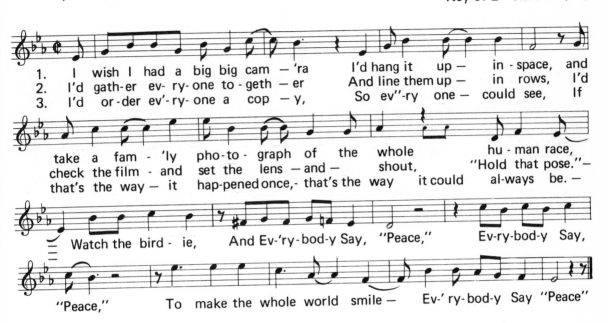

1. I wish I had a big big cam — 'ra   I'd hang it   up —   in - space, and
2. I'd gath-er ev- ry-one to-geth — er   And line them up —   in rows, I'd
3. I'd or-der ev'-ry-one a cop — y,   So ev"-ry one — could see, If

take a fam - 'ly pho-to- graph of the whole   hu - man race,
check the film - and set the lens — and — shout,   "Hold that pose."—
that's the way — it hap-pened once,- that's the way it could   al-ways be. —

Watch the bird - ie, And Ev-'ry-bod-y Say, "Peace,"   Ev-ry-bod-y Say,

"Peace,"   To make the whole world smile — Ev-'ry-bod-y Say "Peace"

104. LET THERE BE PEACE ON EARTH

Words and music by Sy Miller and Jill Jackson

Program song
Level: U
Key of C: start C (do)

The action

Since these two songs are related to peace and brotherhood, it seems appropriate to group them together with suggestions for incorporating them into a program rather than to separate and associate each with classroom activities, although the latter is possible, of course. The following is merely a suggested framework within which such a program might be built.

Musical opening: "Everybody Say Peace" (chorus)

Narrator: Short narration setting the theme of the program by pointing up some of the "universals" among human beings.

Musical selections from each of the following categories, interspersed with narration where background information or a setting would be helpful:

lullabies (from several countries; dramatize if desired)

work songs (songs and movements reflecting various occupations around the world)

play songs (dances and game songs with actions from around the world)

humorous songs (songs with humor, from around the world, pointing up whether or not people around the world laugh at the same things)

love songs (songs of love, unrequited and otherwise, from around the world)

Closing narration leading into need for love of fellow man and for living peacefully together, etc.)

Finale: "Let There Be Peace on Earth" (sung by all participants)

Titles such as "Brother Man," "Music Around the World," "Around the World in Sound," or "Sounds of the World" would reflect the desired emphasis. Costumes and authentic instruments should be included in the presentation whenever possible. Other alternatives are:

1. A simple program of songs and dances from all parts of the world, in a United Nations framework.
2. "National Anthems of the World," backed by a display of flags of all nations. The narration might include facts about the origin of each flag, each anthem and a brief historical background, if desired.
3. Expansion of any of the categories in the large program framework suggested above:

   "Lullabies Around the World"
   "Children's Games Around the World"
   "Man Dances Around the World"
   "Man Works Around the World" (or "Plays or "Sings," etc.)

PART II
PLANNING FOR ACTION

Planning a Music Period

Planning is often the key word in a teacher's success story, and the music-period planning is no exception.

A meaningful music experience for any given class simply does *not* consist of merely singing a few songs. Rather, it requires a stated direction (objectives), movement in that direction (procedures), and a determining of future direction (evaluation of procedures).

The framework suggested below has been set in specific terms in order to point up the fact that a music lesson should include many *varied* activities, each of which should receive an appropriate portion of the time budgeted. For example, in any given 20-25-minute period, no more than 5 to 7 minutes should be spent on music reading (learning of musical "facts" such as note values, syllables, etc.), whereas ear training as such might be limited to 2 minutes or less (see Ear Training, page 231).

Planning Framework

1. Familiar song
2. Tone-matching games (depending on grade level)
3. Ear training
4. Music reading (sometimes referred to as the "nuts and bolts" of music—basic skills required to read music independently)
5. New song (learned either by rote or music reading, depending on grade level)
6. Other activities as desired, for example, body movement, classroom instruments, etc. as related to the reinforcement of musical learnings set forth in the objectives for the specific lesson
7. Familiar song

Assuming that music is included in the curriculum *each day,* the framework suggested above might be used three times a week. A listening lesson (see Teaching a Listening Lesson, page 230), which requires an entire period, could be scheduled for one of the other two remaining days, while the last day might be used for any number of exciting adventures such as a live concert or combining music with another curriculum area such as art, science, etc.

Despite what at first glance appears to be a somewhat rigid structure, numerous possibilities exist throughout all of the framework for a teacher to use his creative imagination without sacrificing direction, variety of musical experience, accomplishment of specified musical goals, or growth on the part of the learner.

Suggested time allotments for each grade level:

K-1	15 minutes daily
2-3	20 minutes daily
4-5	25 minutes daily
6	30 minutes daily

When a teacher is aware of the total sequence of development, he should be able to plan each day's musical experiences with an eye toward gradually achieving the larger goals appropriate for the level of his class.

Helping Out-of-Tune Singers

Out-of-tune singers may be found at all grade levels, but since immaturity is a factor in out-of-tune singing, the number tends to be higher in the lower grades. Wherever out-of-tune singers are found, it is the teacher's responsibility to try to help them find their "in-tune" singing voices as far as is possible, using devices appropriate for that grade level.

In the lower grades, tone-matching games (in which the child repeats the tune sung or played by the teacher, or "answers" musically), are very helpful. Dramatic improvement is possible when such devices are used daily. Samples include selecting a portion of a song, such as "Baa baa black sheep," repeated after the teacher at different pitch levels by individual children. Calling the roll, using the minor third interval, is frequently done:

Other areas of curriculum may be included in this game by passing out shapes or colors or numbers.

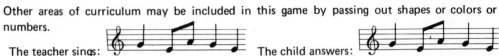

The same procedure may be used, substituting names of rhythm instruments for the colors, shapes, or numbers.

In the upper grades, where tone-matching games as such might be inappropriate, the emphasis should be on securing good tone quality from all of the children. To this end, calling attention to posture, diaphragm breathing, and formation of words on the front of the mouth for improved diction will help.

Among the many reasons given for children singing out of tune, lack of concentration is the most frequently mentioned. Thus it is vital that a teacher insist on complete attention from the class. The production of a specific musical sound requires thought over and above the usual surface attention frequently evident in the classroom.

Above all, if a child is to be helped in this area, he must feel that the teacher really cares whether he succeeds or fails. The teacher should be generous with praise and encouragement as the child works to improve the sound he produces. A little love goes a long way.

For more information on helping out-of-tune singers, see *Experiences in Music.* *

Teaching a Song

Devices

Songs may be taught through the use of the voice, melody instrument (song bells, piano, recorder, etc.), or record. (All the basic song series are available with accompanying record albums containing the songs in the books for each grade level.) A teacher should choose the method with which he feels most comfortable. Whichever device is used, it is vital that children have the best pattern possible to imitate, with special attention given to tone quality, phrasing, diction, and so forth.

Teaching by voice eliminates the need for attention to running a machine, thus enabling the teacher to exercise more control and maintain closer contact with his class. In addition, when the voice is used, there is more opportunity for flexibility in teaching the song. For example, if the song is long or contains sections that need to be isolated for practice, this is easily accomplished by voice (or melody instrument) but becomes virtually impossible if a record is used.

*Gelineau, New York: McGraw-Hill, 1970, pp. 8–13.

Methods

A song may be taught as a whole or in parts, depending on the song, the level of the children, and the device used for teaching it. In either case, the class should hear the whole song through first. Then, if the song is completely unfamiliar, it may be necessary to break it up into phrases, singing or playing (melody instrument) one phrase at a time, and having the children repeat each phrase after it is heard. Following single phrases, sing or play two phrases and have the children repeat; then sing the entire song through.

If the song is short, repetitious, and/or somewhat familiar, have the class sing the entire song through each time for practice rather than break it up into phrases. A compromise between the *whole* and the *phrase* procedures is sometimes desirable when teaching *partly* familiar songs—those in which children already know a line or two from hearing it sung outside of school but are not sure of the whole song. In such cases, isolate only the unfamiliar parts for needed practice.

When difficulty is encountered with the melody at certain places in any given song or when a new tune is first being learned, it is often helpful to indicate the direction of the melody through the use of hand levels. It is also desirable when presenting a song to have the words in front of the children, either in their open books or on a chart or on the chalkboard. Even with very young children, the words provide a focal point; many find they can learn words that were not included in their reading vocabulary.

When teaching by record, have the class listen to the song played through once while they watch the words. The second time the song is played, they may join in where they can. By the third playing, they will be able to sing along with the record throughout most, if not all, of the song. Save additional playings for another day.

Starting a Song

Some teachers have said that the most difficult part of teaching a song seems to be getting the class started on the right pitch and all together. As a means of establishing the tonality or key (or feeling for the home tone, or feeling for where *do* is—however you choose to say it), try the following:

1. For songs in major keys, sound the key note of the song—*do*. (Key note is given in all songs in this book.)
2. Sing or play the tonic chord *do-mi-sol* from the *do* in number 1.
3. Sound the starting tone of the song for the class. Ask the class to listen while it is sounded, then to repeat the sound they hear, sustaining it until you give the firm command, "Sing!"

Note: For songs in minor keys, sound *do*, think, sing, or play down to *la*, then sing *la-do-mi*. Sound the starting tone of the song for the class and proceed as in number 3.

When teaching by record or melody instrument, let the children get the pitch from the record or instrument.

Singing in Harmony

Partner Songs

The term "partner songs" refers to songs which may be sung simultaneously with a pleasing, harmonious result. Such songs must have parallel chord structure on the accented beats throughout; otherwise they cannot be used as partner songs.

When the songs are used in the classroom, half of the class will sing one song while the other half sings the other. It is important that the groups start together, that the songs are in the same key, and that the tempo is clearly established and maintained throughout to avoid total disaster. The children should be encouraged to listen to the sound of their harmony and discouraged from trying to outshout each other.

The singing of partner songs need not be limited to two songs. As many as four can be sung together. For example, "Farmer in the Dell," "Row, Row, Row Your Boat," "Are You Sleeping?", and "Three Blind Mice" sound fine together, provided that the aforementioned criteria have been met. Partner songs may be introduced as early as second-grade level.

When first being introduced to partner songs, upper-grade children do not mind learning on the simple tunes they already know, such as "Ten Little Indians" combined with "Skip to My Lou," and the four songs mentioned above. Later on, they might be able to handle longer and more difficult ones such as:

"Man on the Flying Trapeze" and My Bonnie" (chorus only)
"Home on the Range" (omit chorus) and "My Home's in Montana,"
"Wait Till the Sun Shines, Nellie" and "When You Wore a Tulip."

Occasionally, some of the pop tunes combine and are fun to sing.

For additional suggestions see Frederick Beckmann, *Partner Songs,* Boston: Ginn and Company, 1958, and *More Partner Songs,* Boston: Ginn and Company, 1962.

Harmonizing with Chord Root Syllables

A simple way to introduce harmony in a class is to have half the class sing the melody of a song while the other half sings the root syllable of the chord or chords designated for the measure. It is suggested that in the beginning, songs for use with chord root syllables be selected from among those that contain only the I, IV, and V, or V^7, chords, thus limiting the choice of the root syllable to either *do, fa,* or *sol,* respectively. This may be expanded later as desired.

To determine which of the three syllables to use, first determine the key of the song, then note the letter names of the chords written above the measure. If the song is in the key of G, for example, the I chord would be indicated by the letter G over any measure. The root syllable of the I chord is always *do*; thus every time the G appears, it means *do* is sung as the root syllable for that measure. Counting up four from G (calling G one) we come to C—the fourth tone of the scale, on which the IV chord is built. The root of the IV chord is always *fa*; thus every time the letter C appears in the song, it means the chord root syllable for that measure is *fa.* The root of the V, or V^7 chord is always *sol.* Counting up five from G, we find that D is the fifth tone of the scale on which the V or V^7 chord is built; thus every time the letter D or D^7 appears, it means the root syllable for that measure is *sol.* In summary, then, in the key of G:

if the chord indicated is:	the root syllable is:
G (I)	*do*
C (IV)	*fa*
D (V) or D^7 (V^7)	*sol*

Chord root syllables in other keys are figured in the same way, using the name of the key as I and proceeding alphabetically and mathematically to IV and V:

key of F	root syllable
F = I	*do*
B$^\flat$ = IV	*fa*
C^7 = V^7	*sol*

key of C	root syllable
C = I	*do*
F = IV	*fa*
G^7 = V^7	*sol*

Vocal Chording

"Vocal chording" is merely the producing of chords by voice rather than by instrument. The beauty of vocal chording is that it results in such a pleasing sound with a minimum of effort and ability on the part of the class. Since the progression from one chord to another is stepwise, smoothness and ease of execution are insured, enabling the children to get the feel and hear the sound of three-part harmony without having to take the time to learn long harmonizing parts. [At the outset it is suggested that the selection of songs for use with vocal chording be limited to those that contain only the I, IV, and V (or V^7) chords.]

In any key:

the I chord always contains *DO mi sol*
the IV chord always contains *FA la do*
the V^7 chord always contains *SOL ti re fa*
the V chord always contains *SOL ti re*

[Note that the V^7 chord has an extra added note (*fa*), which is seven tones above the root, *sol*, thus its name, V^7.] All harmony in this book will use the V^7 chord rather than the V, not only because it is more frequently used in the song literature but also because it produces a more interesting sound.

The capitalized syllables above are the *root* syllables of each chord. When a chord is written so that the root is in the lowest position, the chord is said to be in *root* position. If the root is placed anywhere except on the bottom (lowest position), then the chord is said to be in an *inverted* position. The writing of chords in inversions facilitates voice progression in many instances and is frequently done for that purpose, as will be noted below. Vocal chording may be used as an accompaniment for selected songs, as follows:

1. Divide the class into three groups. Write the following on the board (using colored chalk, if available, for the syllables assigned to each group—a different color for Groups I, II, and III):

Group III sings	*sol*	*la*	*sol*	*sol*
Group II sings	*mi*	*fa*	*fa*	*mi*
Group I sings	*do*	*do*	*ti*	*do*
chord	I	IV	V^7	I

2. Sound the pitch of the desired *do,* according to the key of the given song. Point to Roman numeral I and have Group I sing the given *do.* Group II then sings the *mi* above *do* and Group III sings the *sol.* When the teacher points to Roman numeral IV, Group I will sustain the *do,* Group II will move up to *fa,* and Group III will move up to *la*—sounding the IV chord. Thus the voices will move and the harmony will change as the teacher moves from one Roman numeral to another. Note: by reading up from the Roman numerals as written, we find the notes belonging to the indicated chord—for example, above I are the syllables *do mi sol,* above IV are the syllables *fa la do* arranged in inverted order *do fa la* for smoother voice progression. Above the Roman numeral V^7 the syllables *sol ti fa* are also arranged in inverted order *ti fa sol* with the fifth *re* of the chord omitted to stay within the three-voice limit. This omission does not disturb the feeling of the chord and is frequently done.

3. When the class has had sufficient practice moving from one chord to another, the teacher may then have certain members of the class sing the melody of the song or play it on a melody instrument, while the rest of the class accompanies vocally as the teacher points to the chords. (Obviously, the teacher should familiarize himself with the chord progression for any given song ahead of time, before attempting to point a song for the class.) When the class becomes familiar with the procedure involved, individual children may do the pointing in place of the teacher.

4. The chord-letter names and numbers are indicated for most of the songs in this book. Given the formula for translating letters into numbers (figuring the keynote of the song as I—*do*), the children will eventually be able to sing directly from the chord-letter names indicated in their songbooks without someone having to point them out at the chalkboard. In the key of F, for example, the letter F appearing over any measure in the song indicates that the I chord (*do mi sol*) should be sounded; the letter $B^\flat$ indicates that the IV (*fa la do*) chord should be sounded; the letter C^7 indicates that the V^7 chord should be sounded. In the key of G:

G = I chord
C = IV chord
$D^7 = V^7$ chord

In the key of C:

the letter C = I chord
the letter F = IV chord
the letter $C^7 = V^7$ chord

All other keys may be figured in the same manner by counting the key tone (*do*) as I, then proceeding numerically and alphabetically from the key tone to IV, then from the key tone to V.

Teaching a Listening Lesson

The complete libraries of records designed especially for school use (see Part IV) provide explanatory notes and suggestions for teaching each selection contained within the albums. However, the following general information may also be helpful in conducting a successful listening experience:

1. To insure musical growth as well as continuity, one music period per week (out of the five days) should be set aside for a listening lesson.
2. Only the best sound and visual equipment, checked out beforehand, should be used.
3. To encourage *active* listening, children should be given specific things to listen for in a composition. What these specific things are will depend on the musical purposes or objectives set forth for that piece of music.
4. Planning for active listening requires that a teacher prepare himself adequately by listening to the selection many times and studying all related materials carefully, so that he may extract as many learnings as possible from the music. It also requires that the objectives for the lesson be stated in terms of the *music* (not the story, for example), thus insuring that they are truly *musical* learnings. Furthermore, planning should include devices that will motivate interest, and well-prepared questions which will elicit independent thinking on the part of the children. Deeper involvement in the music may also be achieved by providing opportunities for creative expression as an outgrowth of the listening experience—for example, creative dramatization, body movement, writing, painting, scoring for rhythm instruments, etc. The value of these activities lies not only in their intrinsic worth but also in the fact that they are a means of reinforcing the desired musical learning set up for the piece. Additional listening experiences that illustrate the concept, element, or learning under study in different musical settings provide further means of reinforcing desired learnings.

Ear Training

Exploring sound can be an exciting classroom experience. As a beginning, tape various kinds of sounds for children to identify, for example, environmental (wind, thunder, traffic, rain, etc.) or within the school and classroom (bells, doors, walking, etc.). Discuss the sounds in terms of whether they sounded high or low, fast or slow, short or long, loud or soft, etc.

Have the class find possible sounds of their own, using parts of the body, for example:

a. different kinds of clapping—cupped hands, flat hands, finger tips
b. striking other parts of the body with the hand to make different sounds
c. vocal sounds

then create a sound composition, using only body and vocal sounds.

Interesting sounds can be produced from "junk" found inside and outside the home (see Found Instruments), as well as from new ways of playing traditional instruments, such as "preparing" a piano by attaching various objects to the strings.

The activities suggested below are designed to help improve musical acuity. They may be done with a piano, recorder, bells, or voice. Make sure that the children understand the meaning of the terms in which they will be asked to respond—for example, high-low, same-different, etc.—as they pertain to *musical* sounds.

1. Play two tones. Ask the children to determine whether they sound the same or different.
2. Repeat as in number 1, only using 2 short melodies in place of single tones.
3. Play a short tune, going either up or down. Have the children identify the direction of the melody, whether up or down.
4. Play two tones. Have the children identify whether the second tone sounds higher or lower than the first.

5. Clap or beat melody rhythm of familiar songs for identification of the song.
6. Play snatches of familiar songs for identification.
7. Play a simple melody and have the children draw its upward or downward curve, for example,

8. Identify syllables of a simple melody played. (Give the starting tone syllable name and sound to the class before beginning.)
9. Clap two short rhythm patterns:

$$ \textstyle\int\ \int\ \textstyle\prod\ \int \quad \text{and} \quad \int\ \textstyle\prod\ \int\ \int $$

Have the children identify whether they sound the same or different.

The activities suggested above are merely samples. Children and teachers may wish to initiate others, based on their own imaginations and the understanding of the purpose of the activity.

In the lower grades, teachers may wish to use visuals related to the concept as a means of heightening motivation.

Interpretive Body Movement

The term "interpretive body movement" refers to a type of movement more subtle in character than that which is usually associated with action songs, singing games, etc. As used in the context of this book, it means movement that is created to communicate an idea, thought, feeling, or emotion, or simply beauty of design.

When creating movement for the interpretation of a psalm, poem, song, or larger musical work, the movement should reflect the mood, spirit, and subject matter of the work.

Body movement may be used to reinforce such musical learnings as *form*, for example, by executing repetitive movement on repetitive phrases or by expressing *mood* through changes of level and range. Movement may also be keyed to the *dynamics* of the music, reflecting tension, rest, and/or climax.

Movement with children should begin at the preschool level and be continued throughout the grades, thus building a "vocabulary" of movement to enable children to progress in their compositions from a simple imitation of an activity to a more complex abstraction of an idea. When children move spontaneously as an expression of feeling evoked by having touched or heard or smelled or seen, the result is a variety of interpretations reflecting each child's uniqueness.

Two books specifically related to movement experiences with children, which teachers will find most helpful, are: *Rhythm in Music and Dance for Children,* by Monsour, Cohen, and Lindell, Wadsworth Publising Co., Belmont, Cal.: and *Rhythms Today!* by Doll and Nelson, Silver Burdett Co., Morristown, N.J.

Program Songs and Programs

Songs designated as "program songs" in this book are those which have been used successfully in programs for public performance. They are included for the benefit of anyone who may wish to try them in his own setting.

When planning a performance, try to include as many different activities as possible, not only because variety makes for a more interesting program, but also because this will reflect the many facets of music—proof that music truly has "something for everyone."

The addition of costumes (native where appropriate), instruments, and a simple stage setting will not only help to enhance the effectiveness of any musical presentation but also will provide avenues for parent and community involvement. Inviting parents to attend programs, especially if presented at a time when *both* parents can attend, is a proven means of improving public relations. Furthermore, the necessity for "stretching" just a bit so that the performance is better than merely adequate is a good experience for the children. Many are capable of more professional presentations than are ever required of them.

Several rehearsals consisting only of getting on and off the performance area plus some class discussion on what constitutes good "performer behavior" will help to minimize confusion and insure success. It's interesting to note that an audience at a school production is frequently more impressed with good behavior than with the production itself.

When programs can be planned as outgrowths of regular classroom experiences, the frantic zero-hour overrehearsing and wringing of hands which characterizes so many school programs may be avoided.

In summary, simply use what you've been doing, hang it on a simple framework to tie the whole thing together, dress it up a bit, then pray for good weather, no measles, and a plump PTA.

Don't forget to invite the press!

Playing Classroom Instruments

Playing the Harmonica

Harmonicas may be purchased in several different keys, but if playing is to be done in groups, all must be in the same key. Select metal harmonicas that show the numbers 1 to 10 over the holes.

Hold the harmonica in the left hand between the thumb and forefinger (thumb at the front), with the numbers 1 to 10 reading from left to right. (The right hand may be cupped around the right side, with the fingers extended over those of the left hand.)

Find number 4. Place your mouth on the harmonica and *blow* gently on the hole. A chord should sound. (Sounding *one* tone at a time may be learned later.) Draw the breath in at the same hole. Now move up one hole to number 5 and blow. Draw. Move to number 6 and blow. Draw.

For ease in reading, all numbers that are to be *blown* will be written *plain*: 4 4 6 6, etc. All that are to be *drawn* will be written circled: ④④⑥⑥. Thus a plain number means to blow the note, a circled number means to draw the breath in on the note. Try the following brief portion of "Twinkle, Twinkle, Little Star" (no. 28)

4	4	6	6	⑥	⑥	6
⑤	⑤	5	5	④	④	4

Try "Are You Sleeping?" with the numbers:

4 ④ 5 4 4 ④ 5 4

5 ⑤ 6 5 ⑤ 6

6 ⑥ 6 ⑤ 5 4 6 ⑥ 6 ⑤ 5 4

4 2 4 4 2 4

and "O Susanna":

4	④	5	6	6	⑥	6	5	4	④	5	5	④	4	④
4	④	5	6	6	⑥	6	5	4	④	5	5	④	④	4
4	④	5	6	6	⑥	6	5	4	④	5	4	④	4	④
4	④	5	6	6	⑥	6	5	4	④	5	4	④	④	4
⑤	⑤	⑥	⑥	⑥	6	6	5	4	④					
4	④	5	6	6	⑥	6	5	4	④	5	5	④	④	4

As was mentioned above, harmonicas are manufactured in different keys. As long as the player is reading only numbers—not music—the key of his particular harmonica is relatively unimportant (unless he is playing in a group), because regardless of its key, he can play the songs shown above and others like them by using the numbers given. However, as soon as he wishes to read from the music, where the key is prescribed, he is limited to playing those songs written in the same key as his particular harmonica.

In the following, the key of C harmonica was selected as an illustration. On a C harmonica the scale is shown and played as follows:

The following notes above high *do* may also be played on the 10-hole harmonica:

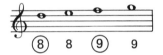

Although the key of C harmonica was used for illustration, the pattern of blowing and drawing to play the scale remains the same in any key:

$$4 \; \textcircled{4} \; 5 \; \textcircled{5} \; 6 \; \textcircled{6}\textcircled{7} \; 7$$
$$d \quad r \quad m \quad f \quad s \quad l \quad t \quad d$$

When these have been practiced sufficiently, the children can play directly from the music without writing in the numbers. Once again, however, a reminder that when the player reads the music written on the staff (and if he expects it to sound as written), he must play it on a harmonica that is manufactured in the same key as the song. In order to play a greater selection of songs, he does not have to buy more harmonicas, but can *transpose* (put into another key) the music he wishes to play into a key suitable for the harmonica he has. Suggestions for transposing are given below.

Transposing a Song

The following short musical passage is in the key of G:

In order to play it on a C harmonica, we must first transpose it into the key of C. This may be done by first writing the syllable names under each note of the melody:

do re mi fa sol mi do

Then write these same syllables in order under another staff with the key signature indicated for the new key. (In this case, it is to be the key of C that has no sharps or flats in key signature; in other keys it differs.)

do re mi fa sol mi do

In the key of C, *do* is on C. Place a note on C, then fill in the other notes according to the given syllable, as follows:

do re mi fa sol mi do

Songs may be transposed into any key by the foregoing method. Simply insert the proper key signature of the new key before placing the notes on the staff.

Additional harmonica instructional material may be obtained from M. Hohner, Inc., Hicksville, New York.

Playing the Autoharp

An Autoharp can provide a great deal of enjoyment for the children, as well as being a satisfying accompaniment for many of the songs. It is simple enough to play that the children can also do their own accompanying.

Autoharps are available in many different models, the difference, for the most part, being in the number of bars on each instrument that must be pressed down to sound the chords. The

12-bar Autoharp has been found adequate for the average classroom. Its key bars are arranged as shown below:

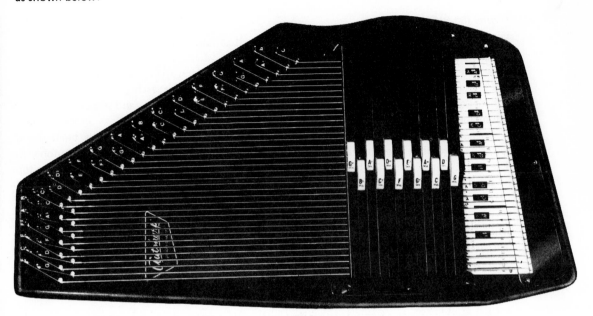

The chord letter names on the bars correspond to the chord letter names found in the music texts. If there is a G *major* chord written above a measure of a given song, the teacher simply presses the G *major* button on the Autoharp and strums. The felt on the bottom of the bar silences all other strings except the ones contained in the G major chord.

Note that the three principal chords of *each* of the keys C, F, and G are arranged conveniently close together, so that they may be manipulated easily with the fingers of the left hand. While the left hand presses the designated bars down *firmly,* the right hand reaches over across the left hand and strums the strings, beginning the strum from the low strings of the instrument and proceeding to the high. A plastic or felt pick may be used, or the player may simply prefer to use his hand. Whatever device is used for strumming, the strum should be a firm one, encompassing all the strings so that the sound is full and resonant. Placing the Autoharp on top of the closed carrying case has been found to enhance the sound. A banjo-type sound is produced by strumming on the section of the strings located to the right of the bars.

The learning of accent and meter can often be reinforced through different types of strumming on the Autoharp. In $\frac{3}{4}$ time, for example, a teacher might wish to strum one long strum on the first beat and two short ones on the second and third beats. Children may move their hands in strumming motions in the air—one long strum and two short ones—to get the feeling of the meter.

The strings may be plucked as well as strummed, using the picks provided with each Autoharp. When used in combination with the strumming, the plucking produces a delightful sound, but it does take practice!

If the children cannot read letters, the buttons may be color coded to the song (four red circles on the song chart mean press the bar with the red circle on it and strum four times, etc.).

Tuning the Autoharp

Tuning the Autoharp is actually a simple process. It should be done with the pitch pipe to be accurate, but if it is to be used with the piano or some other instrument such as the song bells, then tune to the instrument. Some people prefer to tune each string separately, starting with the lowest and proceeding to the highest, blowing the pitch for each one as they go along. Others prefer to tune by octaves—all the Cs first, then all the Ds, etc.—and still others tune by listening to the sound of individual chords.

Strings may be tightened to make them sound higher or loosened to make them sound lower, using a little wrench that comes as part of the standard equipment with all Autoharps. The inside of the wrench is hollow and fits over the silver pins that hold each string at the top of the instrument. Fit the wrench over the pin and turn in the desired direction. Take heart if you're not sure which *is* the desired direction. This comes with practice and experience.

Playing the Ukulele

The ukulele may be used by children and teachers as an accompanying instrument. Because of its smaller size, it is easier to handle than a guitar, and four strings are less confusing than six for a beginner.

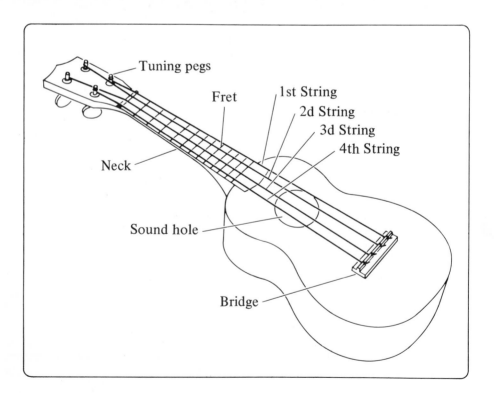

The two most common tunings are the keys of G and F. Using various finger positions, it is possible to play in more than one key without retuning, for example, when tuned as follows:

TUNING FOR KEY OF G

one can play in the key of:

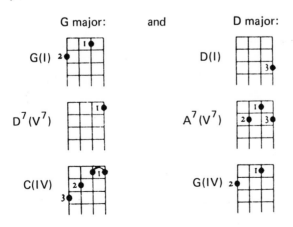

When the ukulele is tuned one tone lower on each string—G C E A (rather than A D F♯ B) we can play in the key of:

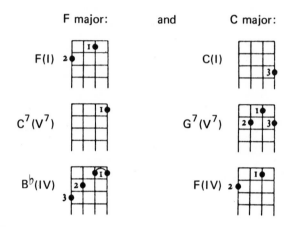

F major: and   C major:

F(I) 2

c⁷(V⁷)

B♭(IV) 2 3

C(I) 3

G⁷(V⁷) 2 3

F(IV) 2

Other chords are possible, of course. Note in the chords below that the tablature remains the same although the names of the chords differ according to which tuning is used.

Key of G tuning (A D F♯ B)   Key of F tuning (G C E A)

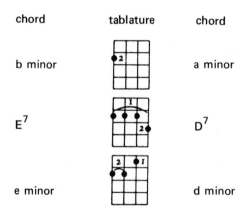

chord   tablature   chord

b minor   2   a minor

E⁷   1 2   D⁷

e minor   2 1   d minor

chord   tablature   chord

$F\sharp^7$

E^7

B^7

A^7

Finger positions may be color coded for children to facilitate learning. Use colored self-sticking tape cut into desired shapes and pressed on the body of the uke within the frets (not the strings), for example, two red circles showing the position of the index and third fingers for the G chord (in the key of G tuning) and one green circle showing the position of the index finger for the D^7 chord.

Playing the Guitar

Tuning the Guitar

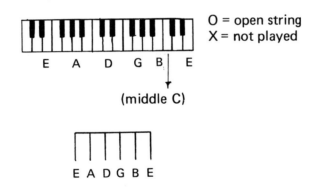

O = open string
X = not played

E   A   D   G   B   E

(middle C)

E A D G B E

Chords

C

G

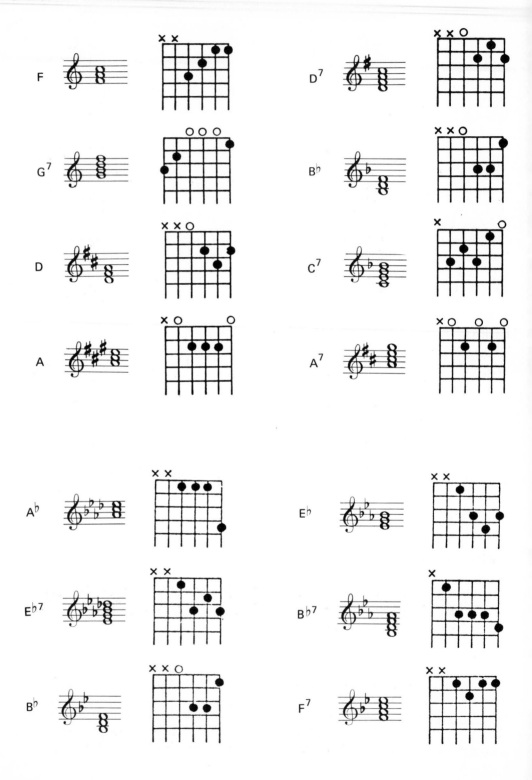

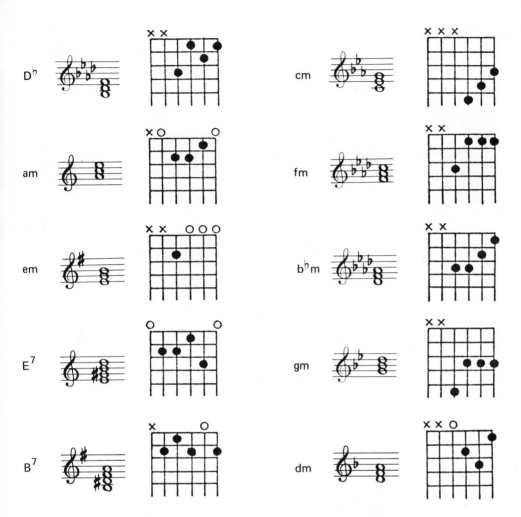

Playing the Piano

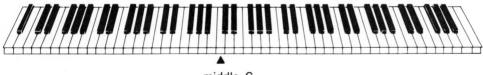

▲
middle C

A piano keyboard is made up of 88 keys, 52 white and 36 black. Throughout the entire keyboard the black keys are arranged in alternate patterns of twos and threes. The white key located immediately to the left of each group of *two black keys* is always C. (The term "middle C" refers only to that C shown in the location noted in the diagram above.) The white key located immediately to the left of each group of *three black keys* is always F. The location of the note on the staff, as well as the clef used, determines where on the keyboard the note is to be played.

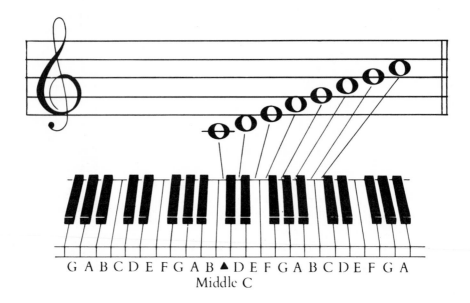

G A B C D E F G A B ▲ D E F G A B C D E F G A
Middle C

Piano Chording

When used for accompaniment, chords are usually played in the left hand, while the right hand plays the melody.

A chord may be built on each tone of any given scale. When the scale tone on which the chord is built appears in the lowest position, the chord is said to be written in "root" position. The term "inversion" refers to those chords in which the root appears in a position other than the lowest on the staff. Chords are numbered (Roman numerals) according to where the scale tone on which each is built appears in the scale sequence. For example, a chord built on *do* is a I chord because *do* is the first tone of the scale. A chord built on *fa* is a IV chord because *fa* is the fourth tone of the scale, and so on.

In the piano chords which follow, note that not all chords appear in the "root" position. To facilitate easier fingering, some are written in inversions. Note also that the finger movements to and from the given progressions remain the same regardless of key. In the progression I to IV for example, the little finger remains where it is. while the thumb and index finger move upward. In the progression I to V^7, it is the thumb that remains in place, while the little finger moves down and the index finger moves up. From IV to V^7 the index finger remains stationary, while the outside fingers (thumb and little finger) move down. These movements remain the same for *all* keys.

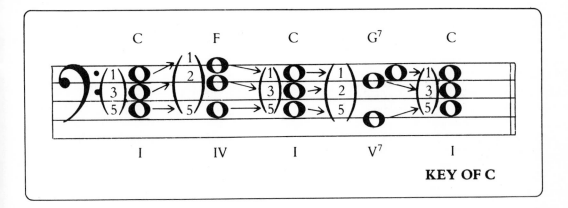

I IV I V⁷ I

KEY OF C

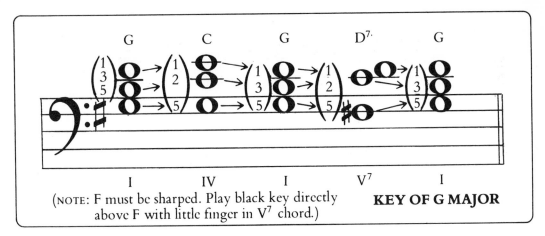

I IV I V⁷ I

(NOTE: F must be sharped. Play black key directly above F with little finger in V⁷ chord.) **KEY OF G MAJOR**

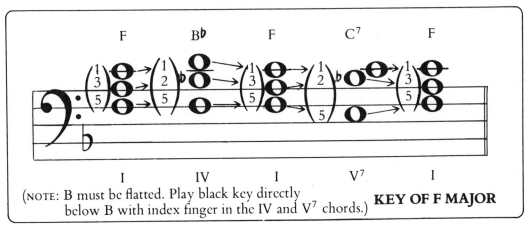

I IV I V⁷ I

(NOTE: B must be flatted. Play black key directly below B with index finger in the IV and V⁷ chords.) **KEY OF F MAJOR**

1 = Thumb   2 = Index finger   3 = Middle finger   5 = Little finger

PIANO CHORDS IN ADDITIONAL KEYS (LEFT HAND)

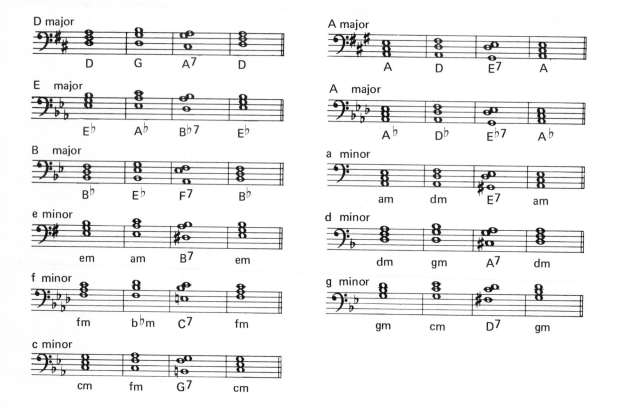

Playing Resonator Bells

The term "resonator bells," as used in this book, refers to a set of thick, rectangular blocks of wood with a hole in the center over which a small metal bar is attached. When the metal bar is struck with a mallet, each bell produces a different pitch according to the size of the bell—the longer the bell, the lower the pitch.

These bells may be handled and played separately and thus may be used to play chords (by striking several bells simultaneously) or single tones as desired.

To play chord accompaniments, pass out the required number of bells for playing all of the chords indicated in any given song. In a song containing the I, IV, and V^7 chords, 10 bells should be passed out, one bell for each of 10 children. The proper bells for each chord are struck simultaneously at prescribed times on signal. The selection of the bells is dependent upon the *key* of the song, as well as the *chords* that are indicated above each measure of the song. For example, in the key of F, the I chord would be indicated by the letter F over the measure, the IV chord by the letter B♭, and the V^7 chord by the letter C^7. Bells to be selected are:

for F	F A C
for B♭	B♭ D F
for C^7	C E G B♭

Bells for the I, IV, and V^7 chords in other keys may be found with the songs as well as below.

Resonator Bells for I, IV, and V^7 Chords in Selected Keys

Key	I chord	IV chord	V^7 chord
C	C E G	F A C	G B D F
D	D F♯ A	G B D	A C♯ E G
E♭	E♭ G B♭	A♭ C E♭	B♭ D F A♭
F	F A C	B♭ D F	C E G B♭
G	G B D	C E G	D F♯ A C
A♭	A♭ C E♭	D♭ F A♭	E♭ G B♭ D♭
A	A C♯ E	D F♯ A	E G♯ B D
B♭	B♭ D F	E♭ G B♭	F A C E♭

Other:

chord	bells
a min	A C E
c min	C E♭ G
d min	D F A
g min	G B♭ D
e min	E G B
f min	F A♭ C
A^7	A C♯ E G
B^7	B D♯ F♯ A

Playing the Recorder

In the following recorder chart it should be pointed out that, unlike the traditional diagrams usually drawn for recorder, the fingering chart here is shown from the *player's* view (rather than the observer's). Thus when the recorder is held in the position shown, all holes on the *lower* section of the chart should be played with the *left* hand, while those in the *upper* section should be played with the *right* hand. The numbers refer to fingers:

1	index finger
2	middle finger
3	ring finger
4	little finger

When playing the recorder, take care to blow gently and cover all holes completely except where indicated that the hole is left half open.

Soprano Recorder

Note: see page 247 for interpretation of this chart.

○ = hole open
● = hole closed
◐ = hole half open
x = alternate fingering

Rhythm Instruments

Rhythm instruments provide not only pleasure, but also serve as a valuable teaching tool. Through the use of rhythm instruments, the meaning of musical terms such as form, timbre, etc. may be reinforced, as may other musical learnings. In addition, these instruments are dramatically effective when used with poems and stories, as well as with songs and as accompaniment for body movement.

When instruments are first introduced to children, each instrument should be identified by name and sound, and the holding and playing position should be demonstrated. (Some may be played several different ways.) The beginning is also the time to lay down a few ground rules about care in handling instruments as well as the need for "ensemble etiquette," to help avert what could be chaos in the future.

As children gain experience with the instruments and the sounds they produce, they should be encouraged to create their own percussion scores by selecting instruments based on the mood, tempo, rhythm patterns, and other considerations within the piece. For example, a short-sounding instrument (sticks, woodblock) might be used for notes of short duration, with a longer-sounding instrument (finger cymbals, triangle) for notes of longer duration. Ascents to musical climaxes can be heightened by increasing dynamicism in the instruments selected.

The following list of rhythm instruments represents those most commonly found in the classroom:

rhythm sticks	six pairs
triangles (include striker and holder when ordering)	four
bells (jingle type)	four
cymbals	two pairs
tambourines	four
finger cymbals	two pairs
drums (include mallet for beating when ordering)	two
sandblocks	two pairs
castanets on a stick	one pair
woodblocks (sometimes referred to as "tone blocks")	two
jingle clogs (optional)	two pairs

Also appropriate for classroom use are lummi sticks, Calypso instruments (conga drum, bongo drums, cowbell, maracas, guiro), and Hawaiian instruments ('I Pu —a gourd drum; 'Illi-Ili —volcanic rocks; Pu'ili —fringed bamboo sticks).

If desired, children can make simple instruments of their own from materials such as the following:

sticks	½- or ¼-inch dowels cut to 12-inch lengths.
triangles	A large nail suspended on a string, or a horseshoe suspended on a string.
cymbals	Pot covers.
tambourines	Metal disks or flattened bottle caps attached to paper or aluminum plates.
sandblocks	Small blocks of wood with sandpaper attached to the bottom and sides and a knob (of the drawer-pull type) attached to the top.
large drums	Nail kegs or barrels made of various materials.

small drums	Oatmeal, cornmeal, or salt boxes. Metal coffee, shortening, or other canister-type cans with plastic covers. When a plastic cover is unavailable, use an old inner tube stretched and laced or attached in some other way over the top (or over both ends if desired). Wooden bowls with rubber stretched over the top. Skin may be purchased from an instrumental supply dealer and used instead of rubber. Ice cream cartons. Large, round plastic containers often found in delicatessen shops.
shakers	Dried gourds. Paper cups placed mouth to mouth, taped together with masking tape, and filled with rice. Fruit juice or other small cans (attach handle), paper plates taped or sewed together with yarn, small milk cartons, and small boxes all may be filled with dried beans, peas, rice, etc. A large light bulb can be covered with papier-mâché, decorated as desired, and then struck hard enough to break the globe inside.
jingle clogs	Metal disks or flattened bottle caps attached to a flat stick at one end.

More sophisticated melodic percussion instruments can be made from graduated pieces of pipe suspended and hit with a tack hammer for a chime effect, while wooden bars of varying lengths attached to a frame and struck with a mallet can make a very acceptable xylophone.

Even graduated sizes of flower pots produce various pitches when suspended by a large knot through the bottom hole of the pot and struck with a wooden mallet. Water glasses may be tuned to different pitches by filling them with water to various levels; they are sounded by hitting a silver knife or spoon against the side of the glass. Simple tunes can be played in this manner. Tuned bottles are another possibility (see Bottle Bands, below). The infinite number of ways in which rhythm instruments may be used make them an invaluable classroom resource.[*]

Found Instruments

The term "found" instruments refers to any object or combination of objects which one might find anywhere in the environment on which a sound might be made by striking, blowing, plucking, shaking, scratching, etc. Junkyards, railroad yards, and backyards yield particularly exotic found instruments. The student is encouraged to try the kitchen, basement, beach, and garage as well (cans, pipes, shells, wheels, etc.).

As much joy may be derived from the search and exploration for found instruments as from eventually playing them, so it would defeat the purpose of the activity to make a list of found instruments here. However, merely as a guide to the kinds of things on which sounds have been produced (and might be overlooked, otherwise), the following are a few possibilities:

shampoo hose	remove spray attachment, fold back end which attaches to faucet, and blow through. Tighten lips for higher sound, loosen lips for lower sound
sink drain	invert, let hand free by a string, strike with any desired striker—metal, wood, or hard rubber, depending on sound preferred
lengths of pipe	laid over an empty (fairly deep) box and struck with any desired striker

[*]The use of rhythm instruments in the classroom is explored extensively in R. Phyllis Gelineau, *Experiences in Music,* New York: McGraw-Hill, 1970, pp. 223–38.

Have the children bring their found instruments to class. Explore the kind of sound each instrument produces, as well as various ways to play it. Divide the class into small groups and suggest that each group create a "composition" to perform for the others. There should be a "mix" of different kinds of instruments assigned to each group in order to produce more interesting creations. Allow all groups sufficient "rehearsal" time.

Following the experimentation with instruments, suggest to the class that they explore further possibilities through the addition of body sounds and/or vocal sounds.

Whistles and Strings, published by Elementary Science Study of Education Development Center, Inc., 55 Chapel St., Newton, Mass. 02160, contains some intriguing ideas for actual *construction* of various sound-producing instruments.

Bottle Bands

1. Select eight soft drink bottles of the same size.
2. To sound, press the rim of the bottle just under the lower lip and blow gently in such a way that the air will be directed down as well as across. Tightening both lips around the teeth, while bringing the upper lip slightly out and over will help to direct the air stream properly. Air should be expelled easily and evenly, not in explosive bursts.
3. Leave the first bottle empty. Blow across as suggested above. This will be the *do* of the scale. (Never mind the key at present.)
4. In the second bottle add a half inch or more of water, enough to produce the sound of *re* when blown.
5. In the third bottle add water as in number 4, enough to produce the sound of *mi* when blown.
6. In all remaining bottles add water as before, enough to produce the sound of each of the remaining tones of the ascending scale—*fa sol la ti do.* When children are doing their own "tuning," they will discover that not as much water is needed between *mi* and *fa* and *ti* and *do* as between other tones of the scale because of the half-step interval between these tones.
7. When all bottles have been tuned, have the players stand in a row. As the "conductor" faces the row, low *do* should be to the conductor's left and high *do* to his right, with tones of the ascending scale in order between the low *do* and the high *do.*
8. Each player blows his bottle as the conductor points to him. Try simple tunes at first in this manner, then more difficult ones.
9. When children have mastered the technique, let them play from "score" by color coding the bottles to correlate with the color of the written notes—for example, *do* might be red, *re* green, *mi* yellow, and so on. The child with the red bottle plays all the notes that are colored red, the child with the green bottle plays all the notes that are colored green, etc.

By the method suggested above, obviously the key of any song will be determined by the sound of the empty (*do*) bottle, with all others being tuned accordingly to the remaining tones of the scale. If one wishes to play in a specific key, it will be necessary to add enough water to the first (*do*) bottle to sound the *do* of the desired key and tune the others in turn to that key. When small bottles are used, it is possible to run out of space in which to add more water for the higher tones (depending on the key, of course). When this happens, use larger bottles. Note: tuning several bottles to the same pitch will enable an entire class to play, rather than just the eight children.

Playing Chords with Bottles

Blowing the tones of a given chord on several bottles simultaneously will produce a pleasant sound of harmony, for example:

sound *do mi sol* together for a I (tonic) chord
sound *fa la do* together for a IV (subdominant) chord
sound *sol ti re fa* together for a V^7 (dominant seventh) chord

In this way bottles may be used to provide a chord accompaniment for songs in which the melody is carried either by voice, melody instrument, or other bottles. Accompaniment variations are possible through the use of such devices as the "oom-pah" rhythm, in which the lowest tone of the chord (*do fa* or *sol*) plays the "oom" and the remaining tones of the same chord play the "pah." If the music moves in twos or fours, use oom-pah. If it moves in threes, use oom-pah-pah.

Appropriate chording letters and numbers have been indicated in most of the songs in this text. Younger children may take their cue for chord changes from the teacher, using a prearranged signal such as one finger up for the I chord, four fingers up for the IV chord, and five fingers up for the V^7 chord. If desired, these numbers may be written on the blackboard and indicated by pointing. Obviously the teacher must have prepared ahead so that he is aware of where the chord changes occur in order to cue the children at the proper place in the music. Given the information as stated above (I chord contains *do mi sol,* IV chord contains *fa la do,* etc.) and a bit of practice, older children may soon learn to play chord accompaniment without cues from the teacher. Additional "instruments" added to the bottles, such as washboards, spoons, gallon jugs (also played by blowing), plus a combination of a washtub, broomstick, and string, known as a "one-string bass," produce a "jug band."

PART III
GETTING DOWN TO FUNDAMENTALS

Review of Fundamentals
Staff

	fifth line
fourth space	fourth line
third space	third line
second space	second line
first space	first line

A staff has five lines and four spaces. The first line is on the bottom and the fifth line on top. The first space is on the bottom and the fourth space on top, etc.

Clefs

Every staff has a *clef* sign at the beginning. Below is a *treble clef,* sometimes called a *G clef*:

Below is a *bass clef,* sometimes called an *F clef*:

Music played from the treble, or G, clef sounds higher than music played from the bass, or F, clef. Some instruments play from the treble clef and others play from the bass clef, depending on the range (highness or lowness) of the instrument. Children's songs are usually written on the treble clef.

Bar Lines

Throughout a staff may also be found a series of equally spaced vertical lines. These are called *bar lines* and serve to divide any given staff into *measures.* A *double bar* is usually found at the *end* of any given piece of music to indicate the completion of the selection:

bar line   measure   double bar

Lines and Spaces

Every line and space of the staff has a letter name:

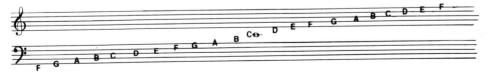

Note that the lines and spaces of the bass clef have different letter names from those of the treble clef. Note also that in both the bass and the treble clefs, the letter names of the lines and spaces proceed in alphabetical order to G and then begin all over again with A. No letter beyond G is used in music.

Leger Lines

It is possible to add lines and/or spaces above and below the staff through the use of *leger lines.* These must be lettered in proper alphabetical order accordingly:

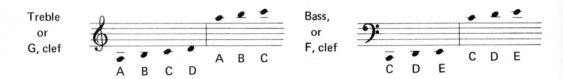

Treble or G, clef   Bass, or F, clef

Note that each preceding line and space must be accounted for when leger lines are used.

Key Signatures

Next ot the clef sign on the staff may be found one or more symbols like these:

♯ a *sharp*:   or ♭ a *flat*:

This group of sharps or flats is called a *key signature.* A key signature contains *either* sharps or flats, or it may contain neither. It cannot contain both.

Placement of sharps and flats on the staff is done in an established order. It cannot be altered. The first sharp, for example, is *always* placed on the *F line.*

Note that in the treble clef, the F falls on the fifth line, while in the bass clef, F is on the fourth line.

In writing a key signature of two sharps, the first sharp must be placed on the F line, and the second sharp on the C space:

In writing a key signature of three sharps, the first sharp must be put in its established place on the F line, the second sharp in its established place on the C space, and the third sharp on the G space:

There may be as many as seven sharps in a key signature, placed in the following order: F C G D A E B

In placing flats on a staff, the first flat has its prescribed place on the B line:

In a key signature of two flats, the first flat must be placed on the B line and the second on the E space:

There may be as many as seven flats in a key signature, placed in the following order: B E A D G C F

Finding do

A *key signature* enables us to determine in what *key* the music is written and/or where *do* may be found. *Do* may be anywhere on the staff, depending on the key signature.

In any given key signature, it is very easy to determine where *do* is through the use of the following simple rules:

1. When there are sharps in the key signature, call the last sharp to the right (the one farthest away from the clef sign) *ti* and count up one place to *do*. If *ti* falls on a space, *do* will be on the line above it.

2. When *ti* falls on a line, *do* will be on the space above it:

3. When there are flats in the key signature, call the last flat to the right (the one farthest away from the clef sign) *fa* and count *down* to *do*, using the notes in the *descending* scale:

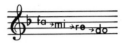

4. It is also possible to count *up* to find *do* in a flat key signature, provided the notes of the *ascending* scale are used:

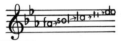

Thus, saying that a song is in the key of D, the key of E, or any other key means merely that *do* is located on the line or space bearing that particular letter name. For example, in a key signature of two sharps, using the aforementioned rule for finding *do* with sharps, we call the last sharp to the right *ti* and count up one place to find *do* on the fourth line. The name of the fourth line on the staff is D; therefore, the name of the key having a signature of two sharps is D.

In a key signature of four sharps, using the same rule, we find that *do* falls on the fourth space, which is E; thus the name of the key having a signature of four sharps is E.

In the case of six or seven sharps, note that the place in which *do* falls has a sharp on it in the key signature. When this occurs, the key must not be called by merely its letter name—the word "sharp" must follow it (or the sharp symbol— ♯).

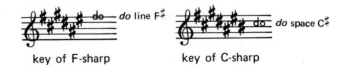

key of F-sharp   key of C-sharp

In naming keys with flats in the signature, using the rule for finding *do* with flats, we call the last flat to the right *fa* and count down to find *do*. In the example below, *fa* is on the third line—*do* is on the first space, the name of the first space is F, and thus it is the key of F:

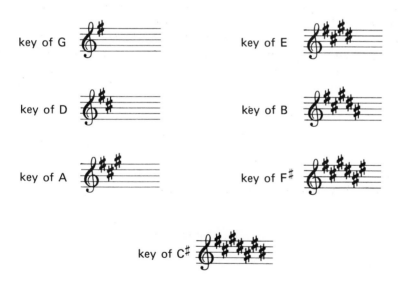

When there are two flats, *do* is located on the third line, on which a flat has already been placed as part of the established order of placing flats on the staff. As with sharps, when this occurs, the key must be called by its letter name followed by the word "flat" or the symbol for flat—♭ — as follows:

In summary, then, the sharp keys (those with sharps in the key signature) are as follows:

The flat keys (those with flats in the key signature) are as follows:

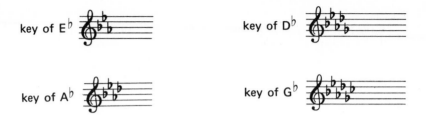

When there are no sharps or flats in the key signature, *do* is always found on the third space (or first line below the staff). This is known as the *key of C*:

key of C

On the bass clef, the method of finding *do* through the use of the last sharp or the last flat is the same as on the treble clef:

In summary—♯ keys:

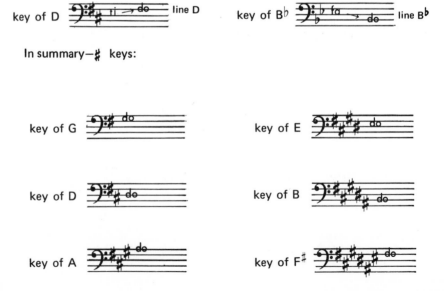

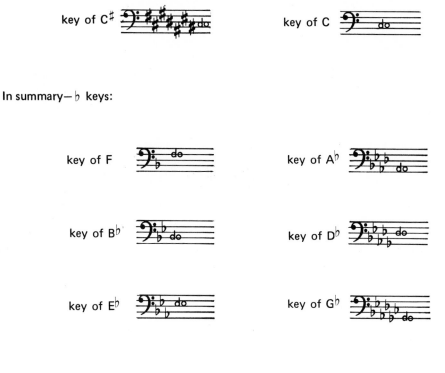

key of C♯

key of C

In summary— ♭ keys:

key of F

key of A♭

key of B♭

key of D♭

key of E♭

key of G♭

key of C♭

Major Scales

Every key has its own scale. A major scale contains the following notes or "syllables," as they are sometimes called:

do re mi fa sol la ti do

When a major scale is written on the staff, it looks like this ascending:

do   re   mi   fa   sol   la   ti   do

And like this descending:

do   ti   la   sol   fa   mi   re   do

It may begin anywhere on the staff, depending on the key signature:

do   re   mi   fa   sol   la   ti   do   do   re   mi   fa   sol   la   ti   do

The relationship of the tones must always remain the same. The pattern for this relationship has been arbitrarily established as follows: Using the C scale (playing C as the first note and proceeding through the musical alphabet until C reappears—C, D, E, F, G, A, B, C) as a model, we note that between E and F and between B and C there is a distance of only a half step (no black key in between), whereas between all other tones there is a distance of a whole step (black keys in between).

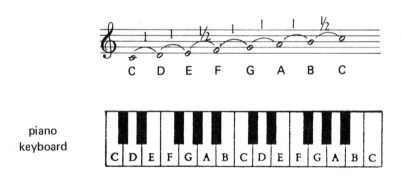

piano
keyboard

Thus the rule for building any major scale is based on the pattern of half steps between the third and fourth (*mi* and *fa*) tones of the scale and between the seventh and eighth (*ti* and *do*) tones of the scale. All the rest must be *whole* steps. As noted above, when starting on C, the half steps and whole steps fall in their correct places; however, when starting on any note other than C, it becomes necessary to alter certain tones in order to maintain the established pattern of whole steps and half steps so that the scale will sound as it should. These alterations are possible through the use of sharps or flats.

For example, in the piano keyboard shown, if one decided to play the scale of D, starting on D as the first note and proceeding through the musical alphabet until D reappears—D, E, etc.—one would notice, if only white keys were played, that the sound of the scale was simply not right. This would be due to the fact that the pattern of maintaining *half steps* between the third and fourth and between the seventh and eighth tones of the scale and of maintaining *whole steps* between all others was not being followed. Let us examine the scale of D and see what alterations would be necessary in order to maintain our established pattern. Marks between the third and fourth and between the seventh and eighth tones indicate that half steps are required here:

D E F G A B C D

All others must be whole steps. On closer inspection, it is apparent that between F and G (third and fourth tones), according to our piano keyboard, there is a whole step. Our rule dictates a half step here. How do we make a needed half step out of a given whole step? Merely by shortening the distance between the two tones—either make the third tone a half step higher by placing a sharp in front of it or make the fourth tone a half step lower by placing a flat in front of it. In this particular case, the *sharp* is called for—in front of the F—because if a *flat* were used in front of the G, it would disturb the relationship (a whole step is required) between the G and A that follows. Looking at the seventh and eighth tones, we find the same problem—a half step is needed, and a whole step is given; thus we must place a sharp in front of the C. Our scale of D, then, would look something like this when written correctly:

When we play it on the piano, we must remember to play the *black* key directly above F (to the right) and the *black* key directly above C (to the right) in place of the white key F and the white key C when we come to them in the scale.

In a longer piece of music, the sharps are not placed in front of these two notes *every* time they occur; rather, they are placed at the *beginning* of the staff to the right of the clef sign, where they become known as the *key signature.* They affect *every* F and *every* C that occurs in that piece of music:

do *re* *mi* *fa* *sol* *la* *ti* *do*

D E F♯ G A B C♯ D

Minor Scales

Just as families are related, so scales may be related also. Every *major* scale has what is known as its *relative minor* scale. The relationship between the two scales is based on a *common key signature*; however, the starting tone of a major scale is always *do*, whereas the starting tone of a minor scale is always *la*.

To find the relative minor scale of any given major scale, simply count down to *la* from the *do* of the major scale:

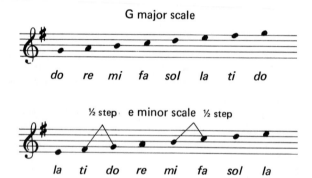

Counting down from *do* (which is G in this example) to *la*, we find that *la* falls on E; therefore E would be the starting tone of the *relative minor* scale of G and would be called the *e minor* scale. Minor scales are usually written in lower case letters. Note that the key signature for the *e minor* scale above is the same as that for the G major scale.

In another example:

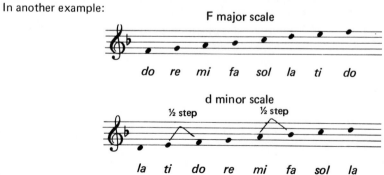

In the scale of F major, *do* is on F and the key signature is one flat. Counting down from *do*, which is on F, to *la*, we find that *la* falls on D; therefore, D would be the starting tone of the *relative minor* scale of F and would be called the d *minor* scale.

Obviously, with a different starting tone in a minor scale, the arrangement of whole and half steps required for a major scale is bound to be different in a minor scale.

Note that in the above minor scales, the half steps occur between the second the third tones and between the fifth and sixth tones of the scale because this is where *ti-do* and *mi-fa* fall, respectively. Minor scales with this arrangement, such as those shown above, are known as *natural* minor scales (sometimes called *pure* minor or *normal* minor). There are, in addition, two other types of minor scales—the *harmonic minor scale* and the *melodic minor scale*.

In the harmonic minor scale, the half steps occur between the second and third and between the fifth and sixth tones, as they did in the natural minor; however, there is also an *additional* half step that occurs between the seventh and eighth tones of this scale. This additional half step is what distinguishes the harmonic minor from the natural minor, and is made possible through the use of some kind of appropriate chromatic sign that will indicate that the seventh tone of the scale is to be sounded a half step higher. Note also that the addition of the chromatic sign increases the distance between the sixth and seventh tones of the scale to one and a half steps (see Chromatic Tones, p. 272).

e minor scale, *harmonic* form

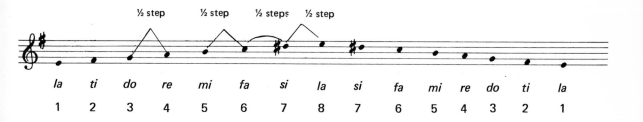

Note that *sol* must be called *si* since the sharp indicates that it is to be sung a half tone higher. The natural minor and the harmonic minor scales maintain the same order in their ascending and in their descending forms. This is not true, however, of the melodic minor scale—a third kind of minor scale, in which the whole and half steps are arranged in an order different from that of the other two types of minor scales.

e minor scale, *melodic* form

In addition to *sol* being sung a half step higher (*si*), note that *fa* is also to be sung a half step higher and thus will be called *fi*. As mentioned previously, the descending form of the melodic minor scale differs from its ascending form. It will be noted in the above example that the descending form is actually the natural minor scale descending.

In summary, then:

natural minor scale	*la ti do re mi fa sol la*
harmonic minor scale	*la ti do re mi fa si la*
melodic minor scale	*la ti do re mi fi si la sol fa mi re do ti la*

A song is considered to be in a minor mode if it ends on *la*; however, minor songs do not always *begin* on *la*. If the tone *si* occurs within a song written in the minor mode, the song is said to be written in the *harmonic* minor. If the two tones *fi* and *si* occur, the song is said to be written in the *melodic* minor. When neither *si* nor *fi* occurs, the song is in the *natural* minor.

Pentatonic Scale

This is the five-tone scale known throughout the world. It contains no half steps between the tones. The syllables are *do, re, me, sol, la,* arranged in the following intervals:

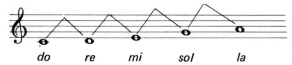

The pentatonic scale may be constructed from any given tone. An easy way to play this scale is to use all black keys:

Whole-tone Scale

The whole-tone scale consists of six notes spaced a *whole* step apart:

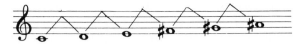

Blues Scale

Blues songs are usually considered to have originated in the United States. The tunes are characterized by the lowered third and seventh tones of the scale. (Sometimes the fifth is also lowered.) Although a given blues melody contains these lowered tones, they need not necessarily be present in the harmonizing accompaniment as well. The slight dissonance that is created as a result contributes to the unique sound of the blues.

Twelve-tone Row

The 12-tone row (or set) was first used by the contemporary composer Arnold Schoenberg. The tones that comprise it are known as the "chromatic scale"; however, no mention is made of a scale when referring to the tone row, for there is no home tone. The tones are usually stated in a given order and are seldom repeated.

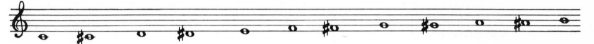

Meter (Time) Signatures

Next to the key signature on any given piece of music may be found what appears to be a fraction (although it is written without the dividing fraction line):

It is a combination of two numbers—one on top of the other. This is known as a *meter* or *time signature.* Just as a key signature denotes what key the music is written in, so a meter signature denotes what kind of time the music is written in. The upper figure of any given meter signature indicates the number of beats that we may expect to find in each measure of the music; the lower figure indicates what kind of note will receive one beat.

For example, in the meter signature $\frac{2}{4}$, the upper figure indicates that there are *two* beats in every measure. In the meter signature $\frac{4}{4}$, the upper figure indicates that there are *four* beats in every measure.

A note is a symbol in music denoting a certain time value as prescribed by the lower figure of the given meter signature. The following are examples of notes commonly found in children's music:

quarter note ♩

half note ♩

whole note ○

dotted half note ♩.

eighth note ♪

sixteenth note ♬

dotted quarter note ♩.

dotted eighth note ♪.

Less common are thirty-second notes (♪) and sixty-fourth notes (♪) which are more likely to be found in instrumental music than in children's vocal music. Each note has a corresponding rest:

quarter rest ╏

half rest ━

whole rest ▃

eighth rest ɣ

sixteenth rest ᛞ

Notes may also be dotted. A dot is worth *half* the value of the note and increases the value of the note by that amount. For example, if a note receives four beats, a dot added to it will receive half of four beats—or two beats—increasing the total value of the note to six beats. If a note receives one beat, a dot added to it will receive a half beat, increasing the total value of the note to one and a half beats.

We have already established the fact that in the meter signature $\frac{2}{4}$ the upper figure indicates that there will be two beats in every measure. The lower figure indicates that the *quarter* note will receive one beat. Using the quarter note as the unit of beat, it naturally follows that

a half note (♩) will receive two beats

a whole note (𝅝) will receive four beats

an eighth note (♪) will receive a half beat

a sixteenth note (♪) will receive a quarter beat

a dotted half note (♩.) will receive three beats

This will always hold true as long as the lower figure of any given meter signature is 4:

$$\frac{2}{4} \quad \frac{3}{4} \quad \frac{4}{4} \quad \frac{6}{4}$$

Lower figures may vary, however. Meter signatures with 8 or 2 as the lower figure are not uncommon:

$$\frac{6}{8} \quad \frac{9}{8} \quad \frac{12}{8} \quad \frac{3}{2} \quad \frac{4}{2}$$

When the *lower* figure is 8, the unit of beat becomes an eighth note (♪), and the other notes change their values accordingly. For example, if an eighth note receives one beat, then:

a quarter note (♩) receives two beats

a half note (♩) receives four beats

a sixteenth note (♪) receives a half beat

a dotted half note (♩.) receives six beats, etc.

When the lower figure is 2, the unit of beat becomes a half note (𝅘𝅥) and the other notes change their values accordingly. For example, if a half note receives one beat, then:

a quarter note (𝅘𝅥) receives a half beat

a whole note (𝅝) receives two beats

an eighth note (𝅘𝅥𝅮) receives a quarter beat

a dotted half note (𝅘𝅥.) receives one and a half beats, etc.

It is to be noted here that regardless of the lower figure of the meter signature, the relationship between the notes remains the same. For example, a quarter note is always held twice as long as an eighth note, a half note is always held twice as long as a quarter note, and a whole note is always held twice as long as a half note. Keeping this fact in mind will prove most helpful in learning to read new rhythms, regardless of what meter signatures are indicated.

In summary, then, when the meter signature $\frac{3}{4}$ appears in any given piece of music, it means that there are *three* beats in every measure (upper figure) and that every *quarter* note (lower figure) gets one beat.

When the meter signature $\frac{6}{8}$ appears, it means that there are *six* beats in every measure (upper figure) and that every *eighth* note (lower figure) gets one beat.

When the meter signature $\frac{3}{2}$ appears, it means that there are *three* beats in every measure (upper figure) and that every *half* note (lower figure) gets one beat.

The upper figure of the time signature also determines how many beats a whole rest (𝄻) receives since a whole rest occupies the whole measure.

A meter signature also determines in which direction a conductor may move his hand when conducting an orchestra or chorus. The following patterns are the most commonly used and are considered basic conducting patterns:

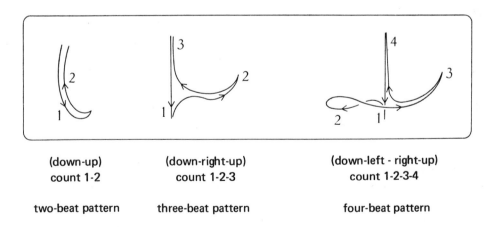

(down-up)	(down-right-up)	(down-left - right-up)
count 1-2	count 1-2-3	count 1-2-3-4
two-beat pattern	three-beat pattern	four-beat pattern

Note that on the count of *one,* the direction is always *down,* meaning that the *first beat* of every measure will always be indicated by a *downward* motion of the hand.

Slow $\frac{6}{8}$ time calls for the following conducting pattern:

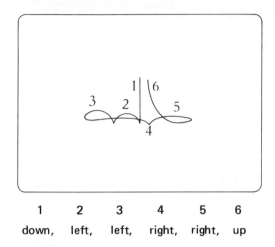

1	2	3	4	5	6
down,	left,	left,	right,	right,	up

When the music is written in fast $\frac{6}{8}$ time, the *two-beat* pattern above may be used.

Simple and Compound Meters

$\frac{6}{8}$, $\frac{9}{8}$, and $\frac{12}{8}$ meters are often referred to as *compound* meters since they may be evenly divided into smaller units. To determine whether music is written in simple or compound time, simply divide the number 3 into the *upper* figure of the meter signature. If it will go more than once, evenly, the music is said to be written in *compound* meter; if 3 will *not* go into the upper figure of the meter signature more than once, evenly, the music is written in *simple* meter. Therefore, the upper figures of 6, 9, 12, etc., indicate compound meter, whereas the upper figures of 3, 4, 2, 5, etc., indicate simple meters. The lower figure of the meter signature is *not* a factor in determining whether the music is written in simple or compound meter; however, it can provide a clue as to kind of rhythm patterns one might expect to find in the given song. When the lower figure of a given meter signature is 8, then eighth notes are commonly found grouped in threes:

dotted quarter notes follow one after the other:

and the quarter note followed by the eighth note is frequently used:

On the other hand, when the lower figure is 4, eighth notes more often are grouped in twos rather than threes:

dotted quarter notes are usually followed by or preceded by either an eighth note or a corresponding eighth rest:

and seldom if ever in basic song series is there found a succession of dotted quarter notes one after the other.

See Classified Index for songs in each of the meters in this book.

Rhythm patterns for practice in simple and compound meters may be found on pp. 277, 278, 279.

For further information regarding musical terms, symbols, and definitions, see the Glossary.

Major and Minor

The terms *major* and *minor* refer to the *mode* of a song, a mode being an arrangement of whole and half steps in specified places.

The fixed arrangement of the major mode, or scale, is half steps between 3 and 4 and 7 and 8 in the scale progression (see Major Scales). The arrangement of tones for the minor mode is dependent upon which of the three forms (natural, harmonic, or melodic) is used (see Minor Scales):

Minor scales may appear in any one of the three forms:

The "natural" minor (sometimes called "normal" or "pure"):

la   ti   do   re   mi   fa   sol   la   la   sol   fa   mi   re   do   ti   la

The "harmonic" minor (the *seventh* tone is a half step higher):

la   ti   do   re   mi   fa   si   la   la   si   fa   mi   re   do   ti   la

The "melodic" minor (the *sixth* and *seventh* tones are a half step higher *ascending only*):

When singing a song with syllables, the minor mode is easy to recognize, for the song will most likely end on *la*. Songs in the major mode frequently end on *do, mi,* or *sol.* The keynote for any given minor song is *la*; when sounding a chord to establish tonality before singing the song, the chord sung should be *la do mi* rather than *do mi sol,* as it is in the major mode. The interval from *mi* to *la* is characteristic of many minor songs.

Throughout this book are examples of familiar songs, traditionally heard in the major mode, with suggestions for playing or singing them in minor to hear the change in general character. Major chords can be made minor by playing or singing the third of the chord a half step lower.

For practice in distinguishing major from minor, try playing the Autoharp chords marked "MAJ" and those marked "MIN," or using the left-hand piano chords given on the song pages, changing them from major to minor by lowering the third of the chord as suggested above.

(See For Study, p. 309, for songs in minor in this book.)

Chromatic Tones

A chromatic tone may be defined as one that is not native to the given key or scale. In the melody below, for example, the second tone is A♯. Since the song is written in the key of G, which has only one sharp (F♯), the A♯ does not belong to the key of G; thus it is designated as a "chromatic" tone in this melody.

One common misconception is that all of the black keys on the piano are chromatic tones. This is true only in the key of C, which normally has no sharps or flats in its key signature. The tones affected by sharps or flats found in the key of C, within the context of a given song, would all be played on the black keys, to be sure, but this is not true of the other keys.

The tones affected by the sharps or flats found in other key signatures cannot be classed as chromatic tones because they *belong* to those keys. In the melody above, the F♯ found in the key signature is *not* to be considered a chromatic tone because it is the scale tone *ti* native to the key of G. Scale tones are those in any given major scale—*do re mi fa sol la ti do.* When they occur as scale tones within the body of a given song, they usually appear on the line or space of the staff unaccompanied by any other signs. Chromatic tones, on the other hand, are always accompanied by any one of these chromatic signs:

a sharp ♯
a flat ♭
a natural (also called a "cancel") ♮

The presence of any one of these signs before a note within the body of the song indicates that it is being altered in some way. Whether the alteration calls for it to be sung a half step higher or a half step lower is determined by the chromatic sign used and the key signature of the song.

A *sharp* (♯) indicates that the tone is to be sounded a half step higher.
A *flat* (♭) indicates that the tone is to be sounded a half step *lower.*
A natural or cancel (♮) may mean *either,* depending on the key signature. For example, if the affected tone has been *sharped* in the *key signature,* then the presence of a natural or cancel placed before it in the melody would indicate that it should be sounded a half step *lower.* If, however, the tone has been *flatted in the key signature,* then the natural or cancel indicates that it should be sounded a half step *higher.*

When one is singing syllables, chromatic tones a half step higher are named in the following manner: add the sound of "ee" (spelled "i") to the first letter of the syllable name—for example, *sol* becomes *si* (see). All other chromatic tones a half step higher than the scale tone are named in the same way—*di, ri, fi, si.*

Chromatic tones a half step *lower* are named by adding the sound of "ay" (spelled "e") to the first letter of the syllable name; for example, *la* becomes *le* (lay). All other chromatic tones a half step lower are named in the same manner—*le, se me, te*—with the exception of *re,* which already has the "ay" sound. *Re* becomes "rah."

For more information in this area, see Introducing Chromatic Tones in *Experiences in Music.* *

Transposition

Transposing simply means shifting a song from one key to another. Although the ability to transpose may not be a requirement for entrance into heaven, it is mighty handy to have here on earth when accompaniment is desired with instruments such as the Autoharp, for instance, whose range of keys is limited. Finger positions for principal chords on the ukulele and guitar are also less difficult when played in certain keys than they are in others.

Transposing may be done in several different ways—by interval, by number, or by syllables, to name a few. The procedure shown below for transposing the familiar song "Skip to My Lou" from the given key of E♭ to the new key of G uses syllables, but any of the other ways mentioned will yield the same outcome. It comes down simply to a matter of choice.

*R. Phyllis Gelineau, New York: McGraw-Hill, 1970, pp. 163–73.

Procedure

1. Insert syllable names under each note of the song in the given key:

Choose	your	part - ner	skip	to my	lou	Choose	your	part - ner	skip	to my	lou
mi	*mi*	*do* *do*	*mi*	*mi mi*	*sol*	*re*	*re*	*ti* *ti*	*re*	*re re*	*fa*

Choose	your	part - ner	skip	to my lou	Skip	to my lou	my	dar - ling
mi	*mi*	*do* *do*	*mi*	*mi mi sol*	*re*	*mi fa mi*	*re*	*do* *do*

2. Select the new key. Selection of key will be determined by the range of the song, the instrument on which it is to be played, and in some instances, the ability of the player. For purposes of illustration here, the new key chosen is G—key signature of one sharp. *Do* in the key of G is located on the second line. Whenever a key is changed, the position of *do* changes also. In the original key (E♭) shown above *do* was on the first line. In the new key (G) *do* falls on the second line.

3. Draw a staff and G clef, insert the appropriate key signature for the new key, then write the syllables of the song below the staff as follows:

> *mi   mi   do   do   mi   mi   mi   sol   etc.*

4. Insert the corresponding note above each syllable in the line or space on which it will now fall in the new key:

> *mi   mi   do   do   mi   mi mi sol etc.*

5. For chord letter names, see Selecting Chords for Accompaniment below.

Selecting Chords for Accompaniment

Some songs do not have chord letters indicated. If they are desired, they must be inserted by the reader.

The selection of the appropriate chord (or chords) for any given measure is based on the notes of the melody in that measure, which in turn, prescribe the harmony. Although the following method of choosing chords for accompaniment may not result in the most exotic sound, it is suggested here as a basic beginning for the inexperienced learner.

The following is true in all keys:

> the I chord always contains *do mi sol*
> the IV chord always contains *fa la do*
> the V7 chord always contains *sol ti re fa*

To select appropriate chords for any given measure, simply determine the syllable names of the notes in the measure, then refer to the above chord information to determine in which of the chords the notes are found. In the song "Skip to My Lou," note that the first and second measures contain all tonic chord tones; thus the tonic, or I, chord would be appropriate for accompaniment in both of these measures. The second and third measures contain the tones of the dominant seventh (V7) chord, so that would be the accompanying chord for these measures. In measure 7, despite the presence of *mi,* which is not contained in the V7 chord, the V7 is still used because the V7 harmony predominates, with the *mi* occurring in an unobtrusive place. While it is possible to sound a chord on every note in a song, the result may prove rather unmusical; thus it is more desirable to limit the chords to one or two per measure.

Once a learner has gained some experience with harmony and chord structure, he will be able to select them by ear rather than the foregoing procedure.

Developing Rhythm Skills

The accurate execution of rhythm patterns in various meters has proven to be one of the most difficult skills to master in the area of music. As a result, various approaches to the problem are constantly being explored.

The following suggested procedures represent a sampling of devices for introducing and developing a feeling for rhythm:

1. Have the class listen for sounds in the environment, then discuss which of the sounds could be defined as "rhythmical" and why.
2. Clap the melody rhythm of a song while the feet beat the basic meter of the measure. In lower grades, divide into two groups, one clapping, the other tapping.
3. Make one sound or movement on the accented beat of each measure, and a different sound or movement on the unaccented beats.
4. Have a child or teacher clap the melody rhythm of a familiar song for identification by the class.
5. Have the teacher clap or beat a short rhythm pattern. Class imitates.

6. Have the teacher clap the melody rhythm of the first line of any familiar song (without singing or playing the melody), class claps the second line, teacher claps the third, alternating throughout the song.
7. Clap or beat the rhythm pattern of names of children in the class for recognition. Have children discover other names in the class that have the same rhythm pattern.

8. Write the rhythm pattern of different children's names, using long lines to represent the long sounds and short lines to represent the short sounds: for example:

BET-SY BLAKE

Transcribe the long and short lines into music notation:

BET-SY BLAKE

9. Substitute the names of places or subjects under study in other areas of the curriculum, such as tools, food, cities, etc., and proceed as in No. 8 above:

SAW   HAM-MER   AP-PLE PIE

10. Put several rhythm patterns on the board, in long and short lines: for example:

a. Have teacher or child clap one of them and have class try to identify which one was being clapped.
b. Have class clap or beat, chanting "long short short long long," etc., as lines occur.
c. Chant long sounds on "ta," short sounds on "tee."
d. Translate long lines into quarter notes, short lines into eighth notes and chant as in "c" above.

11. Teacher or child claps a "question" in a rhythm pattern. Another child tries to clap an answer.

Ex: Q: A.

12. Clap a rhythm canon. Teacher is always one measure ahead of class in his pattern; thus the class is clapping one pattern while watching the teacher clap a different pattern, which they will imitate immediately upon completing the first pattern. Ex:

Teacher:

Class:

etc.

13. Substitute other body movements for clapping in number 12.

The following rhythm patterns are intended to be used for practice in learning the rhythms before applying in songs. Be sure to establish the tempo and basic beat before attempting any of the rhythms. It is also helpful to learn the conducting patterns for various meters, then conduct the meter. This aids in apportioning the proper number of sounds within each beat, depending on the rhythm pattern.

Rhythm Patterns for Practice—Simple Time

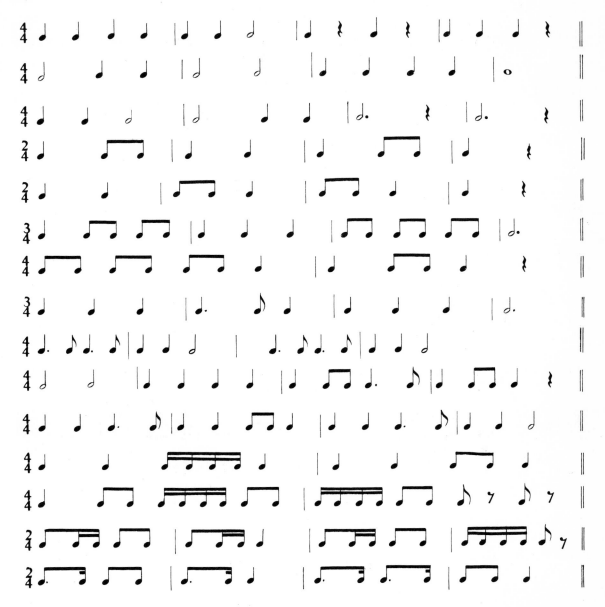

Melodies for Practice—Simple Time

Rhythm Patterns for Practice—Compound Time

Melodies for Practice—Compound Time

PART IV
RESOURCE MATERIALS

Spirituals

The spiritual has its roots in the hearts of those who were taken away from their African homeland and brought to America to be sold as slaves over 300 years ago. It is religious in character and may express sorrow as well as joy.

Characteristic of its African origin is the "call and response" song form, the complex rhythm patterns, and the interval structure. For example, syncopation is frequently found in spirituals, as is the minor 3rd interval.

Spirituals may be classed into three groups: those in slow tempo, whose melodies are full of long, sustained phrases; the highly rhythmical type whose melodies are more segmented; and the call-and-response type. The call-and-response type, of course, refers to the singing of a verse or short section of the song by a leader, followed by a response from the chorus, with alternate calling and responding throughout the song. Historically, the spiritual was sung unaccompanied; thus the leader was most important, for it was he who set the pitch and tempo for the song.

The Fisk Jubilee Singers from Fisk University were responsible for bringing the spiritual to public concert. Attempting to raise money for the school, they sang all over the United States and Europe from 1871 to 1878.

Records

"I Wish I Knew How It Would Feel to Be Free," Leontyne Price, RCA, LSC 3183.
" 'Deep River' and other Spirituals," Robert Shaw Chorale, RCA, LSC 2247.
"I'm Goin' to Sing," Robert Shaw Chorale, RCA, LSC 2580.
"America: A Singing Nation " (FS and record), Keyboard Publications.
"Spirituals and Hymns" from "Songs of Many Cultures," Silver Burdett.
"Afro-American Symphony," Still, in "Enjoying Music" album, NDM series, American Book Company.

Song Collections

Spirituals and Folk Hymns Proof Book, Cooperative Recreation Service, Delaware, Ohio.
American Negro Songs and Spirituals, edited by John W. Work, Bonanza Books (division of Crown Publishers), New York, 1940.
The Book of American Negro Spirituals, edited by James Weldon Johnson, Viking Press, 1925, Edward Marks Music Co.

Background

The Music of Black Americans, Eileen Southern, W.W. Norton Co., New York, © 1971.

The American Indian

Books

North American Indians in Historical Perspective, edited by Eleanor B. Leacock and Nancy O. Lurie, Random House, 1971.
The Native Americans, Robert F. Spencer, Jesse D. Jennings, et al., Harper & Row, 1965.
The New Indians, Stan Steiner, Harper & Row, 1968.

Bibliographies

Frances Densmore and American Indian Music, compiled and edited by Charles Hofman, New York Museum of the American Indian, Heye Foundation, 1968. Lists 175 books and articles on American Indian music, 7 recordings, 8 completed unpublished manuscripts.

Films and Filmstrips (see also Records below)

"How the Indians Lived " (set of five filmstrips on various tribes), Scott Education Division, Holyoke, Mass.

"Charley Squash Goes to Town," 5 min., color, National Film Board of Canada.

"Indian Ways," Denoyer-Geppert AV.

"We Learned from the Indians," Denoyer-Geppert AV.

Records

"Man and His Music: The American Indian " (FS, record), Keyboard Publications.

"North American Indian Songs" (FS and record), Bowmar.

"Music of the Sioux and Navajo," Folkways Records.

"Night and Daylight Yeibichai," Indian House.

"Indian Music of Mexico," Folkways Records.

"Indian Music of the Upper Amazon," Folkways Records.

Principal Sources of American Indian Recordings

Archive of Folksong
Music Division, Recording Laboratory
Library of Congress
Washington, D.C. 20540

American Indian Soundchief (Plains)
1415 Carlson Drive
Klamath Falls, Oregon 97601

Canyon Records (Southwest)
(Arizona Recording Productions)
834 North Seventh St.
Phoenix, Arizona 85007

Indian House (Plains and Southwest)
P.O. Box 472
Taos, New Mexico 87571

Folkways Scholastic (North and South America)
900 Sylvan Avenue
Englewood Cliffs, New Jersey 07632

Hawaii

Song Collections

"Aloha Sampler," Cooperative Recreation Service, Delaware, Ohio.

"Eight Children's Songs from Hawaii," Carol Roes, Mele Loke Publishing Co., Box 7142,

Honolulu, Hawaii.

"Song Stories of Hawaii," Roes, Mele Loke Publishing Co.

"Folk Festivals in Hawaii," John Kelly, Charles Tuttle Co., Rutland, Vt.

"Folk Songs Hawaii Sings," John Kelly, Charles Tuttle Co., Rutland, Vt.

Films

"The Hawaiian Islands, Their Origin and Nature Today," 16-min., Dowling.

"Hawaiian Native Life," 11 min., EBP.

"Hawaii: The Island State," four 10-min. films, color, EBF.

"Traditional Dances of Hawaii," University of Hawaii Communication Center, AV Services.

"Ula Noweo," Library of Hawaii, Film Service Division, Honolulu, Hawaii.

Filmstrips

"Hawaiian Musical Instruments" (with tape), purchase only, University of Hawaii Committee for the Study and Preservation of Hawaiian Language, Art and Culture, c/o Bishop Museum, Honolulu, Hawaii.

"Hawaii: America's Island State," McGraw-Hill.

Books

Legends of Hawaii, Padriac Colum, Yale University Press, 1937.

Hawaii—For Today's Children, Education Dept., University of Hawaii, Honolulu, Hawaii, 1954.

The Early Hawaiians and How They Lived, Dept. of Public Instruction, Office of Hawaii District Schools, Hilo, Hawaii, 1953.

Hawaii—Music in Its History, Ruth Hausman, Charles E. Tuttle Co., Rutland, Vt.

Mexico

Books

Made in Mexico, Patricia Ross, New York: Alfred Knopf.

Song Collections

"Canciones para la Juventud de America," Pan American Union, Washington, D.C.

"Cantos," Cooperative Recreation Service, Delaware, Ohio.

"Amigos Cantando," Cooperative Recreation Service, Delaware, Ohio.

Records

"Man and His Music: Mexico" (FS, record, teacher's guide, students' booklets), Keyboard Publications.

"Children's Songs of Mexico" (FS and record), Bowmar.

Folkways Records

"Songs of Old Mexico"

"Latin American Children's Game Songs"

"Traditional Songs of Mexico"

"Indian Music of Mexico"

"Toccata for Percussion," Chavez, EM, book 3 record album, Holt, Rinehart and Winston.

"El Salon Mexico," Copland, BOL #74.
Folk Dances
"Los Viejitos," Folk Dances #6, Bowmar.
"El Jarabe Tapatio" (Mexican Hat Dance), Special Folk Dances, RCA World of Folk Dances.
"Mexican Mixer," Special Folk Dances, RCA World of Folk Dances.
"La Raspa," All Purpose Folk Dances, RCA World of Folk Dances.
"La Cucaracha," Festival Folk Dances, RCA World of Folk Dances.

Films

"Discovering the Music of Latin America," 20 min., color, Bailey Film Associates, Los Angeles, Cal.
"Felipa, North of the Border," 17 min., color, Learning Corporation of America.

Filmstrips

"Mexico: Part 1 Northern and Southern Regions," McGraw-Hill.
"Mexico: Part 2 Central and Gulf Coast Regions," McGraw-Hill.
"Mexico: Yesterday and Today," Scott Education Division, Holyoke, Mass.

Israel

Books

A Treasury of Jewish Folklore, New York: Crown Publishers, 1948.
Growing Up in Israel, Desider Holisher, New York: Viking Press, Inc. 1963.

Song Collections

"The Songs We Sing," Harry Coopersmith, United Synagogue Commission on Jewish Education, New York.
"Gateway to Jewish Songs," K. Judith Eisenstein, Behrman, New York.
UNICEF Book of Children's Songs, Stackpole Books, Harrisburg, Pa., 1970.

Records

"Voices from the Middle East" (FS, record, teacher's guide, students' booklets), Keyboard Publications, New Haven, Conn.
"Folk Songs of Israel" (FS and record), Bowmar.
"The Moldau," EIM record album.
Folkways Records:
"Israeli Songs for Children"
"Jewish Children's Songs and Games"
"Holiday Songs of Israel"
Folk Dances (RCA World of Folk Dances series)
"Cherkassiya," LPM-1623.
"Hora," LPM-1623.
"Shiboleth Basadeh," LPM-1622.

Africa

Books

The First Book of Africa, Langston Hughes, New York: Franklin Watts, Inc., 1964.
African Myths and Legends, Kathleen Arnott, New York: Henry Z. Walck, Inc., 1963.
Folktales and Fairy Tales of Africa, L. Green, Morristown, N.J.: Silver Burdett, 1967.
Source Book of African and Afro-American Materials for Music Education, Standifer and Reeder, Contemporary Music Project, MENC, Washington, D.C.
Musical Instruments of Africa, Betty Dietz, New York: John Day Co., 1965.

Song Collections

"Echoes of Africa in Folk Songs of the Americas," Beatrice Landeck, New York: David McKay, Inc.
"African Songs," Cooperative Recreation Service, Delaware, Ohio.

Records

"Folk Instruments of the World," Follett Publishing Co.
Folkways Records:
"Drums of the Yoruba"
"African Musical Instruments"
"Songs of South Africa"
"Folk Music of Liberia"
"African Art and Culture," "Musical Instruments" (FS, record, or cassette), Schloat Productions, Pleasantville, N.Y.
Selections from albums accompanying the following books of the New Dimensions in Music series of American Book Co.:
"Investigating Music"
"Expressing Music"
"Experiencing Music"
"Mastering Music"

Films

"African Dances," 28 min., color, Contemporary Films, Inc.

Filmstrips and Slides

"Traditional African Instruments" (slides, tape), Howard University Project in African Music.
"Folktales Around the World—The Cow Tail Switch," Learning Corporation of America.

Japan and China

Books

China's Gifts to the West, American Council on Education, Washington, D.C.
Facts About Japan, prepared by Public Information Bureau, Ministry of Foreign Affairs,

Japan; pamphlets on: Music in Japan, Gagaku, Kabuki, Bunraku, Chanoyu. Write: Consulate General of Japan, 235 East 42nd St., New York 10017.

Fairy Tales of the Orient, Pearl Buck, New York: Simon and Schuster, 1965.

Chinese Myths and Fantasies, C. Birch, New York: Henry Z. Walck, 1965.

Song Collections:

Children's Songs from Japan, Florence White and Kazuo Akiyama, Edward Marks Music Corporation, 136 W. 52nd St., New York.

A Sampler of Japanese Songs, Cooperative Recreation Service, Delaware, Ohio.

The Pagoda (23 Chinese Songs), Cooperative Recreation Service, Delaware, Ohio.

Records:

"Music of Japan" (record, teacher's guide, student's booklets), Keyboard Publications.

"Japanese Koto Classics," Nonesuch Records.

"Favorite Songs of Japanese Children," Bowmar.

"Ancient Chinese Music," Exploring Music series, Book 6, record album, Holt, Rinehart and Winston.

"Chinese Classics," Folkways Records.

Selections from albums accompanying basic song series:

New Dimensions in Music series, American Book Company.

Making Music Your Own series, Silver Burdett.

Exploring Music series, Holt, Rinehart and Winston.

Films:

"Discovering the Music of Japan," Film Associates, Los Angeles, Cal.

"Painting the Chinese Landscape," 10 min., color, Chinese Information Service.

Filmstrips:

"Five Chinese Brothers," McGraw-Hill.

"Folktales Around the World," Learning Corporation of America, (a) "Tears of the Dragon" (China), (b) "The Crane Maiden" (Japan).

Other:

The Japanese Haiku, Ken Yasuda, Charles E. Tuttle Co., Rutland, Vt.

Chinese Kites, David F. Jue, Charles E. Tuttle Co., Rutland, Vt.

Around the World

Books:

Background:

Primitive Song, Bowra/Mentor Books, New York: New American Library of World Literature.

Music Cultures of the Pacific, Near East and Asia, William P. Malm, Englewood Cliffs, N.J.: Prentice-Hall, 1967.

Folk and Traditional Music of the Western Continents, Bruno Nettl, Englewood Cliffs, N.J.: Prentice-Hall, 1965.

Folk Music of Hungary, Zoltan Kodaly, New York: Macmillan, 1960.

Games

Children's Games from Many Lands, Mellen, New York: Friendship Press.

All Time Games, Cooperative Recreation Service, 1955.

Fun with Folklore (riddles, proverbs, fortunes, games), Cooperative Recreation Service, 1955.

Games of Many Nations, E. O. Harbin, Nashville: Abingdon Press, 1954.

Games and Sports Around the World, Sarah Hunt and Ethel Cain, New York: A.S. Barnes, 1950.

Fun Around the World, Patsy Scarry, Morristown, N.J.: Silver Burdett, 1965.

Holidays and Festivals

The Book of Festivals and Holidays the World Over, Marguerite Ickis, New York: Dodd Mead, 1970.

Holidays Around the World, Joseph Gaer, New York: Fleet Press Corporation, 1962.

The First Book of Festivals Around the World, Alma K. Peck, Franklin Watts, Inc., 1957.

Folklore

A Harvest of World Folk Tales, Milton Rugoff, New York: Viking Press, 1949.

Mythologies of the Ancient World, Samuel Kramer, New York: Doubleday, 1961.

Song Collections

Sing Around the World, Cooperative Recreation Service, Delaware, Ohio. Note: Cooperative Recreation Service has song collections in inexpensive pamphlets from all over the world.

Botsford Collection of Folk Songs, 1922 and 1930, New York: G. Schirmer, 3 vols.: Americas, Asia and Africa, North Europe, South Europe.

UNICEF Book of Children's Songs, Harrisburg, Pa.: Stackpole Books, 1970.

Around the World in Song, Dorothy Gordon, New York: E.P. Dutton, 1966.

Folk Songs of the World, Charles Haywood, ed., New York: John Day, 1966.

Records

"Folk Instruments of the World," Follett Publishing Co.

"National Anthems," vols. 1 and 2, Folkways Records.

"Primitive Music of the World," Folkways Records.

"Music of the World's Peoples," vols. 1-5, Folkways Records.

"Rhythms of the World," Langston Hughes, Folkways Records.

"Songs and Rhythms from Near and Far," Ella Jenkins, Folkways Records.

"Songs of Many Cultures" (10 records in set), Silver Burdett.

"Folks Songs of Many People," Bowmar.

"Folk Songs of Four Continents," Folkways Records.

Dances (books and records)

Folk Dance, Lois Ellfeldt, Dubuque, Iowa: Wm. Brown Co., 1969.
Many Worlds of the Dance, Beth Dean, San Francisco: Tri-Ocean Books, 1969.
Promenade All, Janet Tobitt, Box 97, Pleasantville, N.Y., 1947.
"Folk Dances for Fun," Jane Farwell, Cooperative Recreation Service.
Folk Dancing, Mildred Spiesman, Philadelphia: W.B. Saunders, 1970.
The Book of the Dance, Agnes DeMille, New York: Golden Press, 1963.
"Dances of the World's Peoples," vols. 1-4, Folkways Records.
"Folk Dances from Around the World," Bowmar (record).
"RCA World of Folk Dances" series (7 albums).

Filmstrips

"Folktales Around the World," Learning Corporation of America.
"Getting to Know the World" (set of eight filmstrips relating to homes, games, farming,
    schools, music, food, geography, and families around the world), Denoyer-Geppert AV.
"Music Around the World" (FS and record), Denoyer-Geppert AV.
"Games Around the World" (FS and record), Denoyer-Geppert AV.

Miscellaneous

History of Musical Instruments, Curt Sachs, New York: W.W. Norton Co., 1940.
Make Your Own Musical Instruments, M. Mandell, New York: Sterling Publishing Co. 1968.
UNICEF *Hi Neighbor* books, U.S. Committee for UNICEF.
Around the World in Eighty Dishes, Polly and Tasha van der Linde, Morristown, N.J.: Silver
    Burdett.

Additional resource material on China, Japan, Africa, Israel, Mexico, Hawaii, and the American
Indian may be found elsewhere in this book.

Song Collections

American Folk Songs for Children, * Ruth Seeger, Garden City, N.Y.: Doubleday & Co.
American Folk Songs for Christmas, * Ruth Seeger, New York: Doubleday & Co.
American Song Bag, Carl Sandburg, New York: Harcourt, Brace & World.
Animal Folk Songs for Children, * Ruth Seeger, New York: Doubleday & Co.
Around the World in Song, Morristown, N.J.: Silver Burdett.
Best Loved American Folk Songs, John and Alan Lomax, New York: Grosset & Dunlap.
Folk Songster, Leon and Lynn Dallin, Dubuque, Iowa: Wm. C. Brown.
Get on Board, * Beatrice Landeck, New York: Edward B. Marks Music Corp.
Golden Book of Favorite Songs, Minneapolis, Minn.: Schmitt, Hall, & McCreary.
Heritage Songster, Leon and Lynn Dallin, Dubuque, Iowa: Wm. C. Brown.
Little Calypsos, Krugman and Ludwig, Far Rockaway, N.Y.: Carl Van Roy Co.

*Record available to accompany book.

More Partner Songs, Frederick Beckman, Boston: Ginn & Co.
*More Singing Fun,** Lucille Wood, Glendale, Cal.: Bowmar.
*More Songs to Grow On,** Beatrice Landeck, New York: Edward B. Marks Music Corp.
Partner Songs, Frederick Beckman, Boston: Ginn and Co.
*Sing a Song,** McLaughlin and Wood, Englewood Cliffs, N.J.: Prentice-Hall.
*Singing Fun,** Lucille Wood, Glendale, Cal.: Bowmar.
*Songs to Grow On,** Beatrice Landeck, New York: Edward B. Marks Music Corp.

Cooperative Recreation Service of Delaware, Ohio has an abundant library of song collections of all kinds available in inexpensive paperbacks. Catalogue on request.

Professional Reading

General

Beers, Alice. *Teaching Music: What, How, Why.* Morristown, N.J.: Silver Burdett, Division of General Learning, 1973.

Bergethon, Bjornar, and Boardman. *Musical Growth in the Elementary School.* New York: Holt, Rinehart and Winston, 1963.

Cheyette, Irving, and Cheyette, Herbert. *Teaching Music Creatively in the Elementary School.* New York: McGraw-Hill, 1969.

Gelineau, R. Phyllis. *Experiences in Music.* New York: Macmillan, 1970.).

Marsh, Mary Val. *Explore and Discover Music.* New York: MacMillan, 1970.

Music Educator's National Conference. *The Study of Music in the Elementary School: A Conceptual Approach.* Washington, D.C.: NEA Center, 1967.

Nye, Robert E., and Nye, Bernice T. *Music in the Elementary School,* 3rd ed. Englewood Cliffs, N.J.: 1970.

Raebeck, Lois, and Wheeler, Lawrence. *New Approaches to Music in the Elementary School.* 2nd. ed. Dubuque, Iowa: Wm. C. Brown, 1969.

Runkle, Aleta, and Erikson, Mary L. *Music for Today's Boys and Girls.* 2nd ed. Boston: Allyn and Bacon, 1970.

Schubert, Inez, and Wood, Lucille. *The Craft of Music Teaching.* Morristown, N.J.: Silver Burdett, Division of General Learning, 1974.

Swanson, Bessie. *Music in the Education of Children,* 3rd ed. Belmont, Cal.: Wadsworth, 1969.

Specialized

Andrews, Gladys. *Creative Rhythmic Movement for Children.* Englewood Cliffs, N.J.: Prentice-Hall, 1954.

Doll, Edna, and Nelson, Mary Jarman. *Rhythms Today!* Morristown, N.J.: Silver Burdett, 1964. (Correlated record also available.)

Monsour, Sally, Cohen, Marilyn, and Lindell, Patricia. *Rhythm in Music and Dance for Children.* Belmont, Cal.: Wadsworth, 1966.

Wheeler, Lawrence, and Raebeck, Lois. *Orff and Kodaly Adapted for the Elementary School* Dubuque, Iowa: Wm. C. Brown, 1972.

*Record available to accompany book.

Basic Song Series*

Birchard Music Series, Summy-Birchard Company, 1962.
Discovering Music Together, Follett Publishing Company, 1967.
Exploring Music, Holt, Rinehart and Winston, 1966.
Growing with Music, Prentice-Hall, 1963.
Magic of Music, Ginn and Company, 1960.
Making Music Your Own, Silver Burdett, 1965.
Music for Living, Silver Burdett, 1956.
Music for Young Americans, American Book Company, 1966.
New Dimensions in Music, American Book Company, 1970.
Our Singing World, Ginn and Company, 1950.
Silver Burdett Music, Morristown, N.J., Silver Burdett, Division of General Learning, 1974.
This Is Music, Allyn and Bacon, 1962.
Together We Sing, Follett Publishing Company, 1959.

Note: When ordering books for children, be sure to specify one copy of the teacher's edition for yourself.

Addresses of Publishers

Books

Allyn and Bacon, Inc., 150 Tremont St., Boston, Mass.
American Book Company, 55 Fifth Avenue, New York.
Boston Music Co., 116 Boylston St., Boston, Mass.
Wm. C. Brown Publishing Co., 135 South Locust St., Dubuque, Iowa.
Cooperative Recreation Service, Delaware, Ohio.
Follett Publishing Company, 1010 West Washington Boulevard, Chicago, Ill.
Ginn and Company, Lexington, Mass.
Holt, Rinehart and Winston, 383 Madison Avenue, New York, N.Y.
Jan-Lee Music Co., 260 El Camino Drive, Beverly Hills, Cal.
Keyboard Publications, 1346 Chapel Street, New Haven, Conn.
Macmillan Co., 866 Third Ave., New York, N.Y.
McGraw-Hill Book Company, 1221 Avenue of the Americas, New York, N.Y.
Edward B. Marks Music Corporation, 136 West 52nd St., New York, N.Y.
MENC (Music Educator's National Conference), 1201 Sixteenth St. N.W., Washington, D.C.
Prentice-Hall, Inc., Englewood Cliffs, N.J.
G. Schirmer, Inc., 609 Fifth Avenue, New York, N.Y.
Shawnee Press, Delaware Water Gap, Pa.
Silver Burdett Company, Division of General Learning, Morristown, N.J.
Summy-Birchard Company, Evanston, Ill.
Charles E. Tuttle Company, Rutland, Vt.
Wadsworth Publishing Co., Belmont, Cal.

*Related record albums available with all series.

Records

Angel Records, 1290 Avenue of the Americas, New York, N.Y.

Bowmar Records, 622 Rodier Drive, Glendale, Cal.

Capitol Records Inc., 1290 Avenue of the Americas, New York, N.Y.

Children's Record Guild, The Greystone Corporation, 100 Sixth Ave., New York, N.Y.

Columbia Records, 51 W. 52nd St., New York, N.Y.

Custom Recording Consultants, P.O. Box 1618, New Haven, Conn.

Decca Records, 445 Park Avenue, New York, N.Y.

Folkways Records, 701 Seventh Avenue, New York, N.Y.

Keyboard Publications, 1346 Chapel St., New Haven, Conn.

Nonesuch Records, 1855 Broadway, New York, N.Y.

RCA Victor Educational Dept., 1133 Avenue of the Americas, New York, N.Y.

Sing'n Do Records, 214 Godwin Avenue, Midland Park, N.J.

Films and Filmstrips

Coronet Films, 65 E. South Water St., Chicago, Ill.

Denoyer-Geppert, 5235 Ravenswood Ave., Chicago, Ill.

Educational Audio Visual (EAV) Inc., Pleasantville, N.Y.

Encyclopedia Britannica Films (EBF), 1150 Wilmett Ave., Wilmett. Ill.

Eye Gate House Inc., 146-01 Archer Ave., Jamaica, N.Y.

Film Associates of California, 11559 Santa Monica Boulevard, Los Angeles, Cal.

Learning Corporation of America, 711 Fifth Avenue, New York, N.Y.

National Film Board of Canada, Toronto, Canada.

Society for Visual Education (SVE), 1345 West Diversey Parkway, Chicago, Ill.

WASP Filmstrips, Palmer Lane West, Pleasantville, New York, N.Y.

BOWMAR ORCHESTRAL LIBRARY

SERIES 1

ANIMALS AND CIRCUS (BOL #51)
CARNIVAL OF THE ANIMALS, Saint-Saens. (Introduction, Royal March of the Lion, Hens and Cocks, Fleet Footed Animals, Turtles, The Elephant, Kangaroos, Aquarium, Long Eared Personages, Cuckoo in the Deep Woods, Aviary, Pianists, Fossils, The Swan, Finale)

CIRCUS POLKA, Stravinsky
UNDER THE BIG TOP, Donaldson. (Marching Band, Acrobats, Juggler, Merry-Go-Round, Elephants, Clowns, Camels, Tightrope Walker, Pony Trot, Marching Band.)

NATURE AND MAKE-BELIEVE (BOL #52)
MARCH OF THE DWARFS, Grieg
ONCE UPON A TIME SUITE, Donaldson. (Chicken Little, Three Billy Goats Gruff, Little Train, Hare and the Tortoise.)
THE LARK SONG (Scenes of Youth), Tchaikovsky
LITTLE BIRD, Grieg
DANCE OF THE MOSQUITO, Liadov
FLIGHT OF THE BUMBLE BEE, Rimsky-Korsakov
SEASON FANTASIES, Donaldson. (Magic Piper, The Poet and his Lyre, The Anxious Leaf, The Snowmaiden)
TO THE RISING SUN (Fjord and Mountain, Norwegian Suite 2), Torjussen
CLAIR DE LUNE, Debussy

PICTURES AND PATTERNS (BOL #53)
PIZZICATO (Fantastic Toyshop), Rossini-Respighi
MARCH-TRUMPET AND DRUM (Jeux d'Enfants), IMPROMPTU-THE TOP (Jeux d'Enfants), Bizet
POLKA (Mlle. Angot Suite), GAVOTTE (Mlle. Angot Suite), Lecocq
INTERMEZZO (The Comedians), Kabalevsky
GERMAN WALTZ-PAGANINI (Carnaval), Schumann-Glazounov
BALLET PETIT, Donaldson
MINUET, Mozart
A GROUND, Handel
CHOPIN (Carnaval), Schumann-Glazounov
VILLAGE DANCE, Liadov
EN BATEAU (In a Boat), Debussy
HARBOR VIGNETTES, Donaldson. (Fog and Storm, Song of the Bell Buoy, Sailing)

MARCHES (BOL #54)
ENTRANCE OF THE LITTLE FAUNS, Pierne
MARCH, Prokofieff
POMP AND CIRCUMSTANCE #1, Elgar
HUNGARIAN MARCH (Rakoczy), Berlioz
COL. BOGEY MARCH, Alford

MARCH OF THE LITTLE LEAD SOLDIERS, Pierne
MARCH (Love for Three Oranges), Prokofieff
CORTEGE OF THE SARDAR (Caucasion Sketches), Ippolitov-Ivanov
MARCHE MILITAIRE, Schubert
STARS AND STRIPES FOREVER, Sousa
THE MARCH OF THE SIAMESE CHILDREN (The King and I), Rodgers

DANCES, PART I (BOL #55)
DANCE OF THE CAMORRISTI, Wolf-Ferrari
DANCA BRASILEIRA, Guarnieri
GAVOTTE, Kabalevsky
SLAVONIC DANCE #1, Dvorak
HOE-DOWN (Rodeo), Copland
FACADE SUITE, Walton (Polka, Country Dance, Popular Song)
HUNGARIAN DANCE #5, Brahms
SKATER'S WALTZES, Waldteufel
MAZURKA (Masquerade Suite), Khatchaturian
GALOP (Masquerade Suite), Khatchaturian

DANCES, PART II (BOL #56)
FOLK DANCES FROM SOMERSET (English Folk Song Suite), Vaughan-Williams
JAMAICAN RUMBA, Benjamin
BADINERIE, Corelli
DANCE OF THE COMEDIANS, Smetana
CAN CAN (Mlle. Angot Suite), Lecocq
GRAND WALTZ (Mlle. Angot Suite), Lecocq
TRITSCH-TRATSCH POLKA, Strauss
TARANTELLA (Fantastic Toyshop), WALTZ (Fantastic Toyshop), Rossini-Respighi
ESPANA WALTZES, Waldteufel
ARKANSAS TRAVELER, Guion
RUSSIAN DANCE (Gayne Suite #2), Khatchaturian

FAIRY TALES IN MUSIC (BOL #57)
CINDERELLA, Coates
SCHERZO (Midsummer Night's Dream), Mendelssohn
MOTHER GOOSE SUITE, Ravel (Pavane of the Sleeping Beauty, Hop o' My Thumb, Laideronette, Empress of the Pagodas, Beauty and the Beast, The Fairy Garden)

STORIES IN BALLET AND OPERA (BOL #58)
SUITE FROM AMAHL AND THE NIGHT VISITORS, Menotti (Introduction, March of the Three Kings, Dance of the Shepherds)
HANSEL AND GRETEL OVERTURE, Humperdinck
NUTCRACKER SUITE, Tchaikovsky (Overture Miniature, March, Dance of the Sugar-Plum Fairy, Trepak, Arabian Dance, Chinese Dance, Dance of the Toy Flutes, Waltz of the Flowers)

LEGENDS IN MUSIC (BOL #59)

DANSE MACABRE, Saint-Saens
PEER GYNT SUITE #1, Grieg (Morning, Asa's Death, Anitra's Dance, In the Hall of the Mountain King)
SORCERER'S APPRENTICE, Dukas
PHAETON, Saint-Saens

UNDER MANY FLAGS (BOL #60)

THE MOLDAU, Smetana
LAPLAND IDYLL (Fjord and Mountain, Norwegian Suite #2), Torjussen
FOLK SONG (Fjord and Mountain, Norwegian Suite #2), Torjussen
LONDONDERRY AIR, Grainger
FINLANDIA, Sibelius
LONDON SUITE, Coates (Covent Garden, Westminster, Knightsbridge March)

AMERICAN SCENES (BOL #61)

GRAND CANYON SUITE, Grofe (Sunrise, Painted Desert, On the Trail, Sunset, Cloudburst)
MISSISSIPPI SUITE, Grofe (Father of Waters, Huckleberry Finn, Old Creole Days, Mardi Gras)

SERIES 2

MASTERS IN MUSIC (BOL #62)

JESU, JOY OF MAN'S DESIRING, Bach
BOURREE FROM FIREWORKS MUSIC, Handel
VARIATIONS (from "Sunrise" Symphony), Haydn
MINUET (from Symphony #40), Mozart
SCHERZO (from Seventh Symphony, Beethoven
WEDDING DAY AT TROLDHAUGEN, Grieg
RIDE OF THE VALKYRIES, Wagner
TRIUMPHAL MARCH (Aida), Verdi
HUNGARIAN DANCE #6, Brahms
THIRD MOVEMENT, SYMPHONY #1, Mahler

CONCERT MATINEE (BOL #63)

CHILDREN'S CORNER SUITE, Debussy, (Doctor Gradus ad Parnassum, Jumbo's Lullaby, Serenade of the Doll, The Snow is Dancing, The Little Shepherd, Golliwog's Cakewalk)
SUITE FOR STRING ORCHESTA, Corelli-Pinelli (Sarabande, Gigue, Badinerie)
MINUET (from "Surprise" Symphony), Haydn
ANVIL CHORUS, Verdi ("Il Trovatore")
NORWEGIAN DANCE IN A (#2), Grieg
TRAUMEREI, Schumann

MINIATURES IN MUSIC (BOL #64)

CHILDREN'S SYMPHONY, Zador
THE BEE, Schubert
GYPSY RONDO, Haydn
WILD HORSEMEN, Schumann
HAPPY FARMER, Schumann
LITTLE WINDMILLS, Couperin

ARIETTA, Leo
MUSIC BOX, Liadov
FUNERAL MARCH OF THE MARIONETTES, Gounod
DANCE OF THE MERRY DWARFS (Happy Hypocrite), Elwell
LITTLE TRAIN OF CAIPIRA, Villa-Lobos

MUSIC, USA (BOL #65)

SHAKER TUNE (Appalachian Spring), Copland
CATTLE & BLUES (Plow that Broke the Plains), Thomson
FUGUE AND CHORALE ON YANKEE DOODLE (Tuesday in November), Thomson
PUMPKINEATERS LITTLE FUGUE, McBride
AMERICAN SALUTE, Gould
POP GOES THE WEASEL, Cailliet
LAST MOVEMENT, SYMPHONY #2, Ives

ORIENTAL SCENES (BOL #66)

WOODCUTTER'S SONG, Koyama
THE EMPORER'S NIGHTINGALE, Donaldson
SAKURA (Folk tune), played by koto and bamboo flute

FANTASY IN MUSIC (BOL #67)

THREE BEARS, Coates
CINDERELLA, Prokofieff (Sewing Scene, Cinderella's Gavotte, Midnight Waltz, Fairy Godmother)
MOON LEGEND, Donaldson
SLEEPING BEAUTY WALTZ, Tchaikovsky

CLASSROOM CONCERT (BOL #68)

ALBUM FOR THE YOUNG, Tchaikovsky. (Morning Prayer, Winter Morning, Hobby Horse, Mamma, March of the Tin Soldiers, Sick Doll, Doll's Burial, New Doll, Waltz, Mazurka, Russian Song, Peasant Plays the Accordion, Folk Song, Polka, Italian Song, Old French Song, German Song, Neapolitan Dance Song, Song of the Lark, Hand-organ Man, Nurse's Tale, The Witch, Sweet Dreams, In Church)
OVER THE HILLS, Grainger
MEMORIES OF CHILDHOOD, Pinto. (Run, Run, Ring Around the Rosie, March, Sleeping Time, Hobby Horse)
LET US RUN ACROSS THE HILL, Villa-Lobos
MY DAUGHTER LIDI, TEASING, GRASSHOPPER'S WEDDING, Bartok
DEVIL'S DANCE, Stravinsky
LITTLE GIRL IMPLORING HER MOTHER, Rebikov

SERIES 3

MUSIC OF THE DANCE: STRAVINSKY (BOL #69)

FIREBIRD SUITE (L'Oiseau de Feu). (Koschai's Enchanted Garden, Dance of the Firebird, Dance of the Princesses, Infer-

nal Dance of Koschai, Magic Sleep of the Princess Tzarevna, Finale: Escape of Koschai's Captives.)
SACRIFICIAL DANCE from "The Rite of Spring" (Le Sacre du Printemps)
VILLAGE FESTIVAL from "The Fairy's Kiss" (Le Baiser de la Fée)
PALACE OF THE CHINESE EMPEROR from "The Nightingale" (Le Rossignol)
TANGO, WALTZ AND RAGTIME from "The Soldier's Tale" (L'Histoire du Soldat)

MUSIC OF THE SEA AND SKY (BOL #70)

CLOUDS (Nuages), Debussy
FESTIVALS (Fêtes), Debussy
MERCURY from The Planets, Holst
SEA PIECE WITH BIRDS, Thomson
OVERTURE TO "THE FLYING DUTCHMAN" (Der Fliegende Holländer), Wagner
DIALOGUE OF THE WIND AND SEA from The Sea (La Mer), Debussy

SYMPHONIC MOVEMENTS, No. 1 (BOL #71)

FIRST MOVEMENT, SYMPHONY No. 40, Mozart
SECOND MOVEMENT, SYMPHONY No. 8, Beethoven
THIRD MOVEMENT, SYMPHONY No. 4, Tchaikovsky
SECOND MOVEMENT, SYMPHONY No. 4, Schumann
THIRD MOVEMENT, SYMPHONY No. 3, Brahms
FOURTH MOVEMENT, SYMPHONY No. 3, Saint-Saens

SYMPHONIC MOVEMENTS, No. 2 (BOL #72)

FIRST MOVEMENT, SYMPHONY No. 9, ("From the New World"), Dvorak
FIRST MOVEMENT, SYMPHONY No. 5, Beethoven
FIRST MOVEMENT, (Boisterous Bourrée), A SIMPLE SYMPHONY, Britten
SECOND MOVEMENT, SYMPHONY No. 2, Hanson
FIRST MOVEMENT, SYMPHONY No. 2, Sibelius

SYMPHONIC STYLES (BOL #73)

SYMPHONY No. 99 ("Imperial"), Haydn (Adagio: Vivace Assai, Adagio, Minuetto, Vivace)
CLASSICAL SYMPHONY, Prokofieff (Allegro, Larghetto, Gavotte: Non troppo allegro, Molto vivace)

TWENTIETH CENTURY AMERICA (BOL #74)

EL SALON MEXICO, Copland
DANZON from "Fancy Free," Bernstein
EXCERPTS, SYMPHONIC DANCES from "West Side Story," Bernstein
AN AMERICAN IN PARIS, Gershwin

U.S. HISTORY IN MUSIC (BOL #75)

A LINCOLN PORTRAIT, Copland
CHESTER from NEW ENGLAND TRIPTYCH, Schuman
PUTNAM'S CAMP from "Three Places in New England," Ives
INTERLUDE from FOLK SONG SYMPHONY, Harris
MIDNIGHT RIDE OF PAUL REVERE from Selections from McGuffey's Readers, Phillips

OVERTURES (BOL #76)

OVERTURE TO "THE BAT" (Die Fledermaus), Strauss
ACADEMIC FESTIVAL OVERTURE, Brahms
OVERTURE TO "THE MARRIAGE OF FIGARO," Mozart
ROMAN CARNIVAL OVERTURE, Berlioz
OVERTURE TO "WILLIAM TELL," Rossini (Dawn, Storm, Calm, Finale)

SCHEHERAZADE BY RIMSKY-KORSAKOV (BOL #77)

The Sea and Sinbad's Ship, Tale of the Prince Kalendar, The Young Prince and the Princess, The Festival at Bagdad

MUSICAL KALEIDOSCOPE (BOL #78)

ON THE STEPPES OF CENTRAL ASIA, Borodin
IN THE VILLAGE FROM CAUCASIAN SKETCHES, Ippolitoff-Ivanoff
EXCERPTS, POLOVTSIAN DANCES FROM "PRINCE IGOR," Borodin
RUSSIAN SAILORS' DANCE FROM "THE RED POPPY," Gliere
L'ARLESIENNE SUITE No. 1, Bizet Carillon, Minuet
L'ARLESIENNE SUITE No. 2, Bizet Farandole
PRELUDE TO ACT 1, "CARMEN," Bizet
MARCH TO THE SCAFFOLD, from Symphonie Fantastique, Berlioz

MUSIC OF THE DRAMA: WAGNER (BOL #79)

"LOHENGRIN" (Overture to Act 1, Prelude to Act 3)
"THE TWILIGHT OF THE GODS" (Die Götterdämmerung) (Siegfried's Rhine Journey)
"THE MASTERSINGERS OF NUREMBERG" (Die Meistersinger von Nürnberg) (Prelude, Dance of the Apprentices and Entrance of the Mastersingers)
"TRISTAN AND ISOLDE" (Love Death)

PETROUCHKA BY STRAVINSKY (BOL #80)

COMPLETE BALLET SCORE WITH NARRATION

ROGUES IN MUSIC (BOL #81)
TILL EULENSPIEGEL, Strauss
LIEUTENANT KIJE, Prokofieff
Birth of Kije, Troika
HARY JANOS, Kodaly
(Viennese Musical Clock, Battle and Defeat of Napoleon, Intermezzo, Entrance of the Emperor)

MUSICAL PICTURES: MOUSSORGSKY (BOL #82)
PICTURES AT AN EXHIBITION
(Promenade Theme, The Gnome, The Old Castle, Tuileries, Ox-Cart, Ballet of Chicks in their Shells, Goldenberg and Schmuyle, The Market Place at Limoges, Catacombs, The Hut of Baga Yaga, The Great Gate of Kiev)
NIGHT ON BALD MOUNTAIN

ENSEMBLES, LARGE AND SMALL (BOL #83)
YOUNG PERSON'S GUIDE TO THE ORCHESTRA, Britten
CANZONA IN C MAJOR FOR BRASS ENSEMBLE AND ORGAN, Gabrieli
CHORALE: AWAKE, THOU WINTRY EARTH, Bach
FOURTH MOVEMENT, "TROUT" QUINTET, Schubert
THEME AND VARIATIONS FOR PERCUSSION QUARTET, Kraft
THEME AND VARIATIONS from SERENADE FOR WIND INSTRUMENTS, Mozart (K361)

CONCERTOS (BOL #84)
FIRST MOVEMENT, PIANO CONCERTO, Grieg
FOURTH MOVEMENT, PIANO CONCERTO No. 2, Brahms
THIRD MOVEMENT, VIOLIN CONCERTO, Mendelssohn
SECOND MOVEMENT, GUITAR CONCERTO, Castelnuovo-Tedesco
THIRD MOVEMENT, CONCERTO IN C FOR TWO TRUMPETS, Vivaldi

MUSICAL IMPRESSIONS: RESPIGHI (BOL #85)
PINES OF ROME (Pines of the Villa Borghese, Pines Near a Catacomb, Pines of the Appian Way)
FOUNTAINS OF ROME (The Fountain of Valle Giulia at Dawn, The Triton Fountain at Morning, The Trevi Fountain at Midday, The Villa Medici Fountain at Sunset)
THE BIRDS (Prelude)

FASHIONS IN MUSIC (BOL #86)
ROMEO AND JULIET (Fantasy-Overture), Tchaikovsky
LITTLE FUGUE IN G MINOR, Bach
SUITE No. 2 FROM "DAPHNIS AND CHLOË," Ravel
ROMANZE FROM A LITTLE NIGHT MUSIC (Eine Kleine Nachtmusik), Mozart
PERIPETIA FROM FIVE PIECES FOR ORCHESTRA Schoenberg

RCA ADVENTURES IN MUSIC FOR ELEMENTARY SCHOOLS

ALBUM 1 (Grade 1, Vol. 1)
(LC # 71-750850) **LES-1000(stereo)**

Gluck: Iphigenie in Aulis—AIR GAI; Massenet: Le Cid—ARAGONAISE; Moussorgsky: Pictures at an Exhibition—BALLET OF THE UNHATCHED CHICKS (Orch. by Ravel); Kabalevsky: The Comedians—PANTOMIME; Prokofieff: Summer Day Suite—MARCH; Bizet: Children's Games—CRADLE SONG, THE BALL, LEAP FROG; Stravinsky: The Firebird Suite—BERCEUSE; Berlioz: The Damnation of Faust—BALLET OF THE SYLPHS; Delibes: Coppelia—WALTZ OF THE DOLL; Thomson: Acadian Songs and Dances—WALKING SONG; Tchaikovsky: Swan Lake—DANCE OF THE LITTLE SWANS; Ibert: Divertissement—PARADE; Rossini-Britten: Soirees Musicales—MARCH; Bach: Suite No. 3—GIGUE; Gretry: Cephale et Procris—GIGUE (Arr. by Mottl); Shostakovich: Ballet Suite No. 1—PIZZICATO POLKA

ALBUM 2 (Grade 1, Vol. 2)
(LC # 71-750850) **LES-1010 (stereo)**

Arnold: English Dances—GRAZIOSO; Stravinsky: Petrouchka—RUSSIAN DANCE; Khachaturian: Gayne Ballet Suite—DANCE OF THE ROSE MAIDENS; McBride: Punch and the Judy—PONY EXPRESS; Tchaikovsky: Nutcracker Suite—DANCE OF THE SUGAR PLUM FAIRY, DANCE OF THE REED PIPES; Hanson: For the First Time—BELLS; Menotti: Amahl and the Night Visitors—MARCH OF THE KINGS; Grieg: Peer Gynt Suite No. 1—ANITRA'S DANCE; Saint-Saens: Carnival of the Animals—THE ELEPHANT; Milhaud: Suite Provencale—MODERE No. 1; Moussorgsky-Ravel: Pictures at an Exhibition—PROMENADE; Rossini-Britten: Matinees Musicales—WALTZ; Bartok: Mikrokosmos Suite No. 2—FROM THE DIARY OF A FLY; German: Henry VIII Suite—MORRIS DANCE; Moore: Farm Journal—HARVEST SONG; Delibes: The King Is Amused—LESQUERCARDE; Mozart: THE LITTLE NOTHINGS, No. 8; Kabalevsky: The Comedians—WALTZ; Liadov: Eight Russian Folk Songs—BERCEUSE

ALBUM 3 (Grade 2, Vol. 1)
(LC # 71-750850) **LES-1001 (stereo)**

McDonald: Children's Symphony (3rd Movement)—FARMER IN THE DELL, JINGLE BELLS; Ibert: Histories No. 2—THE LITTLE WHITE DONKEY; Shostakovich: Ballet Suite No. 1—PETITE BALLERINA; Moussorgsky: Pictures at an Exhibition—BYDLO (Orch. by Ravel); Faure: Dolly—BERCEUSE; Rossini-Respighi: The Fantastic Toyshop—CAN-CAN; Handel: Water Music—HORNPIPE; Milhaud: Saudades do Brazil—LARANJEIRAS; Kodaly: Hary Janos Suite—VIENNESE MUSICAL CLOCK; Herbert: Babes in Toyland—MARCH OF THE TOYS; Prokofieff: Winter Holiday—DEPARTURE; Gretry: Cephale et Procris—TAMBOURIN (Arr. by Mottl); Elgar: Wand of Youth Suite No. 2—FOUNTAIN DANCE; Bartok: Mikrokosmos Suite No. 2—JACK-IN-THE-BOX; Meyerbeer: Les Patineurs—WALTZ

ALBUM 4 (Grade 2, Vol. 2)
(LC # 71-750850) **LES-1011 (stereo)**

Arnold: English Dances—ALLEGRO NON TROPPO; Prokofieff: Lieutenant Kije—TROIKA; Schuller: Seven Studies on Themes of Paul Klee—THE TWITTERING MACHINE; Copland: The Red Pony Suite—DREAM MARCH; Elgar: Wand of Youth Suite No. 1—SUN DANCE; Rimsky-Korsakoff: The Snow Maiden—DANCE OF THE BUFFOONS; Delibes: Coppelia—SWANHILDE'S WALTZ; Bach: Suite No. 2 in B Minor—RONDEAU; Pierne: Cydalise Suite No. 1—ENTRANCE OF THE LITTLE FAUNS; Respighi: The Birds—PRELUDE; Rossini-Britten: Soirees Musicales—BOLERO; McBride: PUMPKIN EATER'S LITTLE FUGUE; Cimarosa-Malipiero: Cimarosiana—NON TROPPO MOSSO; Gluck: Armide Ballet Suite—MUSETTE; Bizet: Carmen—THE DRAGOONS OF ALCALA; Howe: SAND; Webern: Five Movements for String Orchestra—SEHR LANGSAM

ALBUM 5 (Grade 3, Vol. 1)
(LC # 71-750850) **LES-1002 (stereo)**

Hanson: Merry Mount Suite—CHILDREN'S DANCE; Rossini: William Tell Overture—FINALE; Herbert: Natoma—DAGGER DANCE; Villa-Lobos: Bachianas Brasileiras No. 2—THE LITTLE TRAIN OF THE CAIPIRA; Offenbach: The Tales of Hoffmann—BARCAROLLE; Kabalevsky: The Comedians—MARCH, COMEDIANS' GALOP; Elgar: Wand of Youth Suite No. 1—FAIRIES AND GIANTS; Tchaikovsky: The Sleeping Beauty—PUSS-IN-BOOTS AND THE WHITE CAT; Copland: The Red Pony Suite—CIRCUS MUSIC; Gounod: Faust Ballet Music—WALTZ No. 1; Vaughan Williams: The Wasps—MARCH PAST OF THE KITCHEN UTENSILS; Debussy: Children's Corner Suite—THE SNOW IS DANCING; Bach: Suite No. 2—BADINERIE

ALBUM 6 (Grade 3, Vol. 2)
(LC # 71-750850) **LES-1003 (stereo)**

Bartok: Hungarian Sketches—BEAR DANCE; Bizet: Carmen—CHANGING OF THE GUARD; Grieg: Peer Gynt Suite No. 1—IN THE HALL OF THE MOUNTAIN KING; Handel: Royal Fireworks Music—BOURREE (from 2nd Movement), MENUETTO No. 2 (from 6th Movement); Lully: Ballet Suite (from "Thesee")—MARCH; McDonald: Children's Symphony (1st Movement)—LONDON BRIDGE, BAA, BAA, BLACK SHEEP; Prokofieff: Children's Suite—WALTZ ON THE ICE (from "Winter Holiday"); Rossini-Respighi: The Fantastic Toyshop—TARANTELLA; Saint-Saens: Carnival of the Animals—THE SWAN; Sousa: SEMPER FIDELIS; Taylor: Through the Looking Glass—GARDEN OF LIVE FLOWERS (Five Pictures from Lewis Carroll); Thomson: Acadian Songs and Dances—THE ALLIGATOR AND THE 'COON (from "Louisiana Story")

ALBUM 7 (Grade 4, Vol. 1)
(LC # 71-750850) **LES-1004 (stereo)**

Cailliet: POP! GOES THE WEASEL—Variations; Tchaikovsky: The Sleeping Beauty—WALTZ; Lecuona: Suite Andalucia—ANDALUCIA; Respighi: Pines of Rome—PINES OF THE VILLA BORGHESE; Rimsky-Korsakoff: Le Coq d'Or Suite—BRIDAL PROCESSION; Mozart: Eine kleine Nachtmusik—ROMANZE; Grofe: Death Valley Suite—DESERT WATER HOLE; Grieg: Lyric Suite—NORWEGIAN RUSTIC MARCH; Chabrier: MARCHE JOYEUSE; Ginastera: Estancia—WHEAT DANCE

ALBUM 8 (Grade 4, Vol. 2)
(LC # 71-750850) **LES-1005 (stereo)**

Bizet: L'Arlesienne Suite No. 1—MINUETTO; Dvorak: SLAVONIC DANCE No. 7; Grainger: LONDONDERRY AIR; Khachaturian: Masquerade Suite—WALTZ; Kodaly: Hary Janos Suite—ENTRANCE OF THE EMPEROR AND HIS COURT; Menotti: Amahl and the Night Visitors—SHEPHERDS' DANCE; Milhaud: Saudades do Brazil—COPACABANA; Ravel: Mother Goose Suite—LAIDERONNETTE, EMPRESS OF THE PAGODAS; Scarlatti-Tommasini: The Good-Humored Ladies—NON PRESTO MA A TEMPO DI BALLO; Schumann: Scenes from Childhood—TRAUMEREI; Sousa: STARS AND STRIPES FOREVER

ALBUM 9 (Grade 5, Vol. 1)
(LC # 71-750850) **LES-1006 (stereo)**

Chabrier: ESPANA RAPSODIE; MacDowell: Second (Indian) Suite—IN WAR-TIME; Schubert: Symphony No. 5—FIRST MOVEMENT; Charpentier: Impressions of Italy—ON MULEBACK; Gottschalk-Kay: Cakewalk Ballet Suite—GRAND WALKAROUND; Ravel: Mother Goose Suite—THE CONVERSATIONS OF BEAUTY AND THE BEAST; Sibelius: Karelia Suite—ALLA MARCIA; Gould: AMERICAN SALUTE; Bach: Cantata No. 147—JESU, JOY OF MAN'S DESIRING

ALBUM 10 (Grade 5, Vol. 2)
(LC # 71-750850) **LES-1007 (stereo)**

Anderson: Irish Suite—THE GIRL I LEFT BEHIND ME; Bartok: Hungarian Sketches—EVENING IN THE VILLAGE; Brahms: HUNGARIAN DANCE No. 1; Carpenter: Adventures in a Perambulator—THE HURDY GURDY; Coates: London Suite—KNIGHTSBRIDGE MARCH; Copland: Rodeo—HOE-DOWN; Humperdinck: Hansel and Gretel—PRELUDE; Mozart: Divertimento No. 17—MENUETTO No. 1; Respighi: Brazilian Impressions—DANZA; Stravinsky: Firebird Suite—INFERNAL DANCE OF KING KASTCHEI

ALBUM 11 (Grade 6, Vol. 1)
(LC # 71-750850) **LES-1009 (stereo)**

R. Strauss: Der Rosenkavalier—SUITE; Borodin: ON THE STEPPES OF CENTRAL ASIA; Bach: LITTLE FUGUE IN G MINOR (Arr. by Cailliet); Beethoven: Symphony No. 8—SECOND MOVEMENT; Copland: Billy the Kid Ballet Suite—STREET IN A FRONTIER TOWN; Falla: La Vida Breve—SPANISH DANCE No. 1; Griffes: THE WHITE PEACOCK; Bizet: L'Arlesienne Suite No. 2—FARANDOLE; Wagner: Lohengrin—PRELUDE TO ACT III

ALBUM 12 (Grade 6, Vol. 2)
(LC # 71-750850) **LES-1008 (stereo)**

Corelli-Pinelli: Suite for Strings—SARABANDE; Debussy: La Mer—PLAY OF THE WAVES; Gliere: The Red Poppy—RUSSIAN SAILORS' DANCE; Guarnieri: BRAZILIAN DANCE; Holst: The Perfect Fool—Ballet Suite—SPIRITS OF THE EARTH; Smetana: The Bartered Bride—DANCE OF THE COMEDIANS; Vaughan Williams: FANTASIA ON "GREENSLEEVES"; Walton: Facade Suite—VALSE; Tchaikovsky: Symphony No. 4—FOURTH MOVEMENT

KEYBOARD PUBLICATIONS

1. **MAN AND HIS MUSIC** series (All of the following include two filmstrips, narrated recording or cassette, listening recording or cassette, teacher's guide, and student booklets.)

Now Sound of the classics	Japan
USSR	China
Country Music	Africa
Japan	Middle East
From Jazz to Rock	American Indian
Rock	American Scene
Electronic Music	Latin America (Mexico, Brazil, Argentina)

2. Other selected boxed units are also available under the following titles: (These include record, theme charts, teacher's guide, student booklets and bulletin board pictures.)

ELEMENTS OF MUSIC	MUSIC AND SOCIAL STUDIES	SCIENCE AND LITERATURE
MUSICAL INSTRUMENTS	NATURE AND MUSIC	PERIODS IN MUSIC
MUSICAL STORIES	COMPOSERS	FORM IN MUSIC

3. **CREATING MUSIC** through the use of the Tape Recorder (Contains two filmstrips, record, and instruction book.)

4. **REP** (Reading Enrichment Program. Includes eight composers, self-testing materials, listening records and filmstrips.)

Glossary

Absolute music: Nondescriptive music.

Allemande: A fairly lively dance in $\frac{4}{4}$ time; also the first movement of dance suites of the seventeenth and eighteenth centuries.

Alto: The lowest treble voice. May also refer to a part within a certain range played by an instrument or sung.

Atonal: Lacking a fixed reference point such as a home tone or key.

Augmentation: An imitative device by which the second melody moves in notes of longer duration than those in the first melody, but in the same proportion to one another.

Band: A group of performers or a certain specified group of instruments. A band does not include string instruments, as a rule.

Bar lines: Vertical lines drawn at measured distances on the staff for the purpose of dividing it into measures.

Baroque: Refers to the period from about 1600 to 1750, characterized by grandeur and heavy elaboration of design in music.

Bass: The lowest male voice. May also refer to a part within a certain range played by an instrument or sung.

Binary form: Two-part form; the structure of a musical composition consisting of two main sections.

Bourrée: A fast dance of the baroque period of French and Spanish origin, usually in $\frac{2}{4}$ or $\frac{4}{4}$ meter; also a movement in early suites.

Cadenza: A brilliant passage for a solo instrument, designed to display the virtuosity of the performer.

Canon: A musical form in which a given melody is imitated by two or more voices beginning at different times.

Cantata: A short lyric form dealing with either secular or sacred subject matter.

Chant: A repeated group of notes sung against (and usually below) the main tune of a song.

Chanteys: British and American sailor songs.

Chord: Three or more tones combined and sounded simultaneously.

Chorus: A number of persons singing together. May also refer to a composition written for combined voices.

Chromatic: Refers to tones foreign to a given key or scale; also pertains to all tones of the chromatic scale.

Chromatic scale: A twelve-tone scale within any given octave that includes the diatonic scale tones *(do re mi fa sol la ti)* plus the five intermediate half steps *(di ri fi si li)*.

Classical: Refers to that period from approximately 1750 to 1800, characterized musically by objectivity of the composer, emotional restraint, and simple harmonies.

Coda: Literally "tail." An added ending on a musical composition.

Composer: One who writes music.

Computer music: Music composed by describing sounds mathematically and then feeding the sequence of numbers into a computer.

Concerto: A symphonic composition written for a solo instrument (or group of instruments) and orchestra; usually consists of three contrasting movements, with a cadenza often occurring near the close of the first movement.

Conductor: One who directs a musical group (chorus, orchestra, band, etc.).

Consonance: A simultaneous sounding of tones that produces a feeling of rest, i.e., a feeling that there is no need for further resolution.

Contemporary: Refers to the period from about 1900 to the present, characterized by the use of old sounds in new ways, as well as the introduction of new sounds.

Da capo: From the beginning. A direction to repeat the entire composition from the beginning to the place where the word *fine* appears or to the end.

Dal segno: A direction to repeat from the sign to the word *fine.*

Descant: A melody that is sung or played against the main melody of a song.

Diatonic: Pertaining to a standard major or minor eight-tone scale.

Dissonance: A simultaneous sounding of tones that produces a feeling of tension or unrest and/or a feeling that further resolution is needed.

Duet: A musical performance by two voices or instruments.

Duple meter: Meter in which there are two beats or some multiple of two to the measure.

Dynamics: Varying intensities of sound throughout a given musical composition.

Electronic music: Music produced by distorting or modifying various sounds through the process of electronic devices.

Fine: The end of a piece.

Folk song: A song, usually of unknown origin, arising as an outgrowth of a people.

Form: The basic structure of a musical composition, which results from the arrangement of repetition and contrast in the material.

Fugue: Literally "flight." A contrapuntal form involving two or more voices in which a subject (theme) is introduced and developed through a series of imitations.

Galop: A vigorous nineteenth-century round dance in $\frac{2}{4}$ time.

Gavotte: A French peasant dance of the baroque period, modified for use by court nobility; usually in $\frac{4}{4}$ time with steps beginning on the third beat. Also a movement of an early suite.

Gigue: "Jig." A lively dance in compound time. Also a movement of a baroque suite.

Glissando: A sweeping motion up or down a keyboard in which all tones are sounded in rapid succession.

Harmony: The sound resulting from the simultaneous sounding of two or more tones consonant with each other.

Hold: Indicated by the sign ⌒ over the note, meaning to hold longer than the given rhythm of the note would ordinarily require. Also known as a *fermata.*

Hornpipe: An English sailor dance of the baroque period, accompanied by an instrument known as a "hornpipe," from which the dance derives its name. It was done first in three-beat meter and then in four-beat meter.

Imitation: The reproducing of a given melody by several voices at different times.

Instrument: An implement with which musical sounds are produced.

Interval: The distance between two tones.

Inversion: (1) In contrapuntal forms, the movement of a second voice in the same melody pattern as the first, but in the opposite direction. (2) In harmony, the presence of any tone other than the root as the bass note of a chord.

Jazz: A twentieth-century musical style characterized by double meter, syncopation, and improvisation. Considered to be typically American.

Mazurka: A Polish national dance in triple meter with a stongly accented second or third beat.

Measure: A space on the staff enclosed between two bar lines.

Melody: An arrangement of single tones in a meaningful sequence.

Minuet: A stately French dance of the baroque period in $\frac{3}{4}$ time. Also included in larger symphonic works in modified forms. From the French word *menu*, meaning "small."

Mixed chorus: A group of male and female singers.

Musical comedy: A musical show with songs, dances, etc., unified by a plot, which is usually light in character.

Musique concrète: Electronic music based on natural sounds.

Opera: A musical drama consisting of recitatives, arias, choruses, orchestral music, etc., using scenery and costumes.

Operetta: A light musical drama with action, costumes, and scenery. Dialogue is usually spoken.

Oratorio: A large dramatic production using narrator, soloists, chorus, and orchestra but no costumes, staging, or scenery. Also contains an overture, arias, and recitatives, plus small vocal ensembles. The text is always biblical.

Orchestra: A group of instrumental performers or a certain specified group of instruments.

Ostinato: A repeated melodic fragment.

Overture: An instrumental selection which is usually performed before the curtain goes up on a musical play and which contains tunes that will be heard later in the production.

Phrase: A small section of a composition comprising a musical thought. Comparable to a sentence in language.

Pitch: The highness or lowness of a tone, determined by the frequency of vibration of sound waves. The larger the number of vibrations, the higher the resulting pitch.

Polka: A lively nineteenth-century Bohemian couple dance in duple meter.

Polonaise: A moderately slow eighteenth- and nineteenth-century Polish dance in triple meter. Also a movement of a baroque suite.

Polyphonic music: Music in which two or more melodies sound simultaneously.

Polyphony: Literally "many voices." The combining of a number of individual harmonizing melodies.

Polyrhythms: Two or more contrasting rhythms sounding simultaneously.

Polytonal music: Music in which two or more keys are used simultaneously in a given composition.

Program music: Music of a descriptive nature that tells a story, sets a scene, paints a picture, sets a mood, or describes an event.

Quartet: A musical group of four voices or instruments. Also refers to a composition written for four parts.

Retrograde: A form of contrapuntal imitation in which the melody is played backward.

Romantic: Refers to the nineteenth century musical period characterized by subjectivity on the part of the composer, emotionalism in music, longer musical forms, and richer harmonies.

Rondo: An instrumental form consisting of three different themes in which the recurring main theme (A) alternates with the other two secondary themes (B and C). The rondo was originally a dance form, which came out of round singing.

Root: The tone of the scale upon which a chord is built.

Root position: The position of a chord in which the root appears as the lowest tone.

Round: A form of imitative singing in which each voice enters at measured intervals and sings its part as often as desired.

Sarabande: A slow Spanish court dance in triple meter. Also a slow movement of a baroque suite.

Scale: From the Italian word *scala,* meaning "ladder." A graduated series of tones arranged in a specified order.

Scherzo: Literally "joke." A sprightly movement in larger symphonic works, light and humorous in nature. Usually in triple meter.

Sequence: A succession of melodic figures repeated on various degrees of the scale.

Slur: A curved line drawn over two or more notes of different pitches, indicating that they are to be executed in a smoothly connected manner, without a break:

Solo: A musical performance by one voice or instrument.

Soprano: The highest treble voice. Also refers to a part within a certain range played by an instrument or sung.

Staff: Five equally spaced horizontal lines upon which music is written.

Subject: The principal theme on which a musical composition is based.

Suite: An instrumental form that may consist of a group of dances, a group of descriptive pieces, or a group of pieces from a ballet or opera. It is often unified through a story or idea.

Symphony: A large musical work in sonata form for full orchestra.

Syncopation: The rhythmic result produced when a regularly accented beat is displaced on to an unaccented beat.

Tarantelle, tarantella: A fast dance, usually in $\frac{6}{8}$ time. The name is derived from the word "tarantula." It was believed that doing a wild dance would cure the bite of the tarantula spider.

Tempo: The rate of speed at which a musical composition is performed.

Tenor: The highest male voice. Also a part within a certain range played by an instrument or sung.

Ternary form: A three-part structure of a musical composition consisting of three sections, the middle section of which contrasts with the first and last sections.

Theme: A short musical passage that states an idea. It often provides the basis for variations, development, etc., in a musical composition.

Tie: A curved line connecting two or more notes of the same pitch. When played or sung, the first note in the series is sounded and held for the duration of the combined beats of all the others throughout the length of the tie:

Timbre: The quality of a musical tone that distinguishes voices and instruments.

Tonal music: Music in a definite key, in which one pitch is used as a reference or home tone.

Tonality: The feeling of the presence of, and a tendency to be drawn toward, a certain home tone or key in a musical composition—a feeling produced by the musical scheme of the composition.

Tone: (1) A musical sound. (2) The quality of a musical sound. (3) The larger interval between adjacent sounds of a scale—a whole tone (step) as opposed to a semitone (half step).

Tone Poem: An orchestral piece in one movement, usually descriptive in nature.

Tonic: The keynote of a given key.

Transpose: To transfer a musical composition from one key into another.

Trio: A musical group of three voices or instruments. Also a composition written for three parts.

Triple meter: Meter in which there are three beats or some multiple of three to the measure.

Triplet: Three notes performed in the time of two of the same value.

Twelve-tone row: All twelve tones contained in any given octave, as in a chromatic scale.

Variations: Different treatments of a given theme or melody through changes in rhythm, mood, tempo, meter, etc.

Waltz: From the German word *walzen,* meaning "to roll about." Original waltzes were much heavier and less graceful in character than those we know today.

Whole-tone scale: A scale of six tones in which all intervals are whole steps.

Dynamics Terms

Crescendo: gradually growing louder

Diminuendo: gradually growing softer

Forte (f): loud

Fortissimo (ff): very loud

Mezzo forte (mf): moderately loud

Mezzo piano (mp): moderately soft

Pianissimo (pp): very soft

Piano (p): soft

Sforzando (sf): explosively

Expression Terms

Legato: smoothly connected

Maestoso: majestically

Sostenuto: sustained

Spirito: spiritedly

Staccato: disconnectedly

Vivace: vivaciously

Tempo Terms

Accelerando: gradually growing faster

Allegretto: rather fast

Allegro: fast

Andante: slow

Andantino: rather slow

Largo: very slow

Lento: slow

Moderato: at a moderate pace

Presto: very fast

Ritardando: gradually growing slower

ALPHABETICAL INDEX OF SONGS

CLASSIFIED INDEX OF SONGS

FOR STUDY

INDEX